CROSSING INTO
MEDICINE COUNTRY

ALSO BY DAVID CARSON

Medicine Cards:
The Discovery of Power Through the Ways of Animals

2013 Oracle:
Ancient Keys to the 2012 Awakening

CROSSING INTO
MEDICINE COUNTRY

A Journey in Native American Healing

David Carson

COUNCIL OAK BOOKS

TULSA & SAN FRANCISCO

www.counciloakbooks.com

Originally published by Arcade Publishing

FIRST PAPERBACK EDITION, 2007
COUNCIL OAK BOOKS

The author of this book does not dispense medical advice or prescribe the use of any technique or substance as a form of treatment for physical or medical problems, either directly or indirectly. The intent of the author is only to offer information of a general nature, based on his experience, about traditional Native American healing. In the event you use any of the information in this book for yourself, the author and the publisher assume no responsibility for your actions.

Library of Congress Cataloging-in-Publication Data

Carson, David, 1937–
    Crossing into medicine country : a journey in Native American
    healing / by David Carson. — 1st paperback ed. 2007
    p. cm.
    ISBN1-57178-208-7
    ISBN-13: 978-1-57178-208-3
    1. Shamanism — United States.   2. Carson, David, 1937–.
    3. Shamans — United States — Biography.   4. Indians of North
    America — Medicine.   5. Indians of North America — Religion.
    I. Title.

    BF1611.C39 2005
    299.7—dc   222005010303

ISBN-13: 978-1-57178-208-3

For Jason

Contents

Acknowledgments

*T*HIS BOOK WOULD HAVE NEVER BEEN WRITTEN without the amazing human, plant, and animal teachers in my life. With affection, I bow to all.

With love to my family, to Sara, Greta, and my wife, Nina Sammons, for their continual encouragement and suggestions all along the line. To all my relatives.

Special acknowledgments and thanks to Gershon Winkler and Lakme Batya Elinor, M. J. Bogatin, D. H. Latimer, and Gary Heidt.

Deep gratitude to Cal Barksdale, who inspired me and helped beyond all measure on this work. Thanks are due also to Tessa Aye.

Prologue

Looking for My Teacher

*A*LONG TIME AGO ALL THE STARS CAME DOWN TO EARTH for a visit, at least that is what I was told as a child. When the stars flew back up to be in the midst of the night sky, the country where the Big Dipper had been became Oklahoma.

The Great White Father in Washington said, "We're going to put all the Indians in that big skillet and cook them. That will be their land." So they did. And after all the Indians were cooked, the Great White Father said, "Now we're going to take your skillet. You don't need it anymore." Soon Oklahoma was no longer Oklahoma, land of red people. Now the state belonged to practically everybody and their dog.

I'm one of the mix-ups, called an Okie coyote or breed. Though of Choctaw descent, I don't qualify to be an FBI — full-blood Indian. And I've found a lot of things that disqualify me from being white, too. We breeds are different, a bunch of coyote mix-ups out barking at the moon. Some people call coyote a half-breed, and some say he has no breeding at all. Oklahoma is full of such mix-ups as me. The trick if you are a coyote is just to be one. Be proficient. Be a coward when others are brave. Be brave when others are cowardly. Tell lies when others speak truthfully. Tell the truth when others are lying. And so on until everyone is mixed up. When that happens it will be the same for everyone. There'll be no more mix-ups.

I have long been interested in various occluded aspects of the ancient legacies of Native America. When I was growing up, my aunts Ruby and Agnes along with my mom, Opal, belonged to Native women's circles that were devoted to preserving secret knowledge and unwritten practices. For instance, these circles cleansed and fed power objects. During the lunar year, there were times to open and close sacred medicine packs and perform life-enhancing ceremonies. Many power songs were sung and the memory kept. These oral teachings were closely guarded and passed from women to men, then from men to women. The sacred information and training flowed over time in this manner from one generation to another. Some awareness of this rubbed off on me, but I certainly didn't know it then. I was too busy being a kid and having fun. From my aunts, I learned to observe animals in the wild and about their powers. My mom taught me to be proud of my Indian heritage and to respect the beating heart of its traditions. When I grew older, I sought to gain some of this secret knowledge through formal apprenticeship and by going to live among the indigenous people of Montana and Canada.

But now, here I was back in home country — back in the Choctaw nation. I was driving my old clunker pickup truck. My daughter Sara sat next to me. We were just outside of Talihina, a town situated on the periphery of the Ouachita mountain chain in the southeastern part of the state. The Ouachitas go due east almost to Little Rock, Arkansas. A segment of the Choctaw Trail of Tears is a part of their sad history, and the mountains are considered holy and big medicine. At the turn of the century, there were doctoring enclaves up here and some say cabals of wizards and witches. They say Rolling Thunder, the famous medicine man, obtained his power in these mountains when he was a young man, and he was one of the few conjures willing to share it and treat white people and scientific types who had no faith in it.

"I don't think I'd like to live here," Sara said. "It's too remote."

"You ain't seen nothing yet," I said. "We're going out where the hoot owls make love to the chickens. And the chickens like it."

Sara laughed. She was my light in a fog bank of trouble. She lived the ancestral way pretty much impeccably. Her face was full of health, life, and beauty. But we had just been through the proverbial meat grinder of the American justice system, and were pretty beaten up inside.

I always go back to Oklahoma when I am spiritually malnourished, or in times of great trouble. Outsiders never understand how such a historical hornet's nest of rigidity and intolerance can also be the source of truth and light, yet it can. And here I was with Sara back in the red land that was my heritage. We were on a sad mission. My son Jason had recently been sentenced to fourteen years in prison for vehicular homicide. This had happened in Iowa City, Iowa.

I wanted to find my old teacher, whose name was Mary Gardener. Mary was a snake-skirted woman, as they are called. In olden times, snakes symbolized the umbilical cord, and snakeskirts were midwives. But that isn't all they were. They were keepers of highly secret knowledge. I wanted to get a certain kind of medicine from Mary Gardener to slip to my son for protection while he was serving time. Snakeskirts have the knowledge to capture and empower this medicine. It was the only thing I could think of to do since I had turned his life, not to mention my own, over to lawyers. Mistake. Things had gone downhill ever since.

Anyway, that was my mission. Even if I was unable to locate a snakeskirt, perhaps I could get the medicine from someone else. I still had a few friends in lowly and lonely places. This particular medicine was not talked about much, the holders believing in secrecy. The medicine is called *hagee* or *sabeeha*, and is a kind of charm or ally. Most people in southeastern Oklahoma who know of this medicine call it either *sabeeha* or *hag*, but the original word was *hagee*. I know of no exact translation other than "charm" or "helping medicine." I do know that there is no association whatsoever with the English word *hag*.

Sabeeha were always carried for a particular purpose. There were sports *sabeeha* to help in stickball playing. *Sabeeha* were used in hunting, war, love, acquisition, the chase, divination, for good luck, and so on. Snakeskirts could empower a *sabeeha* for virtually any purpose. *Sabeeha* are so powerful that the owner would rarely keep them indoors. They were often hidden in the hollow of a tree.

Since *sabeeha* are varied, they are difficult to describe. Each is unique. Each is a small, magical buckskin bundle containing a buckshot-sized charm that looks like glass or crystal. Both the tiny bundle and its contents are called *sabeeha*, but the contents are often called *sabeeha* stones. *Sabeeha* stones all sparkle, except for black ones, which are opaque and matte-colored and look rather like the burnt end of a kitchen match. Black *sabeeha* are mysterious and are called rainbows. They serve as a kind of general all-purpose medicine, bringing luck and authority in most endeavors.

Red *sabeeha* are male and used in competition such as sports and warfare. They are the *minko* or chief *hags*. This is the *hag* to use in any act where force or rashness is exerted, such as the slaying of men or animals. In the old days they were used in horse stealing. They were also popular as a love medicine.

The yellow *sabeeha* is also male. It is typically used for health, well-being, and longevity. It sometimes gives relief to the dying. Yellow *hag* is also a good grieving medicine.

Blue *sabeeha* are female and offer total protection from a power gaze or evil eye. If you own a blue *hag*, no evil spirit can harm you. People will call on you to remove hexes or curses. Evil curses are rendered powerless. Evil people or evil magical beings will avoid you at all cost.

White *sabeeha* are said to bring reasonableness into any conflict. They are grounded woman medicine. They give great charisma to the owner. People want to help and serve the owner of this *sabeeha* without reservation.

My aunt Ruby once gave me a red *sabeeha* when I joined the marines. A few days before I had to report for duty, I stopped at a diner on the way home to get a hamburger and a Coke. I was sitting in a booth waiting for my order, when I impulsively unsealed the round of buckskin. The *sabeeha* stone seemed to light up instantly. As I gazed at it, my eyes started playing tricks on me. The tiny rock appeared to swim around, and I had to blink tightly to make it stop.

I took the straw from my glass of Coke. Using the tip, I began to coax and prod the stone. When I did, the little guy changed shape and trembled atop the buckskin wrapping. It would glitter and dim like an ignited pellet. Even without making contact, the straw tip would cause it to roll. Obviously, it didn't want to be fooled with.

The waitress came and set down my burger and fries, causing the *sabeeha* to cut a different path. It seemed interested and went toward her.

"Damn my eyes," she said in a frightened voice. "What is that? It's alive."

By this time, the *sabeeha* stone was bouncing around on the table. I tried to act nonchalant and at the same time catch it. As I made a grab for it, though, it appeared to break the law of gravity by floating in the air longer than necessary, and my hand missed. Did I look silly. I was attempting to sweep it back to its wrapping with my right hand while reassuring the waitress with my left. Meanwhile, people in the diner were starting to turn their attention our way.

I managed to shoo the *sabeeha* back to the tabletop and onto the buckskin, but not before I knocked over my glass of Coke. The liquid covered the table, and the glass went smashing to the floor. I quickly bundled up the *sabeeha* and put it in my shirt pocket.

All the customers — there weren't more than eight or so — were gawking at me. You haven't experienced anything until you've had a room full of hayseeds checking you out. There was silence all around. The waitress was holding her abdomen with both hands and beginning to hyperventilate.

"I'll take this to go," I said, putting the burger and fries into a napkin. I halfway stood up and slid out of the booth. "Sorry I made a mess. Here." I left enough money to cover the check and included a big fifteen-cent tip.

The cook was walking toward the waitress as I exited. "Wanda June, are you all right? What was that kid doing?" I heard him ask as I was going out through the front door.

When I told my aunt Agnes about the incident that night, she laughed and said, "*Sabeeha* are a grave responsibility. They can easily be fatal if kept incorrectly. They can drive you to do desperate acts or even destroy you with lust. Ruby gave you a warrior medicine, and best you act like one from now on." I think it was at that moment I learned to truly respect medicine. I learned that medicine was dangerous and never to be offended or simply taken for granted.

Though most people believe that *sabeeha* stones are crystals, they aren't. One may encounter a *sabeeha* on a wilderness walk, twirling around in a dust devil. It must be captured while tumbling around in the air, because once on the ground, it becomes barely visible.

There must be hundreds of stories about the powers of *sabeeha*. Some tell of *sabeeha* following a person for days, hovering just above and behind the person's head, and at night darting and zigzagging about the bedroom. Snakeskirts maintain that if you are meant to carry a *sabeeha*, it will find you.

The wrapping in which *sabeeha* are kept is a small piece of brain-tanned skin that has a smoky smell. Songs are sung to the *sabeeha* while it is unwrapped, and each song has special words that must be said. To acquire a *sabeeha* without the empowering songs is to acquire nothing. When a *sabeeha* is unwrapped, a small dot of specially prepared red paint is pressed with a flicker quill below the left eye of the owner.

Let me tell a story I heard from an old man who lived over in Wilberton. His name was Pritchlynn. He was going blind because of cataracts and took his problem to the water, as they say. He had gone out into the forest until he stood facing a boiling, rushing stream. "Oh holy living one, oh long one," he prayed to the torrent. "You are a great wizard, oh ancient one. You fail in nothing that you attempt. My eyes are covered over with film, and I am going blind. I ask the little green frog to help me preserve my sight. I ask the dragonfly. Mink, help my eyes stay alive. Now listen. There is nothing you can't do. You promised my clan you would always help. Give me some relief."

As he was praying, he felt a strange presence, but when he looked, he saw nothing. His eyes were drawn to the ground, where there was a strange-looking plant he didn't recognize. He turned back to the water to continue praying.

In the middle of his prayer for good eyesight to return, he felt the presence again, and again he shifted his gaze to look. There stood a small traditionally dressed Native girl. She was pretty, and she was smiling at him.

Thinking he had lost his mind, the old man stepped away from the child. She addressed him in the Choctaw language. "I can help you," she said. "Bend forward and look me in my eyes."

The old man, still in a state of bewilderment, bent and did as he was instructed. He was completely mesmerized by the little girl's exquisite face and shiny black eyes. She stared at him intently. Suddenly, she spit in both of his eyes. The old man stumbled backward. He rubbed his eyes and blinked. It was as though a new light flooded the morning. By degrees, he began to see better. He stood up, dumbfounded. The little girl said again in Choctaw, "Put out your hand."

When he did so, she spit once more. But this time she spit out a tiny *sabeeha* stone the size of a seed. It glowed with an inner light. "Ho," she said, smiling. "You are a humble man and devoted to the spirits. This stone will allow your new eyes to see into the future. What is hidden from others will now be in your sight. Use this power wisely, and keep this stone with integrity." After she said this, her shape imploded downward. Where she had stood was a wilted, dead plant.

Pritchlynn became a famous diviner, and people from Oklahoma and other nearby nations consulted him. He was known as the man who could tell where your road would lead. The *sabeeha* gave him this extraordinary power.

As Sara and I drove up into the maze of mountains, the dusk turned to night and I cut on the headlights. I was headed for a certain secluded cabin that belonged to a friend who could help me find out what was going on, catch up on gossip, and learn who had died and who was still living. The man I was looking for had a long name that ended in "tubby." Everyone who knew him called him Tub.

When I saw my road, I slowed and left the pavement for gravel. We were going gradually uphill. Three miles later the road dipped abruptly, then climbed. My pickup coughed and chugged desperately, and the spinning rear tires showered a rooster tail of stones behind us. Sara yelled out a curse, which was followed by another caustic remark mumbled under her breath. I finally made it over the hump and took a quick right down a dirt path lined by tall pines. Crossing a field, I parked on the other side near a fenceline.

I got out. "Sara, you stay here. Hand me that flashlight in the glove box."

Sara handed it to me, and I clicked it on. I shut the truck door. "See you in a few minutes," I said.

"Don't leave me stranded out here all night," she called after me.

I climbed the barbed-wire fence and started down the path that led to Tub's cabin. The night was full of animal sounds and phantomlike shapes that were accentuated by the flashlight. The moon was so low in the star-spangled sky that it added no light. A soft wind came up, or perhaps I just became aware of it. On either side loomed tall trees, with the trail forming a long corridor between them. Soon, though, the path veered away from the trees and sloped through a ravine. I tripped and slid a little going down. After climbing up a steep incline to the other side, I fumbled with the flashlight on top and reclaimed my bearings. It was a straight shot along Neshoba Creek to Tub's place.

The knoll of a hill and thick trees sheltered the cabin from the north wind. It was only a little ways now, and I could make out a mellow light coming from the irregular windows. I walked past a stand of red oaks and was soon at the threshold. I knocked.

Tub's voice boomed, "Who the hell's out there? Leave me alone before you get capped!"

I was about to answer when the cabin door pulled back and a snarling dark form hit the screen door, which flew open, bowling me over backward onto the ground. I went down with my feet in the air. The snarling form turned out to be a vicious Chowmutt that was now poised on my chest, growling and dripping saliva — ready to tear out my throat.

"Nice dog," I managed to say to the two fiendish eyes staring in my face.

Another large form, a man, appeared suddenly. He was carrying a kerosene lantern extended away from him. I turned toward the light and became aware that I was looking into the barrel of a long revolver. It was pointed carelessly, it seemed to me, between my eyes.

Tub held the lantern higher. I felt a close scrutiny. His face softened. "David Carson. Is that you?" he asked, puzzled.

"Yeah, it's me. Help."

"Ofahoma, get off of him — right now! Friends. We're friends."

Ofahoma wasn't entirely convinced and continued to growl, turning away hesitantly.

"You been feeding that dog gunpowder again, Tub?" I asked. I had to crawl around on all fours before I managed to get to my feet.

"Man, you're lucky I didn't shoot you," Tub said apologetically. "I thought you was some kind of revenuer or something."

"No, it's only me. Why 'Ofahoma'? What kind of name is that? You name that damned dog after me, Tub?"

"Yeah, I did. Come on inside."

"Sara's out in the pickup. I should go get her first."

"Sara — great," Tub said. "How's she doing?"

"We both seen better days," I answered.

Later, Sara and I stowed our gear in a corner. Tub's cabin was surprisingly tidy for him. There were a couple of shotguns, a .30-30, and a bolt-action .22 in the corner nearest the door. The rest of the space looked like a wizard crib. There were various animal skins nailed to the log walls. The three of us were sitting at a battered table. The main table because it was the only one in the cabin, it was littered with all sorts of ammo, a rattlesnake skin and several removed rattles, a jar of some kind of tree sap, a dirty sock, some loose change, a letter in the penciled handwriting of a six-year-old addressed to Tub care of general delivery, jars of various herbs, a bowl of vinegar, and many miscellaneous roots. The splintery old surface was stained with candle wax and had an impossible-to-count number of cigarette burns. I stared silently at the agglomeration of goods. Tub and Sara seemed relaxed and were talking animatedly about mutual friends. I was just thankful that my anguish about my son wasn't contagious.

Tub leaned back on the wooden legs of his chair. "Did you eat? You want a snack?" he asked. "Are you hungry, Sara?"

"Always." I was the one who answered.

"I've made up some son-of-a-gun," Tub offered.

"What kind is it?" I asked. He was referring to a kind of stew made from the organs of an animal — intestines, brains, liver, heart, kidney, and so forth. It is really delicious, if you care for that sort of thing.

"It's deer son-of-a-gun," Tub said. "I shot it about two nights ago. Still fresh."

"I'm a vegetarian," Sara said, a bit annoyed. "And I know why," she added, tossing me a narrow-eyed glance. "One time we kids had to eat crow gut pudding for a week. He fed us kids rattlesnake and said it was pizza. Don't you have some peanut butter?"

"Got that too. Just picked up my commodities," Tub said. "Son-of-a-gun for your dad and a peanut butter and jam for Sara."

He went outside for a moment and came back with a stew-holding gallon jar and sandwich fixings. He didn't have a refrigerator — no electricity. Just the creek and the great outdoors. He puttered around, getting his two-burner kerosene stove going to heat up the son-of-a-gun and making sandwiches.

"What brings you and Sara out in this direction?" Tub asked after awhile.

"I need help from Mary Gardener. I've had several dreams about her lately. I need to see her. It's important. Is she still around these parts?"

Tub shook his head sadly. "Nobody knows what happened to Mary," he said at length. "She just sort of disappeared. No one knows if she's alive or dead. People say they've seen her over in Atoka and Okemah, if that's any help. I don't know. There are all sorts of strange reports about her. One person said she saw her up in Toronto, Canada."

"Sort of like Elvis, huh?" Sara said.

Tub spread some peanut butter on white bread. He gestured with the knife. "Yeah, I guess so. Mary would be in her nineties. I have the feeling she's still alive. I don't think Elvis is. I think I'd know if she had passed on because we were all so close. She's just too damned ornery to die on us."

Tub soon had the food on the table.

"There," he said, taking a seat. "Now, the last thing I heard about you, Carson — you were living with someone named Brenda — a Beverly Hills showman."

"Her name wasn't Brenda," Sara said, frowning. "I think it was Glenda. My dad went completely off his nut for her."

"Neither name," I corrected. "And the word is shaman, Tub. Not showman. She wasn't a shaman, not in my books anyway."

Tub scratched his cheek. "No? Well, what is a shaman?"

"You know. Like a powwower — a conjure. Like Mary Gardener. Like us. Like we were supposed to be, anyway. A shaman is a conjure."

Tub chuckled. "I don't do much powwowing anymore. People are less and less interested. I wish I could get rolling again. What about her? That woman?"

Sara whistled sarcastically, shaking her head in mock pity and disgust while I filled him in.

Tub looked at me with concern. "You sound bitter. It's bad medicine to stay such a long way from the nation, you know." He always referred to southeastern Oklahoma as the nation. He went on, "You'll be back someday."

"I was doing just great until this thing happened with Jason." I told Tub all about Jason's wreck, how at first I didn't know if my son was going to live or die. When I got to the hospital in Iowa City, Jason was disoriented. He had smashed his head pretty hard and had suffered almost complete memory loss. When he learned of his best friend's death, he became dangerously suicidal. It was so unlike Jason, it frightened me. The doctors replaced his hip and screwed two iron rods in his legs, but then, on top of the tragedy of his dead friend and battered body, the judicial system handed him a verdict of guilty. I felt my son needed spiritual and psychological help. "That's why I want to see Mary."

We sat in silence for a few moments. Then Tub began to reminisce about Jason, about the times they had fished together and what a great outdoor person he is. He spoke of Jason's good-heartedness and generous nature. "I had to hide the flyswatter from that boy. I can't believe anyone would ever make Jason a criminal. They should meet some of the people here in the Kiamichis or over in the Big Thicket in Texas. Those are some real bad criminals. They'll shoot your ass for a dime. Hell, they'd probably do it for free."

"You know, Tub, in nature you often see a helpless and beautiful creature go down, get swarmed and ripped apart — law of the jungle. But that doesn't mean I have to accept it when it happens to my son."

Our conversation drifted over old times. We told stories and had a lot of laughs. The first streaks of dawn were in the sky when we walked out of Tub's cabin to my pickup. Tub seemed sad to see us go. "We used to have some good times with Mary, didn't we?" he said.

"Yeah, we did," I agreed. "Mary was the jewel of the Kia-michis. She helped a lot of people. Don't guess anything like conjuring will ever come our way again."

Tub shrugged. "It's ancient history, I think. It's over. No one wants me to do powwowing. They haven't wanted it for better than ten — make it twenty or thirty — years. They all go to white medicine now. Those big horse pills is what they go for."

"It's their loss," I said. "Conjuring had a lot to offer in some instances."

We stood around awkwardly for a few more minutes, toeing the ground and telling jokes, remembering things about Mary Gardener. I looked over at my truck. Sara had some good memories to share about the weeks she and Greta, her sister, had spent on vacation with Mary. It was the first time I had heard her speak of it. I don't know what happened to Sara and Greta that summer. They came home from Mary's greatly changed. They had developed a supercharged sense of humor and, at the same time, seemed a lot more serious. I thought Mary had slipped something in their granola.

Tub frowned, then brightened. "Hey, I've got an idea. Write about powwowing the spirits. Put me in it. Make me a star."

"Ah, too hard," I said after thinking about his suggestion.

"I'll get you a *sabeeha*. Just be sure and say I'm ruggedly handsome, okay?"

"Deal," and I laughed.

"The sun's coming around strong today," Tub said, looking to the east. "Why don't you two stick around awhile longer? What's your big rush? We can all go fishing. Don't you want some blackened catfish? It's better than my son-of-a-gun."

Sara turned green. Tub put his arm around her and squeezed.

"Next time, Tub," I said. "Right now, we've got a long haul and best be on our way."

Sara and I climbed inside the cab, and I drove off slowly. I could see Tub waving in the rearview mirror. It had been good to see this old friend.

One

*I*FIRST HEARD ABOUT MARY GARDENER in Tony's, an after-hours club on the east side of Oklahoma City. The place was owned by two brothers, Jack and Leaford Potts. Both had graduated from Tuskegee. Leaford had been highly decorated for bravery in Korea and was one of the first black officers to lead white troops in combat in that far-off land. Jack, the more gregarious of the two, would greet new arrivals at the club and always managed some clever exchange with them. I had become good friends with both.

No one needs to be reminded that Oklahoma was Little Dixie and had been since the aftermath of the Civil War. I won't forget so soon. One Indian name for the state was Land of Sleeping Giants with Nightmares, which made a lot of sense to me. Those were days of segregation. When Leaford came home from the military, he was a captain and had a chest full of medals, including a Purple Heart. Yet the only place we were able to celebrate in mixed-race company was at the bus station. We had a little dinner party at the cafeteria there, Jack, Leaford, three women, and myself. True, I felt somewhat disconcerted when we had to use different restrooms. But I had seen many No Indians Allowed signs posted in various parts of the state. I would go into those places now and again and have a beer, though I often wondered how they would treat me if the management got wind of my Indian ancestry.

Chet Baker, the famous jazz trumpet player, came into Tony's one night. He had several 45s out. He was probably visiting his parents over in Choctaw. He had picked up a horn when he was a kid and now was making jazz history. I wondered if he was part Indian: he looked it. Jack asked him to leave and he did — no questions, just turn around and get back through the door. Later, I asked Jack why.

"I don't have anything against him," he said. "He's a great musician. I have his records on the box. But he'll bring the heat if he hangs out here. He uses a lot of drugs — it's obvious. The police will close us down. The man is looking for any excuse. They don't like integrated clubs. I just don't want to make it easy for them, that's all."

Tony's had unquestionably the best jukebox in Oklahoma, with tunes ranging from King Pleasure to Phineus Newborn Jr. Small and intimate, the joint was usually hopping. It had a uniquely soulful atmosphere enhanced by fantail goldfish swimming around in a large plastic bubble installed in the ceiling. The tank was made from a surplus jet airplane canopy. In the mellow light, the goldfish cast soft shadows as they slowly transited the bowl. Below them, there was a horseshoe bar along with several booths. Customers were characters, both black and white. The place served a mean coffee and good barbecue sandwiches and ribs.

Late one night, I was having a cup of laced coffee with Chuck Collins, whom I had met a few days before. We were sitting in an out-of-the-way corner booth. Chuck was a beatnik poet complete with a Vandyke beard. He had done a stint in Hollywood and had lived in New York and read his poetry at the Five Spot on the same bill with Thelonious Monk. For me, this was like an astronaut who had gone to Mars and returned to Oklahoma to tell us earthlings about the scene up there. To put it mildly, I was highly impressed. All in all, Chuck had bombed out, but that didn't matter to me. No doubt, he had returned to Oklahoma looking for a handout, but he was older and experienced, and I was interested in both poetry and prose, his chosen fields. When he'd suggested I read various books on writing, I did, but I couldn't understand their rarefied principles. They were gobbledygook as far as I was concerned, so I asked him to explain.

The most important thing a novice writer like me could learn, Chuck said, was to put a sense of space in a story. "Without spatial proportion, you're dead. If you really want to be a writer, study color, visual proportion, mathematics, and geometry. Those are your keys. Study the Greeks."

"Hey, don't you be talking about that Pluto and Aristotle. You make it sound like you have to be Albert Einstein just to turn a phrase. Writing can't be that complicated."

"Well, it is, believe you me. More than you'll ever know. Just look at me. I landed right back here in Oklahoma, where I started. You go places, but that's the kind of thing that can happen to you if you're a writer." He blinked tiredly, gazing upward at the goldfish. He sighed and then looked me squarely in the face. "Listen, there are cryptic levels to writing most people never catch — and to write you have to both catch and throw. Not only that, but you are in competition with newspapers and movies. The market for literature is going to dry up." He stated this with a voice full of emotion.

"I think I'm in the old Pentecostal writing school," I said.

"Oh? And what's that?"

"You just rare back and let 'er rip. Roll on the floor, speak in tongues, whatever."

"Spoken like a true Okie. That just shows how pedestrian you really are."

"Where'd you grow up?" I asked, trying to shift the conversation in another direction. I could see he was getting annoyed with me. I was being too flippant. Writing was obviously Chuck's passion, but his intensity made me anxious. I thought he might be a bit of an oddball, prone to violence or at least violent outbursts. I was probably projecting my own persona, but I didn't like to see it in others.

"I was raised over in McAlester," he said. "You know that town?"

Chuck went on to describe his upbringing. Polio had struck him when he was in his teens. His legs became partially paralyzed, and he couldn't walk without the aid of braces and crutches. His mom took him secretly to see Mary Gardener.

"What did she do?"

"She used a drum. She drummed to my legs, and she did a couple of other things. She used a rattle and did hot hand massage."

"That's it? You mean bang bang on a drum? And she rubbed you. That's what she did?"

"She blew cigarette smoke on me. And she gave me some herbs that helped a lot."

"C'mon?"

"No, I'm telling you. She did things with her mind that shifted me. I don't know how she did it. All I know is that I was able to walk. I got rid of my crutches because of her. I limp pretty bad, but at least I'm not totally crippled. I can get around."

I made up my mind that I wanted to meet Mary Gardener if I ever got half a chance, and I wrote her name down in a little pocket notebook. When I was about seven years old, I too had been suddenly paralyzed. I was taken by ambulance from the southern part of the state to St. Anthony's Hospital and placed in a small, glass-enclosed room. Many doctors wearing white face masks visited me. None of them knew what was wrong with me, but they told my mother that I would be paralyzed for life. And I lay there day after day, unable to move.

The one thing I liked about my predicament was the great deal of interest people showered on me. I was a pet to the doctors and nurses. They all smiled at me. I knew it was because they felt sorry, but I didn't care. I must have craved attention. Many visitors brought me presents. My brother, Rex, gave me a chameleon that he had gotten at a carnival in Ardmore. The tiny creature was able to run about on a thread leash that a nurse pinned to my pillow. I spent a lot of time in communion with it. Its skin would change color, and I realized this was a kind of language — that this was the chameleon's way of saying, Howdy, big guy, or, You're welcome to look at me, but don't even dream of touching.

My mother, who I called Mama Opal, visited me now and again when she could. She had to drive about a hundred miles in order to see me. Once she came with an old Indian man from down around Carter County. His first name was Oliver, but I don't remember his last name. He was a bit wary in the hospital setting, and first made sure no one was watching us.

He laughed at the chameleon. With a thick accent, he asked, "Where did you get that?"

"My brother gave it to me."

He looked me over and made some hand signs over my body. He blew on me. He said some Indian words and put a little beaded bundle the size of a quarter under my pillow.

When he was done, he said, "Opal, your boy has spider sickness. We're going to do a pray for him, and he's going to be all right. I just told that chameleon to eat the spider causing all the trouble."

"I hope you're right, Oliver," Mama Opal said. "I hate to see him this way. I haven't known what to do."

"I know this spirit. It's a bad one. It comes on like a black widow bite. You just have to give it some time."

Sure enough, just as Oliver predicted, about two weeks later I wanted to get out of bed and did. I was walking to the nurse's station when I fell down, causing a commotion.

A nurse came running up. "You can't walk! You should be in bed! What's the matter with you? What are you doing?"

I knew that my chameleon had eaten the spider spirit, just like Oliver said. But I couldn't tell them that. The doctors remained puzzled. I was an even bigger celebrity for awhile, and everybody came to see the boy who had mysteriously recovered. Pretty soon the novelty wore off, though. I was held for observation for two more weeks, then released.

After saying good night and leaving Tony's that early morning, I went home to dream about a huge spider. Her name was Henrietta, and she was as large as a horse. I called my mom and told her about my dream. She said it was a major good luck sign to dream about such a large spider. She told me to be especially careful not to kill one.

Two

OKLAHOMA IN THE EARLY SIXTIES was a strange place. I had joined a group of about fifteen people who met informally every week and were unofficially known in the community as the "UFO nuts." I was the youngest person to attend. We discussed such topics as poltergeists, Ouija boards, hypnosis, spirits, Nostradamus, astrology, life after death, mind over matter, Zen Buddhism, UFOs, yoga, extrasensory perception, the work of J. B. Rhine at Duke University in parapsychology, LSD-25, as it was called in those prehippie days, as well as various books like the works of Swedenborg and Blavatsky. Often the meetings would degenerate into torrents of absurdity. Was it possible, for instance, to walk through a wall or to walk on water? Such questions today seem hackneyed and a waste of time. Back then they were of enormous philosophical importance to me. I was looking for answers.

Most of the participants, but certainly not all, would have been considered eccentric. It would be normal to assume that as a group they were genial by nature, but that wasn't the case. Some were mean as a coachwhip. Often heated arguments would rage. I wondered now and again if the meeting wouldn't erupt in a fistfight. Some hothead would demand apologies, and when none was forthcoming would walk out — quit and good riddance. So it was a kind of combative group in the end.

One man there greatly interested me. His name was Johnson Bob. He was an Indian. I later learned that he had gone to Central State and graduated with a degree in biology. He had

spent a year or two in medical school but for some reason became disillusioned with medicine and dropped out. Like me, he
never said much — not that he was aloof. He seemed to have
gained a serenity none of the rest of us had achieved. He spoke
in a different manner, not challenging or argumentative. Yet,
upon reflection, it was his words that often stirred the pot and
caused havoc. After observing him carefully, I became convinced
that he was the hidden root of the periodic vicious arguments
that would break out. And I was also more and more certain he
did this on purpose.

"I'd like to talk to you," I said, one night when the meeting
was dispersing. "Do you think you could manage it?"

"Well, sure. When?"

"How about now? Let's go have a beer."

We met at a bar off of 13th on Kelly, not far from University Hospital. It smelled of dank beer and was poorly lighted. It
was a fairly quiet little place frequented by resident medical stu-
dents, nurses, hospital personnel, and a few doctors. Normally, I
liked my bars to be a bit more boisterous. Oddly, though, I didn't
feel out of place.

We both ordered a beer. Johnson looked unblinkingly and
directly into my eyes. His mouth was suspended between a frown
and a smile that could go either way. The expression made me
feel a little nervous.

"Well?" he said.

"I just wanted to ask you a few questions."

"Please, go ahead." Finally, he grinned. "Shoot."

"I was wondering why you attend those meetings," I said
evenly.

He chuckled. "Maybe I'm like a coyote," he said. "The coyote sees everyone going to church. He says to himself, 'I will be
a religious coyote. I will fool the Great One and I will go to
church too.' So coyote joins the party. Those meetings are a sub-

stitute for religious experience, don't you see that? Those folks could just as easily be leaderless communists or nazis. They have a yearning, a need. They're seeking the authoritative voice. They are seeking identity. Holiness is with the coyote always. I realize that. I just want to prove it to myself. It's easy to nudge those know-it-alls into a bone-picking battle. If we handed out knives beforehand, there'd be a lot of carnage. Most religious people will have a good go at each other's throat. You asked me and I've answered you, so it's my turn. Why do you listen to all that horse puckey?"

Johnson did have the appearance of a coyote suddenly. "I had the feeling that you were playing with everyone," I said.

"Maybe I was," he said. "Now you should answer my question."

"Well, I think I go there to learn something. I don't know. I'm seeking, I guess."

"Now look," Johnson said. "About all you are ever going to learn at those meetings is how to act smug and pompous. They really are a bunch of imbeciles, fakers, and bigots. I wouldn't bother to tell you this, but you're really sucking it up. Don't be so serious. If you're that thirsty, I believe I have something better to offer you."

"What's that?"

"Have you ever heard of peyote?"

"Yes, but I've never taken any."

"There's a little group who meet out at my place, and we all take peyote, this medicine. We sing and celebrate. Want to come and try it out?"

Three

A LARGE MOON WAS UP as I drove to the meeting. I was full of anticipation. KOCY was playing the Platters. The night was at hand when I pulled up in the gravel driveway of Johnson Bob's country house and cut the engine. There were several cars parked randomly off to the side. The house and other buildings were nestled in a clearing, but all around was a tangle of high trees, bushes, and vines. I was met by Johnson's wife, who came out to my car. She was a thin, pretty woman in her late twenties, pleasant but rather reserved. Later I found out she was a nurse at one of the local hospitals. Her name was Julie Bob.

She led me down a flagstone path around the main house to a barn in back that had been converted into a kind of meeting place. Julie Bob tapped on the door, and a few moments later Johnson opened it. He greeted me warmly. "We were just getting going," he said. "Come on in and meet everybody."

The mood was quiet and reverential, I thought, as I met the various people. Everyone was unmistakably Indian except for me and Julie Bob. Altogether, there were nine of us — five women and four men. Flat cushions lined the walls, and everyone sat back down. I took a seat on one of the cushions. I didn't realize it, but I had sat next to Mary Gardener. I thought of her only as some new Mary who had come into my consciousness.

Because of the high, arched ceiling, the former barn had a churchlike feeling. The air was spiced with aromatic sage and other incense. The room was long and bare of furniture. Christian pictures hung on the walls. The polished brick floors gleamed. I had never been in a room so spartan. At the far end was an altar with a large poster of Jesus at Gethsemane hanging above it. Guttering candles cast a warm light and infused the picture with life. A burning red lightbulb lit the rest of the room, giving it an eerie tinge.

I kept looking at Mary Gardener out of the corner of my eye. She was striking. I could sense a great power surrounding her. I felt drawn into it, and after awhile I began to think of her as a confidante. I didn't really know any of the people involved in this meeting. We drummed and rattled and sang a few songs. They were all simple Christian songs such as you might hear on a Bible Belt radio station. I wasn't a churchgoing person, and I began feeling slightly uncomfortable. I wondered if I shouldn't just quietly leave.

I leaned over to Mary and asked why there were so many cheap Christian pictures in the room.

"If it offends you, don't think about it," she answered in a low voice. "Christ points the direction in these peyote meetings. Read your Bible — it's full of hidden meanings and words of power. Consider only the inside shadow of the book. Maybe I'll explain to you what that means sometime. Christianity is distorted. You see, the inside shadow is what is real. Let your sweepers clear your path. Christ taught about the shadow land, a within place of great power and beauty. If you look at the world shadow, of course the Bible will be confusing. The Bible has cast a very long and very distorted outside shadow. It's good that you are here. Let the medicine teach you — the grandfather peyote. He's the wise one here and offers help to all who come to meet with him."

Her words struck me as meaningful, except I didn't understand what she was trying to say other than, "Pipe down. Don't panic." Tin plates of sliced peyote medallions were passed around. Mary leaned toward me and told me to eat six no matter how difficult. This medicine was so bitter I could hardly swallow it — bitter as gall. The taste made me shiver with nausea. I thought I was going to have to run outside and throw up, but the wave of nausea seemed to diminish more and more. This took a few minutes. With each passing moment, I felt less sick. It was as though my body had to wrestle with the sickness and lose, then it was better.

I must have sat there for a long while, keeping time with a small turtle-shell rattle and pretending to sing. Warm and soft sensations were coursing through my arms and legs but mostly my stomach. I kept swallowing as if some invisible thing was caught in my throat. A plate of yellow wilted apples came around. I declined. Julie Bob offered me some fry bread and dried apricots. I wasn't hungry. Slices of peyote were again passed, and I ate several more, gagging them down without chewing very well. This was followed by a tin plate of corn-shuck-and-tobacco-leaf cigarettes. Each cigarette was tied together with three pieces of tiny red thread, one at each end and in the middle.

I lit a cigarette and took several breaths. They were strong and quite different from commercial cigarettes, rather like a harsh but sweet cigar. The taste seemed to blend and balance with the peyote. I exhaled several times. There was a distinct layer of smoke hovering about chest height. Then I noticed that spirals of brilliant color were raining down on the room and on all of the people in it. I wondered why it hadn't stuck out before, it seemed so apparent. The religious songs we were singing began to take on a kind of beauty, and I could hear each individual vocalization. The songs were actually miraculous. How could it be that so many distinct sounds blended so perfectly together?

Then I became aware that Mary was staring at me. She looked suddenly like some priestess of long ago. I could see jewel-like veins in her face and arms. Her smile came down over the centuries, and it was as though I saw her for the first time. She was certainly some kind of queen or sacred mother. I was her subject. She motioned with her rattle for me to join in. Evidently, I had been sitting there awhile doing nothing with my rattle except holding it out in front of me. I joined in.

I rattled for perhaps fifteen minutes. When I shut my eyes, I again saw Mary Gardener, as real as at any other moment. She was standing on a hill and wearing sacred garments that had supernatural powers. She had on a tobacco-flowered apron. All about her clung eagle down. Red paint slashed her face. Behind her was lightning, and before her were great whirlwinds. She signed for me to come up to her. I began to climb the hill.

Astonishingly, we were all suddenly in a circle. I hadn't remembered moving into that position. I looked at Mary across the way. She had an eagle feather hanging down from above her left ear. Her face was lovely and impressed me greatly. For some reason, I held my left arm straight out with my fingers pointed upward. Mary did the same. I felt a momentary flash of heat as her energy shot across the circle and connected to my hand. I was sure this connection was visible to everyone. It joined us. I could certainly see it. As I studied a portion of the energy, it flattened out and became a spreading mist. A white light fell from above into the center and settled the mist downward to the floor. It rolled and boiled and became a molten silver pool. This pool became a huge polished mirror filling the circle.

Everyone began to look down into the mirror. Out of it, images would take form and rise up. People were laughing. Some were sobbing. I realized that the mirror was revealing something to each person at the peyote meeting. When I looked down, a beautiful plant grew up and flowered. Then it plunged back in just as suddenly and was sucked into the mirror pool. Books rose up and were swallowed. I didn't know if these were books I would read or write. Other forms were coming, and I became afraid.

My fear jolted the pool. I quickly became aware that I was still holding out my arm, but the pool had disappeared and the trail of energy leading to Mary was weakening. I became very weary and shut my eyes. When I again opened them, everyone had gone outside for some reason. I could hear them singing and rattling somewhere away from the barn. I was still sitting across the glistening brick floor from Mary.

"Where is everyone?" I asked. My voice sounded far away.

"They went out for a sunrise prayer session. I decided to stay and look after you."

"Thanks," I said.

She was smoking and smiled at me between puffs. She seemed very beautiful, like one of those art nouveau Indian maidens. Her age had disappeared completely, and she could have been a young woman. Rays of color poured out of her like strips of ribbon floating in the wind, only they were obviously part of the energy around her. My heart swelled with love.

She took a suck on one of the corn-shuck medicine cigarettes. From where I was sitting, the tip flashed and glowed like a brilliant ruby. When it dimmed, it formed a cat eye and floated in front of Mary's own eye. Then she exhaled the breath of smoke. A billowing cloud rose just above her head, carrying the cat eye in it. The eye seemed to be studying me. Then I recognized the shape of a lynx. It swung its head and looked at me squarely with both of its ruby eyes. This mysterious apparition scared me, but that was nothing compared to what followed.

The lynx began walking toward me, slowly at first. I recoiled and must have gasped out loud. This Mary was some kind of witch, and she was sending this freckled lynx cat to kill me. It was at that moment that it jumped, and when it hit, it somehow slid inside of me and disappeared.

I screamed, "Don't!" I had thrown my arms up to protect myself and fend off the beast. My knees began to jerk involuntarily.

Mary smiled. "What?"

"Don't do that," I cried. I was shaking badly and couldn't control myself. I wondered if I had lost my mind. "Did you see it?" I asked in a frightened whisper. I must have been cowering.

"Yes, I saw the smoke cat. I created it for you. Was there something unusual about it?"

I stammered and realized I was in way over my head. "I guess not," I finally managed to say. "No. It was just a cat — a real pretty one at that."

"Good. It means the smoking lynx is willing to lead you through the sacred villages of the ancestral tobacco. I think you should go with her, for she is a great instructress."

Four

A FEW DAYS LATER, I telephoned Johnson Bob from work. I thanked him for inviting me to the peyote meeting, told him a little bit about what happened, and said I was still reeling from my experience. I was doing my best to objectify it but wasn't having much luck.

"I wouldn't try too hard," he said. "Those sorts of things happen often around Mary Gardener. It was a great honor to have her attend, you know."

"That was Mary Gardener?" I said, putting together what I had been told. I realized she was the medicine woman Chuck Collins had mentioned. "I thought she lived down in the mountains."

"She does. She doesn't often travel far from her home down there in the Kiamichis. People from all over go to see her and later speak of her miraculous powers. She has several male and female apprentices. I've considered asking her to teach me, but my wife doesn't like the idea. Conjuring would complicate our lives too much, and right now we're settled in for the long haul.

"Mary's one of the last authentic practicing snakeskirts in Oklahoma. Many people will testify that her power can be frightening. I noticed you left in a hurry just as soon as the meeting was over. She must have really got to you. You looked like you'd been hit in the head with a ball-peen hammer."

"To put it mildly," I said. "Driving home, the front of my car was a block long. I was absolutely scrambled. That's why I'm calling. I don't think I'll be attending too many peyote meetings, not for awhile. I'm not used to it, and I need to get this first one under my belt before I try any more.

"By the way," I said. "Mary Gardener helped a friend of mine walk after the doctors had given up on him."

"That doesn't surprise me."

I repeated Chuck Collins's story.

"I could tell you a dozen similar stories. I could tell you some that would stand your hair on end. You ought drive down and see her. She liked you. She told me so herself."

"Maybe I will," I said. "Obviously, a person could learn a lot from her — that is, if she were willing to teach them. Do you think she knows any love medicines? You know, something to capture the heart of some gorgeous creature?"

"It's her specialty," Johnson said with a chuckle.

Five

*I*N THE EARLY SIXTIES through the spring of 1965, I was an initiate in a hidden ring of conjure under the tutelage of Mary
Gardener. This book tells of the time I spent with her and of my
formal training in powwowing, a ceremonial method to the healing of sickness. Central to this approach was the use of tobacco
in ritual, curing, and divination.

Mary was a dark-complexioned, beautiful older woman. Tall
and slender, she wore cowboy boots, skirts or jeans, and western
tops, together with beaded Indian jewelry. Despite her age, she
was lively. Like a sapling, she could bend but would never budge
from her center. She had a wonderful feeling of calmness about
her. I wouldn't call her aloof so much as singular of purpose,
which made her seem distant at times. Sometimes her presence
made me slightly uncomfortable. She could get angry but never
perturbed. I felt nervous and awkward in the face of her unaf-
fected responses.

Mary had the curious, birdlike mannerism of cocking her
head to one side as she spoke. Her smile was often ironic, almost
imperceptible. Like many Indians, she used her hands expres-
sively, signing as well as saying. She had beautiful hands with
lovely tapering fingers. When she sat, she held herself rail-
straight, her salt-and-pepper braids hanging down in front of the
rose-embroidered material of her sun-faded shirt. She walked
with a kind of brevity of movement. She could assess you with
her gaze clearly and coldly, then suddenly her black eyes would

light up and beam. This powerful gaze conveyed much more than mere words.

Her lineage and life experience left Mary no doubts about who she was or her place in life's order. Her consciousness was unlike any I was acquainted with. I had a deep thirst for whatever it was she had, which always seemed to be just out of my reach.

Mary lived in a small, clean, humble cabin in the mountains. Her furniture was rough-hewn pine mostly. When I went to see her, she seemed at first reluctant to discuss anything but the most trivial of topics. I realize now that her lack of interest was a subtle test of my character.

"Will you teach me or not?" I finally said in exasperation.

She laughed. "So you want to join my hidden ring of apprentices, do you? You want to know powwowing secrets. I can assure you it's tedious work, work like you've never done before. You must be dedicated. It doesn't happen overnight. I advise you to think about it carefully. What I teach has been around since long before the invaders came here, but it's damned near dead. It's complicated and hazardous, and I can't think of a more useless occupation."

"I still want to learn from you. You're supposed to discourage me, aren't you? Isn't that part of it?"

"If I wanted simply to discourage you, I would tell you to get the hell out of here right now."

"Then why are you letting me stay?"

"If you must know, I saw an omen just before you came. I saw a shooting star streak by. It's a good sign. The Maker of Life is tossing away a doctoring cigarette. Perhaps He had a hand in your coming."

When I kept returning to the subject of initation into conjure practices, she finally said, "There's an art to it. Aspire to its power. It's right here before you. You don't have to go off a long,

long ways. The circle of conjure is right down where your two feet are planted. It's nowhere else.

"Teaching is always indirect. How can I take my being and place it inside of your being? That is what you are asking of me. I can rehearse you and show you the art, but this doesn't make you a power doctor. Take the necessary steps and pick things up, but be aware you will need a power within. Right now, you are running for the borderland. You may be a slow or hasty runner. Who can say? But you are already a healer, a conjure man, or you're not. You may be one of the few who make it inside this conjure house.

"Light a thousand candles for some people, and they still choose to live in darkness. Keen up your eyes. The great lodge is open for everyone. Come over to my mysterious garden. I am waiting for you. I will receive you with open arms.

"The conjure walks a trail of loneliness," Mary said. "It is a road that few others will follow — a solitary occupation. Yet you will see things no other human will see. The night will have day eyes, and the day will have night eyes. Believe me, you will walk through hardscrabble and thorny places. It's a long and difficult trail, but only then will your heart open to all that is. Yes, you must go into the beating heart of the world. By doing that you will go deep into your own heart. In that understanding is your birth as a conjure.

"You have to move carefully and slowly in order to cross the distance. You have to contain — to remember. You must construct an inner map, for without it you will be lost. You must realize, your eyes have ambushed you. You have never seen anything. Most of your life has been spent staring off into space. Your eyes have been starved to death. You might as well have been sitting your whole life in a movie house. With conjure eyes you can see once more. You can see our desperate condition."

She stared at me in silence. When I gave no answer, she

said, "Conjuring and powwowing requires total dedication. You have to keep your medicine laid by, and you have to keep in touch with it all the time. If you fool around, medicine will turn on you or even kill you."

"Yeah, I know about that. My aunt Ruby —"

"How ignorant you are, young man," Mary said, cutting me off. "You don't know what you're saying. I just said this can drive you crazy or kill you. You are confronting eternal power — the power of life and death. It's a risky doing. Would you change the course of a great river? Well, if I teach you, you will open the flood-gates wide.

"The world of the conjure is the magical world. No one commands you to make this journey. Nothing will help you except what I teach. That's the only baggage you can take to the land of the conjure. You have to know what to do on every occasion.

"Doctoring and the conjure arts were once revered. But now even our own community has turned against these things. Friends and neighbors may rile against you if you are stupid enough to tell them what you are doing. If I take you into our hidden conjure circle, you are forbidden to speak of it to anyone. In my own lifetime, this old way has stumbled. Maybe it will never get up again."

Mary opened her hands and spread them wide and empty. "There are infinite trails right here before us. Luckily, our minds can only grasp a few. We see the trails forged by others and we use them. They are the easy ones. To cut an entirely new trail is to admit we don't exactly know how to get there. But we're will-ing to try. A new trail is dangerous, and we strike out alone or perhaps with the help of another. Hopefully, a new trail takes us to a new place, but not always.

"There are so many reasons to warn against this juggling path. It is fraught with ambush and deadfalls. The way is not predictable or habitual. Often the jaws of death are all around us. But if we go on always to forge the new trail, we have lived life to the largest measure. We may be wounded and bleeding, but we don't have anything to be ashamed of. We have cut dead time to a minimum, and we have been alive from moment to moment.

"I am a conjure woman, a snakeskirt, a powwower. It's true. You come to me and say, 'Teach me.' I have traded in medicine since I was a little girl. I learned the way from my mother and my aunts. They said they were going into hiding in the twenties and thirties. Before that, no one bothered them too much as long as they kept it quiet, as long as they didn't reveal too much. People thought conjure and powwowing had something to do with sex orgies and devil worship, and they didn't want to find out any different. Conjures always encouraged the spread of these ideas. They thought maybe it would keep the unknowing away. They left it at that. Maybe it was a mistake. What did anyone care what a bunch of Indians or Negroes were doing out in the bayous and boondocks? But you can believe they came to us soon enough when they were sick or couldn't get any relief from their own black-bag doctors. I was instructed never to tell white people about the powers of powwowing and conjuring and never to treat them. There are many sad stories about what happened to us as a result of misplaced kindness to white people. I won't bother you with them. And besides, I don't want to discourage you.

"There used to be a lot of trading between conjures all the way down into South America and all the way up into Canada. That's mostly gone. Even in my time we could nearly always get what we needed. For some reason, we are now a threat to the authorities. Look around and see for yourself. Am I a big threat? Not just the authorities but even nature, seemingly, has turned against us. Some medicine and conjure plants are no longer dependable. And there are not as many as there used to be. Still, there are literally tens of thousands of plant and animal medicines. A single person can only hope to know a fraction of them. Mark my words, they will try to outlaw the plants of great power once they discover and learn of their miraculous qualities.

"Often I have considered giving up powwowing. I know how it looks from the outside to people who don't know anything about it. It's a joke. They call it hoodoo and quackery. But why should I give up my ancestors and what they taught me? I would have to die before I could do that. I will not dishonor their bones by going the way of the makers of filth. I refuse to live like them.

"My mother said that a lot of people were practicing conjure and juggling who shouldn't have been. It gave us a bad name. True, many conjures were illiterate. I have a fourth grade education at a government school myself. This isn't much book learning, but it's enough so I can read and write and speak your tongue. Most conjures can't. Many couldn't or didn't want to speak English. That's a prejudice I sometimes feel myself. Why should I speak a language the spirit of which I don't agree with?

"There still are many power doctors with wise medicine. Almost all of them have some knowledge to share. Even the worst can lend a hand in time of misfortune. But because a conjure is illiterate certainly doesn't mean they don't know what they're doing. They may know it better than anyone. They often hit the nail right on the head.

"I think the authorities want to destroy everything they can't put in a tin can or take out on the golf course with them. They want to bottle and bag everything, even their lives. They will, you know — in time. It's on their side now. We could swallow them many times over in time as they measure it by their date keeping, yet they are going to get what they want in the end — to eliminate our old ways completely. If it doesn't entertain the white tourists, it's no damned good. If it has real spiritual power, it's dangerous. Let's make a carnival out of it. Let's have the Indians parade around at county fairs and circus tents. To destroy us completely, that's all they want — to laugh and make a joke of us. Not us per se, but our knowledge. Our heritage. They know if they can kill it, they won't have to think about us anymore and that will please them to no end. Our spirits will be gone. Then they can picnic and stand high on the hill towering over us. But sooner or later they will have to clean up after themselves. They may have cheated us time and again. But they won't be able to break a treaty with *lukfi* — our sweet earth. They'll discover she'll slaughter back, and they'll find how swift it can be.

"Did you ever notice how hard it is for some white people to look at us even now — Oklahomans who have been around us all their lives? I sometimes wonder who these people think we are — savages, barbarians? Believe me, we were never as savage as they were. They won, after all, but it took them some doing. They think they've taken most everything, and yes they have. But a few of us are still around who know something more. We're the ones they hate now. We still have a life worth living while they only have premonitions that they will never come untranced.

"It is said that without the conjure, the world will change. Without the conjure, colors will have no spirit. The conjure is able to get the shadow disentangled so that a little conjure world can mix in with theirs. Their world can then sparkle or even dazzle the eye. It is the conjure who is responsible for this. If they succeed in killing us all off, their world will turn dull, gray, and ugly. Perhaps it already is. It will be a world with no heart. There won't be much left of the little rabbit looking up at the stars, just a few feeble thumps."

Six

*T*HAT'S HOW IT STARTED. I should explain that I couldn't just tramp off and take up residence in southeastern Oklahoma in order to be Mary's apprentice. I was living and working in Oklahoma City, socializing and maintaining a normal life. My job allowed me to work ten straight days with six days off. Without fail, I would leave for the Kiamichis on the tenth day after work. I would return to the city as late as possible. With twenty sick or vacation days a year in addition, I spent a lot of time at Mary's cabin. It was a fortunate arrangement.

Looking back, it was in many ways an ideal period for me. I was young, still in my twenties. I had served my larger nation in the military and had few obligations. Life was fresh. I had plenty of friends and enough money for my meager needs. I had a nice Chevy that ran well. I was renting a cheap attic apartment in a large two-story house. Much of the work to convert it I had done myself. It was comfortable, not a box, and had a lot of angles and cubbyholes. It had a fireplace for winter and access to a flat portion of roof, so I could sleep outside under the stars during hot summer nights. The place, along with my scant possessions, made me happy.

Once Mary agreed to teach me the art of conjure, our relationship immediately changed. I would arrive at her cabin as my work schedule allowed. I became her gofer, roady, and chauffeur — slave, in short. Yet there was another, more subtle dynamic involved. It was as though a binding had taken place. I was tied to her but felt sure that she was in no way tied to me. She swallowed me, and I was going to have to fight to get out. Yet I grasped that I would need her help. I had to trust her, but I was afraid of this commitment.

Mary must have sensed my internal struggle, for one day she said out of the blue, "Hold fast to me. I know the way, and I'll get you there."

I might as well confess that by nature I am a lazy person. There are many accounts of hard work and discipline married to spiritual instruction. The first phases of my apprenticeship with Mary Gardener followed this general principle. She worked me like a beast of burden. I thought I'd been through hell in Marine Corps boot camp, and I had, but Mary made my drill instructor look like an angel in comparison. Rather than go into a lot of detail about my labors for her, I will only touch on a couple.

One morning I was carrying rocks to build a wall when Mary came out and brought me some tea. I was filthy and drenched with sweat. We both sat on the wall and I was happy for the break from work.

"Is this what I have to look forward to, Mary?" I asked. "Blood, sweat, and tears?"

She took a sip of tea and smiled. "For a time, yes. Apprenticeship is known as enfoldment. It is a kind of collapsing of the known to the unknown. Once you get there, you will have to have inner strength and this will build it for you."

"You don't seem to work very hard. I mean you're always doing something but . . ."

"True, I never work, never struggle. I don't have to. I'm not addicted to work, nor do I fear it. I do just as I damned well please. But you are quite different from me. You don't know what work is. You like to stir everything up and go in all directions at once so you get nowhere. You create the illusion of work. Now that's a great mismanagement of power."

"What have I been doing? If I'm not working, what?"

"I'm sure you think you are working, but you're not. You're thinking about the pretty girls in Oklahoma City and feeling sorry for yourself because you have to do something you don't want to do. I assure you, it doesn't matter what you are doing. You have to work to get most anything done. If you learned how to care about what you are doing, work would disappear. You would let go of yourself. What you would have in its place is the great joy of accomplishment."

Worn out, I was always happy to leave the Kiamichis and get back to my job in Oklahoma City, where I could sit around and drink coffee with other employees. I listened to their complaints about their hard tasks with a shrug. My job was fun. My boss, Mr. Hart, had become a fine man in my eyes. Before, he had been something of an ogre. Other workers were put off by him. I, on the other hand, wanted to give him a hug each time I saw him and he gave me my assignments.

I was on my fourth trip to the mountains since I had become Mary's apprentice. No sooner had I arrived than Mary came out. Before I could even say hello, she told me to rake up around the place. I wilted on the spot. She said it in such an offensive way, I wanted to get back in the car and go home.

"Don't just stand there. Get busy," she ordered.

"Where's the rake?" I asked.

"What rake?"

"The rake I'm supposed to use."

"I don't have a rake."

"I should have known better than to ask," I said. I was stunned, but it did seem comical in a way. "Okay, I'll drive into town and buy you a rake if you need one. Why didn't you just say you wanted me to give you a rake?"

"I won't have a store-boughten rake on my place. I want you

to make a rake. Don't be so damned dependent. You want every-one to do for you. I want you to learn to do for yourself. Now get busy and make a rake, and use it to clean up around here."

I had never even considered the construction of a rake. About all I knew was that it needed teeth. I didn't know where to begin, but Mary had marched back inside the cabin. It took all day for me to fashion it. I used a dead redbud sapling for a handle, and I weaved some straight pieces of willow for the busi-ness end. I tied it with some silk parachute cord I had in the trunk. I kept this cord to tie items to my car's roof and donated it to the project. The rake fell apart more than once when I used it. Finally, it worked.

I was bent and raking the roots of some old chinaberry trees when Mary came out. She was gussied up, as they say around these parts.

"Don't you look nice today," I said.

Mary was wearing a beautiful hand-sewn ribbon shirt along with several Navajo silver bracelets. She didn't often wear a skirt, but she was wearing a brown cotton twill one now. She looked clean and fresh. I thought she was going to ask me to drive her somewhere. However, she said, "I want to hike up to the top of that mountain." She nodded. It looked a long way off. "You bet-ter bring some water."

I went to the well and got some, submerging my army can-teen in the bucket. I slung the belt holding the canteen over my shoulder and let it hang down my back. We started up the path, walking unusually slowly. It led through short yellow grass and various rock beds above. Grasshoppers sprang off in every direc-tion, taking cover in the scarce shade under the bent grass blades. I could see the low chain of purpling mountains — the Kiami-chis. Up higher, the sun splotched through tree boughs, throw-ing a dappled, flickering light.

The walk got progressively steeper as we neared the crest.

Meadowlarks dived by. A great family of crows in an old dead tree commenced to cawing and squabbling. The birds weren't accustomed to intruders. There were a lot of pretty flowers out, wild roses, buttercups, and other blooming ground flowers. I noticed the three-pronged tip of deer antler among some uneven stones. I picked it up. It was quite weathered and polished by the elements, and had the delicacy of a Japanese sumi ink drawing.

At the top we sat down and had a drink from my canteen. I showed Mary the antler tip.

"I think it's about time I teach you something. That piece of deer antler tells me to do some explaining. Let me see it." She took it from me and examined it carefully, rubbing her fingers on the smooth prongs. She handed it back. "Yes, it's an important omen. I am going to tell you a story, so you can begin to get the feel of doctoring. If you were a young woman, I would tell you a story about Yellow Tobacco Girl. Since you are a young man, I will speak of Yellow Tobacco Boy. The thing to know is that Yellow Tobacco Boy is the early spirit of tobacco. It is the same with Tobacco Girl. You should try to remember this story because it is your first acquaintance with the good enemy. It's your first important secret."

She motioned for the canteen once more and took a small drink. She handed it back and I took it, screwing on the chained lid. I set it between my boots and got comfortable.

Mary, deep in thought, looked out across the rolling mountains. She turned back to me and said, "These are old stories, how old I could only guess. They go back before the dog days. Anyway, it happened that Yellow Tobacco Boy saw a deer. He sent an arrow, and his arrow drove deep into Deer's flesh. Another arrow followed. And another. Deer fell to the soft grass, fainting and in shock, kicking and jerking in spasms. The luster in Deer's large eyes dimmed and smoked over while staring into this new world of death. This was the first killing of a deer.

"Deer spirit said to the young hunter — to Yellow Tobacco Boy — 'You have killed me unfairly. You have brought chaos and disorder to my quiet path. My road stops here. I have not had time to sing a death song or dance a death dance. You have not sung the little lightning song to comfort my departing spirit. For these reasons I am going to give you the first sickness.

"'You have disregarded me and my spirit but I will not disregard you. I will make a cure for the sickness. I will give it to you provided you do as I say.'

"Yellow Tobacco Boy did as he was instructed. Following Deer's advice, he went to a power spot, where he thirsted and fasted for four days. At the end of that time he heard Deer's voice from within and from without. 'You have made trial, and you have cut through it. Medicine I will give to you in keeping for your brothers and sisters. There will be medicine in your medicine.

"'Yellow Tobacco Boy, by killing me you have opened the way for many diseases to flourish. Many other animals will now cause you injury and harm. Each animal will also offer you the remedy.

"'Do not despair. I now bestow upon you soft and quieted medicine eyes with which to see the spirits of the animals. You may speak to them and learn the prevention and cure of these diseases. You must chase down these cures and find them. Let them not be lost or hidden, for they will try to elude you. You will find them near creeks or in rock crevices or other mysterious places. Once found, bundle your medicines up tightly in deer hide and keep it in a sacred and safe place. Keep it wrapped and ready to be lifted out and used for the people. Feed it often with tobacco smoke.

"'Many false people will come and try to steal this medicine. You must hide and protect it. You must keep my medicine honorably at all times because it is holy.

"'One last thing of importance. I am going to give you a

part of my breath — conjure deer's breath. Let all be respectful of this gift, for it is a great blessing. Go and use hollow reeds and blow my breath upon the sick.'

"The deer spirit vanished. Yellow Tobacco Boy found a tiny antler at his feet. It was similar to the one you have found. That deer antler was the first power object ever bestowed upon the people. I want you to begin your doctoring outfit with it, for it is a worthy find."

I sat awhile studying the prongs on the deer antler. Finally I looked up and said, "You say deer disease was first. What are some others?"

"Oh, there are so many. All the animals created sicknesses for humans. And one single animal can cause many kinds of sickness."

"Is there more than one deer sickness?"

"Yes, there are many."

"What are they?"

"Well, there's *minko* deer sickness, whitetail sickness, many deer sickness, wombling deer sickness, deer jinx eye, and jinx throat. Those are the main ones. Deer mimicry is a sure sign of deer sickness."

"What was that word you used: *minko*. What does that mean?"

"The *minko* is chief, in this case, chief of the deer. He is a small magical deer about two feet high. You can be sure he's running around here. The conventional mind does not recognize the existence of this deer. I do. No matter. What is important is that a clash with this deer causes grave illness. A *minko* deer can cripple you for life. White people call this disease arthritis and rheumatism. It's deer sickness nevertheless."

"What do you do when someone gets it?"

"The simplest medicine to use for deer sickness is a root which I will show you. This, and scratching is sometimes necessary. You may rub the area with a mash, a mix of various leaves, bark, and roots. The salve used to be made with bear grease, but now we use canned lard. There are numerous other remedies I will show you how to make and doctor with. During the preparation of most of these remedies, the conjure blows into the medicine four or more times. Deer spirit songs sung by the conjure are necessary. Blue Deer Drinking First Water should be sung first.

"As I have mentioned, deer breath is administered through a piece of hollow cane or a pipe stem. Eventually, I will show you how this is done. The cane is not only used to make animal breaths and to blow into the medicine, it is also used to communicate with spirits. You talk through the cane, pointing it in the right direction. Then you hold it up to your ear and listen for the answer."

"It sounds complicated."

"It's both simple and complex."

"So animals cause disease?"

"You bet they do. Don't ever think otherwise. Insult to animals is the prime cause of imbalance and sickness, and harmony must be restored. Animals have powers most people have never imagined."

"And did all the animals give a part of their breath?"

"Most of them did, but not all. There are many conjure animal breaths."

"Are animals the only cause of disease?"

"No, there are various other spirits which are capable of causing harm — the spirit of war, for example. Elementals can and do cause disease."

"What are the elementals?"

"Earth, wind, fire, water, and tree. They each correspond to a direction. Fire people are daybreak people. South people are dirts people. West people have water as a relative. Air is the main relative of north people. Tree people are centered. They are rare. They may have had a great vision or a traumatic experience."

"Okay, I can see that. Elements can affect your health. What are some of the other causes of disease besides animals and elements?"

"Knifewing causes a disease, a bad one. Little Man Shooting His Arrows from Above — he causes lightning sickness. There is a water sickness called little animals frolicking around in the water. What's in the sea is another. What's near the sea is another still. Many Confused People cause a disease. Sun can cause a disease and so can moon. There are various other sicknesses which I will show you and teach you about soon enough."

"Are they always treated by powwowing?"

"No, not always. Sometimes the remedy is given without it. There is no set rule — whatever works."

I was about to ask another question when Mary used the old sign language and drew two fingers across her mouth, meaning silence. She did it twice, so it meant shut up. She rolled and lit a cigarette, and the smoke winged off to her left. We sat there for a long time, not saying anything. She handed me the cigarette, and I took a couple of drags. I handed it back. She took another couple of puffs and crushed and stripped it. When Mary finally got up, there were many golden grass blades clinging to her skirt. She brushed them off and said, "Like I told you, keep that deer antler for your doctoring outfit. It's your first medicine, as it was the first medicine for the people. Come on. Let's get back."

Seven

MARY'S CABIN was little more than a shack put together from odds and ends. The foundation rose to less than a foot off the ground, and the floors were made of wide old graying planks. The porch ran the entire length of the cabin, its tin roof supported by ground-to-beam stripped cedar posts. Much of the lumber used to construct the inner walls was recycled, or should I say scrounged? The mottled and faded tongue-and-groove boards exposed blotchy remnants of earlier paint jobs, for Mary hadn't bothered to paint over the old wood. The cabin was your basic rectangle that could be divided into two squares, one on the right and one on the left as you entered the front door. The area to the right served as the kitchen and social area. To the left was an ancient iron bed where Mary slept. The bed didn't have a mattress. A wide piece of plywood sat on top of the iron springs. Various ragtag blankets were piled on the wood to cushion it. Mary's clothes hung neatly on cane poles with homemade willow-and-leather hangers. In fact, everything in the cabin was well organized and neat as a pin.

The windows were also scavenged and of various sizes. None matched. As you entered the front door, there was a large wood-burning stove near the opposite wall. To the right, many strings of herbs hung from a beam in the kitchen area. Wooden and cardboard boxes held roots. There were also a dozen or so old gallon pickle jars full of other botanicals.

The first time I drove up to Mary's cabin, I couldn't help but notice a strange shape in her yard, a grotesque tree stump that lay to the right of her front porch. It was gnarled up and gave me a spooky feeling, as though it had an almost human presence. Later, when the moon was up and showed behind it, the stump became even more alive. The weathered wood had a black spot of rot along the bottom.

One night I arrived at Mary's cabin at 11:00 P.M. As I was walking to her door, I stopped. I felt a cold shiver take me. I don't often experience such confusion and fear, but something was wrong. The stump had moved. It was farther from the cabin. It had somehow transported itself in the direction in which I had my tent pitched. The stump was stalking me.

Mary had instructed me to leave my army surplus pup tent standing out front on a permanent basis. I decided right then to move it farther from the stump, no matter how irrational the act. I would do this nonchalantly, and Mary wouldn't notice. It was probably completely stupid, but one thing was for certain: the stump had moved. My mind wasn't playing tricks on me.

I went up to the cabin door and knocked. Mary invited me in, though she had been resting. She lit a candle, and I sat at the table. She poured me a jar of very good mint tea sweetened with wild honey. As my eyes adjusted to the room, I became aware of a form in Mary's bed.

"Who's that?" I asked.

"That's Evangeline. She's my apprentice from Louisiana. Don't talk too loud or you'll wake her up."

"What's she doing up here in Oklahoma?"

"She's Cajun, a *treature*."

"What's a *treature*?"

"A *treature* is a healer."

"I never heard of it."

"There's no reason why you should. Many of the *treatures* learned from Indian healers. Evangeline has studied with me for several years now. She knows well how to prepare medicine and how to doctor with it. She has a practice at home, but she comes to see me often to brush up. Down there in New Orleans, where she's living now, root work is greatly respected."

"I've never been to Louisiana or New Orleans," I said. "I hear it's one big party."

"Until it's over," Mary said. "I grew up close by."

"I didn't know that. I thought you were an Okie like me."

"No, I'm originally from Louisiana, but here I am now. I call Oklahoma my own."

I took a long swallow from the tea jar. I could see a sheaf of blond hair protruding from a long lump of blanket on Mary's bed. "She looks young from what I can see. Is Evangeline in school?" I asked.

"No, she was in nurse's training, but she got fed up and went her own way."

"She didn't like nurse's training?"

"She didn't like getting ordered around, and she hated the business end. She didn't like where she had to work."

"You mean a hospital? I've been wondering why conjures don't have something like hospitals — a place to bring the sick?"

"When you gather together the dying so that they can die in one single place, you only give power to the death spirit. It's better for the dying person to be moved around. That way, at least, the death spirit will have to work and seek you out."

I protested. "Hospitals are there to heal and make you better. You can go there and get cured."

"Not me. I will never die in the dead house of the white doctors. Their lonesome medicine house is white like most of them. They have soft, bending beds. In there it stinks of unnatural medicines and tonics. They will dose you often by a regimen of their clock. Evil spirits like such places. Their doors are the grinning jaws of death. I don't want to be around their needle men and black-bag and blue-bottle men. Who wants medicine that runs out of a tube or is swallowed in the form of pills? Who wants medicine based on money and not on spirit? I don't. I want to die far away from this kind of medicine, with dignity, alone.

"Life has its seasons. We all roll with the tides of coming generations. If you find me dead, it will be in some pretty place. Lean me with my back against a tree. Face me toward the enemy camp, for I have always been at war with intolerance and greed. Put my conjure apron on me. Leave me my drum and rattle. Scatter tobacco over and around me. Smoke a doctoring cigarette and remember my spirit. Dance a death dance and then walk away. Celebrate my journey to the spirit land. Remember, I might be right behind you. Don't look back."

"Good Lord, don't die on me, Mary. I'll be completely lost if you do."

"No, you won't. What I have to teach is simple enough. Tobacco will do the rest. Think of tobacco as your elder brother or sister. It's much wiser than you are. Be a tobacco man. The tobacco man is the red pole man. Red pole led us. Red pole is the center of the nation. Why question or limit yourself? There's nothing so complete as a red pole man. Walk with it and use it in your everyday doings. In times of disharmony, you can lean on this spiritual pole. You will be greatly strengthened and supported by its truths.

"That is what I am trying to show you. Don't be a red pole man in the shadows. Cut to your innermost being. I don't care about the opinions of others. I want you to be a red pole man now. I want to teach so you can be powerful and secure. After all, in awhile there will be no trace of you, David. You'll be trading this world for another."

"Don't remind me. Do you think I'll ever learn?"

"Yes. To learn conjuring takes a great deal of time. Apprenticeships may last ten years. In an actual doctoring ceremony, five or six days can be as nothing for these kinds of powwowing.

Forget it and do your job. You live in a world of hurry-up doctors — I mean no disrespect. The white-robed medicine man of your world may have a good heart and want to help others. Many of them have the responsibility of more than can be humanly accomplished. They only know what their hurry-up doctor teachers have taught them.

"You don't have to look very hard for the whereabouts of sickness. It's everywhere. It is crammed in with the crammed-up way of life now. Relax.

"I will soon teach you about many plants and roots. I advise you not to hurry. If you just scrape the surface, you won't know much. Information and experience shouldn't be at war. Find one plant or root and work with that one. Salute only one flag. Marry it and be faithful to it. Sleep and dream with it. Pray to it. Show it respect and it will teach you. You don't want to be a dilettante with your medicine, do you? A smidgen of this and a smidgen of that. It's dishonorable and unworthy medicine. By little, learn them. If you truly know one medicine plant, then you will know something about all of them.

"A conjure learns of the miraculous life-giving properties all around us and learns how to use them. We note everywhere so many good and natural things, fresh air, sunshine, baths in living water at the correct temperature, fasting, blanket sweats, the human touch, and the touch of spirit. We seek the fullness of life not just for ourselves but for all of life, for the people. Conjures learn medicine. They seek the unity of all and try to instill vitality, happiness, and wisdom. If they don't at least try, they aren't a conjure. They're a hoaxer. We aren't cultists. Powwowing and conjuring are ancient. Our dear ancestors made the discoveries. They weren't floating around in some uncharted ocean. They knew what they were doing. I hope that one day you'll know what you are doing too. Right now, simply learn what you can. Now go to bed. It's getting late."

Eight

THE NEXT MORNING Mary woke me up just as dawn was beginning to break in the east.

"Have you changed your address?" she asked from outside.

"Oh, I was just a little uncomfortable," I said. "I moved my tent."

She told me to get up and get dressed. She said to come in and eat breakfast.

I lay there a minute and then sat up in my bedroll, wiped sleep out of my eyes, and pulled on my boots. When I crawled outside, I walked a little ways off from the ugly stump, then stretched and took a deep breath of the fresh air. The low sky was pink- and coral-colored just above the mountains. I could see everything in a dimmed silhouette. A cold breeze from those higher elevations rustled the tree leaves. I went to the well and pulled a bucket of water, rinsed out my mouth, and drank some. I splashed my face until I was fairly awake. Except for the thinning wind and a few bird chirps, everything was quiet.

Inside Mary's cabin, I met Evangeline. She was a small-boned, beautiful young woman. She wore a flower-print skirt that didn't match her top and she had on men's lace-up work boots. I didn't say much, and neither did she. I was put off by her presence. She seemed totally uninterested in me. I had a bowl of acorn gruel and a hot cup of sassafras root tea. A candle burning on the table augmented the sparse morning light that was coming in through the windows. The serenading birds outside finally started to liven up. A couple of magpies were already fussing.

Mary lit a cigarette and we all shared it, going around to Evangeline and then to me and back again to Mary.

"Well, everyone's up so early," I said, making conversation because of the lull.

"I thought we'd take a little walk today," Mary said.

"Where to?" I asked.

"Nowhere in particular. We'll just follow our noses and have a look around. Maybe I'll show you a root or two."

"Okay by me." As if I had a choice.

"Eva, it might be awhile," Mary said to Evangeline. "I want you to stay here and do the herb soak and make deer tobacco power water."

I was disappointed, for I'd been hoping Evangeline would come with us. I wanted to get to know her in an uncontrived way. I wasn't a very forward person and was bashful around new acquaintances, both men and women. I needed to loosen up and thought I'd be able to out in nature. That hope was quickly dashed. Mary and I were soon out the door. Mary set off at a brisk pace, and I fell in behind her. We were going into the sun in a southeasterly direction. She seemed to be leading me through an obstacle course. Before long, we encountered a tangle of shoulder-high growth. Mary disappeared through it as though admitted by some secret doorway, and I quickly lost sight of her. I was stopped cold after plunging in a slight distance. It was too dense and thorny for me. I had to beat a painful retreat.

"You'll have to climb about a hundred yards up and then come back around," Mary called through the dense foliage. I still couldn't see her. "You're going to need some practice getting through strips of thorn bushes and overgrown places."

I surveyed the difficult climb I was going to have to make in order to circumnavigate the slice-and-dice growth. It wasn't going to be easy, but it was better than getting shredded. I began to climb. The day had grown warmer. I was soon working up a sweat and was wet under the arms. When I finally managed the feat, Mary was sitting on the ground, waiting for me. I was thirsty and realized I hadn't brought any water.

"Your lack of ability cost you over a half hour. If you knew what you were doing, you'd have slipped through there in seconds." Her comment was delivered more like an observation than a scolding.

"I didn't know this was going to be the Oklahoma death march," I said. "I'm getting thirsty."

"There's a spring about half a mile from here. We'll go there."

She got up and moved quickly. She cut off obliquely, and we began going downhill. The path she took was rocky and led through clumps of yellowed grass. I stumbled, nearly losing my footing. When we retuned to level ground, I noticed several cottonwood trees in the distance between two slopes. As we neared the spot, an inviting pool appeared. I followed Mary to it.

"Old Sprinkley," she said, stooping at the water's edge. "This is good water and ought to slake you."

A trickle was seeping out of the hillside. It fell to the pool in twisting rivulets. The water had eroded a pit over time that was about fifteen feet across and maybe three feet deep at most, with a sandy bottom and mossy edges. I could see curving reptilian marks on the wet ground around it, but careful inspection didn't turn up any snakes. I knelt down, cupped some water into my hand, lifted it to my mouth, and sipped. As I did so, a water spider skimmed over the surface of the pool. I noticed some other small water bugs dipping and diving in the cold, sweet water.

"Don't swallow a water bug," Mary warned. "If you do, you'll want to heave. Water bug illness used to be so common. There's another dive-down-into-the-pond sickness, but I don't think it's water bug's fault, so I won't tell you. Water bug was maligned, I think. Nowadays there is wanton disrespect for water, and many illnesses are being hatched. If you don't believe me, ask the dragonfly of the water. Ask Water Bug Maiden."

"I believe you," I said, not exactly sure what I was believing but convinced by Mary's earnestness.

Mary's hand shot down in the water like lightning and came up just as quickly. A water bug wriggled in her palm.

"Do you miss Yellow Tobacco Boy?" she asked the insect. "You do, do you? Well, he'll be back." She smiled and submerged her hand slightly. The water bug swam off and then hit for the bottom.

"Why did you ask that question, Mary?"

"It's an old legend we tell." As Mary spoke the water bug angled back up to the surface and swam toward me.

I pointed and said, "I think she wants to hear about the legend."

"My mother once told me that the bug of the water was formed when the Master of Breath spit in a pool. I can believe it." She pointed. "Look at her. Last night she slept underneath, down on the bottom where it was safe and cool. She could see Moon's face illuminated above her on the shimmering pane of the water.

"Long ago, Water Bug Maiden was very beautiful.

"Yellow Tobacco Boy said to her, 'I'm taking you over. You are mine and you will do what I tell you to do from now on.' She had no choice.

"When Yellow Tobacco Boy got Water Bug Maiden home, he tied her up with a piece of strong deer sinew. He made her work all the time, cleaning up and taking care of him. At night, she would get overcome with weakness. He would bring her a gourd of water from her homeland, so she wouldn't die.

"Each day, Water Bug Maiden grew a little bit stronger. One morning when he woke, Yellow Tobacco Boy found himself all tied up with sinew. He was shocked, and he struggled to get free.

"Water Bug Maiden laughed at him. 'I'm taking you over,' she said. "You're mine, and from now on you will do exactly what I tell you to do.'

"She took him back to her spring and kept him prisoner there. Now his time had come to get bossed around. 'Go out and dig potatoes, wild onions, and turnips and come back and cook for me,' Water Bug Maiden ordered. 'Clean my house and fix up my place the way I like it. Don't do anything until you've done a good day's work. And remember, there's always plenty to do. There's corn to be planted, hoed, and harvested. It will need to be washed and dried and ground up. Then you can store some away. Don't just stand there idly. Hop. Go on, hop to it.'"

I cut in, jokingly, "That Water Bug Maiden sounds like you, Mary."

Mary laughed and karate-chopped the water. It flew up in my face.

"Don't interrupt me," she said, smiling. "I might forget my place."

"Okay, what happened to Yellow Tobacco Boy?" I asked, wiping the water from my eyes.

"He worked hard. He wasn't lazy like you. At night, he would become so tired and weak she would bring him a mussel shell containing fire from his home, so he wouldn't die.

"Actually, he was secretly getting stronger all the time — so strong, in fact, that one day he broke his deer-sinew bonds. He stood dumbfounded for a moment, not quite realizing what had happened. 'I'm free!' he shouted at last, throwing off the broken cords. 'I'm free! I'm free of her. I hate working, and I don't want to do it anymore. She nearly killed me. I'm going home, and, from now on, I'm going to be lazy.' After that, he set off for his own village.

"Halfway there, Yellow Tobacco Boy began to think about Water Bug Maiden. He had been made strong from work. He felt good. She was very beautiful. What would she do without him? How would she get along? Maybe she'd miss him? Maybe she would die of loneliness. But he sensed she had already let him go. The thought made him sad. He stopped in his tracks, thinking to himself. All the time now he would have to figure out what to do with himself without Water Bug Maiden's instructions. 'I did learn a lot from her,' he said to himself. 'Maybe I could learn some more. Maybe I'll return to her for just a little while.'"

"Oh no, that was a mistake," I interrupted. "He should have kept moving on down the line."

Mary splashed me again. I coughed and sputtered.

She waited for me to recover. "Some say, they have remained together in spirit ever since. She brings him fire, and he brings her water. And of course it goes without saying, this is where Yellow Tobacco Boy learned the secrets and the cures of water bug sickness."

"How do you treat this strange-sounding sickness?" I asked.

"It's best treated with pinkroot water. Pumpkin seeds will also help. Don't get it. Watch what you drink. Otherwise, Water Bug Maiden will get hold of you just like she did Yellow Tobacco Boy. You'll be dancing every which way then."

I was about to say something, when all of a sudden she drenched me again. "Come on, let's go," she said.

"What's your hurry?" I coughed. "It's nice here."

"There are watering places it's best to respect. This is one of them. *Oka nahullo*, water babies, live here. They will get annoyed if we stay too long. You don't want to stick around without their permission, believe me. Get another drink, give thanks, and let's get going. I have a great many jobs for you to do."

I drank and then sloshed off behind her.

Nine

THE NEXT DAY I finally got acquainted with Evangeline. I have an Okie twang and am quite familiar with those honey-dripping Southern voices, but this was the first time I had ever heard a Cajun accent up close. It seemed a happy tongue, and when she was at a loss for a word or two she would mutter in French. We talked for a good long time while Mary was collecting snap peas from her garden. She told me about her home. "It's hot and wet down there, you bet. Fantastic food. Great music. Emotions run high. You'll hear the loudest laughter, and you will see the bitterest weeping. You need thick skin to live in New Orleans. You need to be half gator just to get by."

"I thought I might move down there someday — all I've heard about it. You don't advise it?"

"No, it's too raw and damp. It's hot too — unless you're a bullfrog."

I glanced at Mary, who was bending over and seemed to be lecturing her raspberry plants. Evangeline turned and looked too. She gazed at Mary fondly for a long moment. "I owe so much," she said, "because I have been able to stand on my own two legs. I've been able to plant the red pole and learned pow-wowing. With what I already knew, it meshed. I've assisted in healing since I was four years old."

"Oh? How's that?"

"I grew up in the bayous. I didn't wear shoes until my gran died. My first memory is the watery swamp by our shotgun shack. My grandmother was a *treature*, she was."

"Explain that a little, will you?"

"Like a conjure, a powwower — the same. Like Mary. The name is different, that's all."

"How did you learn it?" I asked.

"I helped my gran gather medicines. Them old things I know, that's how come. That old woman knew all there was to know about swamp doctoring. She all the time made up pretty good remedies. Sickly people came to see her. My grandmother is living to a ripe old age. Then she suddenly passed on when I was thirteen. I was right with her when she went over. She told me I could be a *treature* but that I would have to learn some more."

Evangeline's gray eyes lifted to meet mine. Her face was delicate. "Maybe I shouldn't tell you. I am pregnant. The child, he is coming. I am two months now."

"Which do you think it is?" I asked, confused. "A boy or girl?"

"My baby, he is a boy. Mary told me, and she is never wrong in these matters. Mary will come to New Orleans and deliver my baby. I am happy, yes. My life, it will change."

My mouth fell open. While I couldn't say I knew Evangeline well, this bit of information was surprising. I must have stared at her in wonderment. Men never know what to do with this kind of news — it's way beyond us. We go toss a football or shoot a few hoops or do something with some other egg-shaped object. Motherhood is both mystery and magic, material and spiritual. It touches on the very continuum of life. If we're truthful, it makes us adult males feel somehow jealous and threatened, or awestruck and terrified. Pregnant women connect to something deep in consciousness. While we can create nothing really, women can replenish and repeople this world. Men know intuitively that for once we have been demoted to second string. In my conversation with Evangeline I was in some sense both speaking to this and addressing the sacred mother.

"Well, congratulations," I stammered. "I hope it's what you want."

"You bet I do."

"Will you be able to support a child?"

"Now, yes. Easy. But when I first moved to New Orleans, no. I had a lot of problems with men. I missed my kinfolk something terrible. I worked in a laundry and a bar. I didn't like either job. That's when I decided to become a nurse. I wanted to help somebody else for a change and not just please myself. Until I met Mary, I didn't realize how truly selfish and self-obsessed I was.

"Nursing school didn't work out. I came back and lived with Mary for almost a year. I wanted to get away from New Orleans. Mary never quit teaching me. Before you knew it, she was showing me roots and how to make many secret remedies. I was helping her with her powwowing and conjure work just like I did with my gran. I was learning a lot without even realizing it. Now I'm doing conjuring on my own. Mary says I'm a fledgling good conjure. I've had pretty much success. Took awhile before my name leaked out. Now everyone wants to come see me. I'm able to support myself and have a little left over. Sometime I get paid in unplucked chickens and boxes of old clothes. That's all right. She's *bon*. I guess powwowing is against the law. I'm not even sure. But you can do anything in New Orleans, legal or not — that is, if you make friends with the right set of people. I come up here to check with Mary every once in awhile. I often need her advice on curing matters. She helps me store up on the roots and herbs I need. I can always ask her if I'm stumped on a sickness. My friend Betty brings me up here when she comes to see her parents. Her kin live over in the Winding Stairs Mountains, so it's on her way. Me, I still have much to learn. So here I am."

She pulled out a fresh pack of cigarettes from the breast pocket of her flowery blouse. It was a pack of Picayune tailor-mades. She hit the pack on the back of her hand to settle the tobacco, opened it, tapped some out, and offered me one. We both lit up. "And what about you, David?"

I took a drag and coughed. "That's some strong tobacco," I said.

"It's a Louisiana cigarette. You'd never guess it. I like 'em," she said, blowing a breath of smoke. The soft wind scattered it. "If you're going to smoke her, smoke her."

"Yeah, well, you better quit," I said.

"I intend to. Mary said the same. This is my last pack until after the baby he comes, you bet."

I smoked the Picayune down to the nubbins, until it was hot to my fingers. I put it out. Then I told Evangeline a little about myself and about growing up in Oklahoma. I must have talked for half an hour, when I felt her interest level drop. It seemed easy now to talk to her, even though her presence had given me a start. She was charming. I didn't know many people making a living at what I was trying to learn. On impulse, I asked, "Do you ride horses?"

"Like the wind," she answered. "You?"

"Not as much as I'd like to," I said.

"This baby will come. We'll have to go out and ride together sometime afterward, me and you," she said. "Betty's dad has some ropers — they're old quarter horses. They'll still be there when I can again ride, good."

"Let's do it. I'm game, that is if Mary will cooperate." Just as I said it, I heard the engine of an automobile coming up the tote road. "I wonder who that is?"

"That'll be Betty. She's coming to pick me up. We're heading back."

The car came into view, and a dark woman was driving. She

pulled up and parked next to my Chevy. I walked over to the car with Evangeline, and Mary came over from the garden. First I was introduced, and then Mary and Betty hugged warmly.

"Ready to go?" Betty asked Evangeline.

Evangeline shook her head in the affirmative. "I'll get my bags."

"No hurry," Betty called.

Evangeline disappeared inside the cabin. I turned my attention to Betty. She was a tall, wiry Indian woman with laughing black eyes. I stood there awkwardly. Betty appeared to be a very happy person. She seemed on good terms with Mary but didn't pay me even so much as a never-you-mind. Mary informed her that Evangeline was pregnant and expecting a boy. Betty seemed overjoyed. "Well, she will be a great mother," she offered, grinning widely.

Just then Evangeline came out the cabin door carrying two suitcases. One, no doubt, contained her replenished doctoring outfit. I rushed to help her. She set them at my feet. Betty, talking animatedly to Mary about aspects of motherhood, opened the trunk. The outfit was heavier than I expected, and I put both suitcases inside the trunk, one at a time. "Careful," Evangeline warned. And when I was done, "Adieu, David." When I turned to speak with her, she threw herself against me and kissed me on the cheek. I almost fell in the trunk with the suitcases. I was a bit flabbergasted, but before I could say anything, Evangeline was inside the car on the passenger seat, having darted around me to get there. I shut the trunk as Betty was giving Mary a hug. Betty got in and started the engine, backed up, and headed down the tote road to the gravel. Their arms were protruding from the windows, waving. We watched as the car disappeared over the hill.

We stood a moment longer, then Mary turned to me and said, "I want you to water the garden and trench up around the melons. The okra looks good, but the ground needs to be loosened at the stalks." These tasks meant I would have to carry buckets of water from the well for the rest of the day, plus grub around in the dirt.

"Where's the hoe?" I asked a little indignantly. "I suppose you want me to make one?"

"No, you can use my digging stick."

"Okay." I shrugged and headed for the well.

Late that afternoon, I was sitting out on Mary's porch steps reading a popular magazine. My back hurt from pulling buckets of water and bending over and digging. I was busy skimming through the pages, looking at all the grand houses and cars, when Mary came out and sat down next to me. I showed her some of the pictures. My eyes lingered on the image of a curvaceous woman standing on tiptoe and placing a book high on an upper shelf.

Mary shrugged her shoulder, unimpressed. "Live modestly, David. At your age, you should be looking for the ratio of harmony, a perfect place within the great geomancy."

"That sounds like mathematics. Are you telling me to live a mathematically correct life?" I flipped the magazine aside, giving Mary my attention.

"I am telling you to seek a place of balance and non-excess. And yes, it is mathematics. Do you think the scientists of today are the only people to use mathematics? I dare say we, by that I mean Indigenous, know as much or more about sacred numbers as the invaders did. We were quite aware of the trickster maze, and the great round of truth. We knew the foundations of life as well as our celestial errand. I am speaking to you of sacred geometry and the exercise of inner strength. Isn't it clear we go from point to point in this life? We have desire, ambition. We set off to achieve it, no matter how great or small. If the universe cooperates, we achieve our ambition. If we have a false understanding of geometry, the universe crushes us without so much as a ho-hum.

"When you go to the next world, the laws change. Geometry is a tool that can help you in the world to come, one of the few tools you can use. If you are going to read, read something that will feed you, help you. Not trash."

"It's not trash. What harm does it do to wish for a few nice things?"

"Wishing is like one of those wish biscuits. You wish it would hit you in the mouth. It's like an arrow flying to no mark. You could use that arrow for something else. I was up in Tulsa not long ago. I went up there with my cousin who wanted to see a Cherokee friend. We were there for three days. My cousin also had to deliver a shawl she had sold to a rich person. We drove over to an exclusive neighborhood, and I waited inside the car while she went up to the house to get her money.

"Across the street, a fancy car pulled into the driveway. A man and a pregnant woman got out and waited on the lawn. Pretty soon a department store truck pulled up. The man gave some orders, and the woman unlocked the front door. It was a delivery of a bassinet, a baby bed and other nursery furniture, a rocking chair, and many other items. While I was watching this huge assortment of goods being unloaded and taken inside the house, I noticed a bird's nest above the front porch. In an elm tree on the lawn, I saw a swallow with a small twig in its beak. He was patiently waiting for the baby goods caravan to clear off in order to make his own delivery — the twig. It was a lesson in simplicity.

"I watched this proud father-to-be. I knew this man was going to have a long and difficult road even with his wealth and possessions. His money wasn't going to help him in the day-to-day problems of living. I knew the swallow was going to have it much easier because he cooperated with life.

"If you want to be a conjure, don't talk of riches. Don't speak of the expensive hotshot cars you want, your hot-rod clothes. Don't speak of gold watches and diamond cuff links. Do you hear me? You don't know how stupid you sound. Don't insult women by telling me of the movie stars you'd like to go to bed with."

I protested. "What are you, a damned mind reader? I didn't say that."

"Yes, you said it clear enough. Don't tell me of your lavish future estates. It's a joke. You'll never get them. And you wouldn't want them anyway. It's clear that that's your lesson — the shiny stuff. Sink all that pretty rubbish.

"There's a good story about Yellow Tobacco Boy entering the heart of the mountain. Inside, he found a magical snake — some say raven, but no matter. Let's just say he found an animal that could do any sort of magical work. I like snake, and since I'm telling it, snake it will be. His eyes were great jewels and his voice was like the sweet wind, and he asked Yellow Tobacco Boy what he wanted.

"Yellow Tobacco Boy told him about his horrible life, how he was poor, how nobody liked or respected him. The snake listened patiently. 'I'll tell you what,' said the snake. 'It's no big operation for me. I'll give you a new life. Go back home, and you'll be rich. Everyone will love and respect you. You're going to have plenty, and plenty of women too. I'll straighten things out for you. Now go,' the snake ordered.

"Yellow Tobacco Boy dashed back to his village. It was just as the magical snake predicted. Circumstances had changed. Yellow Tobacco Boy was a many-blankets, and the people quickly changed their opinion of him. He had it all, as they say. But in less than one moon, it vanished. Whatever the reason, his life slowly eroded and returned to the same miserable mess it had been before.

"Yellow Tobacco Boy returned to the mountain to see the snake. 'Listen, my life is the same as it was when we first met,' he said in a woebegone tone. 'It was a horrible trick. I believe you've played a joke on me.'

"The snake lay silently. He hissed thoughtfully. 'Look, Yellow Tobacco Boy, that's the most anyone can do for you. I gave you a little vacation. I gave you a few riches, that's all. But the world will never change unless you change.'

"So you change, David. Outward circumstances will follow. True prosperity, peace, and joy are inside of you, not out. Think of what you are asking. You seem to have a great respect for greedy people. You admire them and identify with them. For some reason, you want to be like them. Believe me, they are cursed. What these greedy people don't understand is that enormous wealth is a hindrance. It is another form of obesity. Great wealth is like weighing three hundred pounds. People will get out of your way quick enough and secretly fear you. You inadvertently plow through the crowd. Because of your ungainly nature, you knock over others or even trample an innocent child. There's never enough food. I think Indians are very conscious of this because they are tribal. Greed was always detested. You see, the greedy person never has enough money or material objects, even though they are carrying off everything."

"I just want to be somebody. What's wrong with that?"

"I am saying to use your arrows to good purpose. You're a busybody, and you're letting on a lot more than you think. To reveal is negligent. Don't ever speak of conjuring to anyone unless you are attempting to teach them or treat them. They will only revile you behind your back or else they will make fun of you and you will deserve it for being so foolish. The humans of this generation have forgotten the good things of old. I pity the generations that believe we are machine-nourished, for it is the green gash of the living that sustains us. The knowledge passed down through the ages has slipped to the ground and disappeared like a snake in a hole.

"You cower before the great silence. Believe me, it is not silence at all and can be deafening. A lot of people around here call the mouth a trap, and that's exactly what it is. Don't be a babbler. Keep your composure. Be a snake in a hole. Speak only a little bit, and hiss when you do it. Let your silence be as mysterious as the stillness of night — no telling what is stirring in deep unknown places. It is emptiness you fear, not silence. Silence is pregnant with life, and not saying is its only birthing. A conjure's mouth should be closed most of the time. Don't ever say anything, no matter how they coax you — not even the dregs. Save your words for swamp jacks and spirit helpers. If you must speak to another, say it without saying it is the best way: by example.

"Silence has more power than words," said Mary. "You talk way too much. It was a magpie that wanted the entire world to come out of its mouth. Magpie has been trying ever since. You're like a magpie. It's fine to talk if you really have something to say. But you're a real bull artist. If you want to be a conjure, keep your big mouth shut. You drive me crazy with all your foolish gibberish."

"I don't remember saying so much," I said apologetically.

"There are plenty of other ways of shouting other than using your voice. And get your mind off Evangeline. You would greatly complicate her life and your own, so don't even think about it. You are so transparent, you think right out loud. Learn to be less forthright."

"No one ever told me that before," I said. I sat back and lit a commercial cigarette, then blew out a puff of smoke. "So the lesson today is, don't read or even look at pictures and keep my mouth shut, right? And further, quit thinking so loudly."

"If you want to put it that way. That's correct."

Ten

AFTER BREAKFAST, Mary led me to a field not far from her cabin. She pointed out various wild plants. She described their uses and told me legends about each one. I discovered a mushroom close to some scrub oak and asked her what it was.

"We call this mushroom the ravaging black wolf."

"Oh, it looks harmless enough."

"That's what you think. Another name for it is shiny black coffin. I never want you to experiment with anything like this until you first check with me. You are too inexperienced, especially in this field. Even now it is calling you. If I weren't with you, you'd probably taste it."

"I might. What would it do to me?"

"First, your lips would turn blue, and then your entire body. But this is only the beginning. Next, you would be led by the wolf to the sacred last hunting grounds and be devoured. Hungry spirits would rip you to pieces and then they would eat you. You would convulse and die. If this happens, you better hope I'm around with the remedy."

"What is the remedy?"

"There are many I could use."

"Give me an example."

"It depends, but a strong root medicine brewed with belladonna can be used. There are many easy ways to destroy the power of this fungus."

Mary leaned forward and moved her hand around the periphery of a small weed as though caressing the area around it.

She suddenly began to sing. She told me to repeat the words to this song as she sang it. I'm not a very good singer, but I soon got into the spirit. When she was done, she said, "A conjure must learn the words and learn them exactly. And you must learn them not in the head but in the heart. You must love all of plant life and show your acknowledgment and compassion for their gifts. The remedies are practically worthless without the medicine songs and words. The roots, barks, berries, leaves, and grasses will know if you are faking. Their truth was revealed to the ancestors long ago. If you don't honor the plant, you disrespect your ancestors. Always sing to them the proper song. That is what makes them stand up with power. Without them, the cures are about as good as old dishwater. In fact, dishwater might even be better, depending on what you had for dinner."

"From what you tell me, many of the plants around here are quite dangerous," I said.

"Yes, many will put you right in the dirt," Mary said. "Like that one." She pointed toward a vine with a white flower that was growing along the ground. I recognized it at once as a datura plant, rare in Oklahoma. "Used properly, this plant has many faces and much to teach you. Used improperly, you will have swallowed certain death. No earthly power can save you. You must learn to speak to plants in order to settle them down. Otherwise, it's risky to even be near them."

"What's so risky?"

"The old ones say this plant was married to the invaders and can be treacherous. Think of this jimsonweed as you would a tornado. That's what it is. A cool wind from the tornado teases you. How nice. The cool wind blows over you, caressing you. Wind is one aspect of the tornado. Too much tornado, and you will be flung like an old rag doll to smithereens. You will lose all your old stuffing.

"Treated in haste and with improper respect, almost any

plant becomes angry and hazardous. Many live in hazardous dirt, which may cause illness."

"Dirt meaning earth?"

"Yes, there is a many-kinds-of-dirt sickness."

"How does this sickness manifest?"

"It comes from going about stupidly and walking on unsafe dirt. It can cause sores over the body. And walking barefoot on uncomplimentary dirt is bad. This can cause swollen feet. Dirt is either healthy or not. It might contain fevers or other dirt sicknesses. There are good and bad dirts for every tribe of men and women. One dirt might be good for one tribe but not for another. Dirts can cause bad bones and teeth. We ate dirt not so long ago, and rocks and clay and the liquid produced from them. It would be good if we still did. Dirt can be big medicine if you know what you are doing."

"Will you show me the various dirts?"

"Watch the animals carefully. They'll show you. They know good dirts both to live on and die on. Animals know where to burrow and where to hide. Conjures have always used dirts the animals have shown. Some dirts can make us invisible. Some can give us courage. Some can knock down the enemy."

"Knock down the enemy?" I repeated.

"Yes, some can kill, and some can heal."

"Well, I hope I'm on good terms with the dirt."

"You're not. You are courting dirt sickness. You are calling it to you like calling an old hound dog. That's why I mention it. Your dirts are not comrades, not friends. And some bad ones are headed your way."

"Why? I mean, why aren't they my friends?"

"Why? I'm not sure yet. Maybe because you think you walk alone but we walk hand in hand with everything. Dirts are mad as hell at you. It may be city dirts. They can be the worst, the angriest."

"Ah, c'mon?"

"Absolutely. Really furious. Here. Come here."

Mary led me over to some level ground and told me to sit down. The earth was warm from the heat of the day yet soft. However, it was not a place I would normally choose to sit down, left to my own devices. It felt unusual. The dirt here was red and sandy — real Oklahoma dirt. Mary began to circle me and chant. She took a handful of dirt and threw it in the air. She repeated this again and again. It made a red puff and scattered. She went around me several times, letting a thin trickle of the dirt drop from her hand. The purpose of all this eluded me.

When she had finished the dirt circling operation, she came over and squatted down. She seemed to be examining me using that birdlike cock of the head. She grasped both of my hands and placed them palm up, extended out from my shoulders. I felt she was using me like a human scale, because she lowered my right hand and raised my left one. She scooped up some dirt and put it in both hands and told me to hold it.

"Sit like so, and don't move from your position."

"Okay."

"Be quiet and shut your eyes."

"Okay."

The next thing I knew, Mary was throwing dirt on me — barrage after barrage — all over me, everywhere. I began to cough softly and wanted to sneeze. I didn't think I could bear it much longer. The rain of dirt suddenly stopped.

Mary said, "Open your eyes."

I did. She was sitting directly in front of me, smiling.

"Thanks," I said, unamused. There was grit on my lips and in my mouth. My hair and eyelids also felt laden with crud. I felt like a chicken drumstick floured and ready for frying. I needed an immediate soapy shower.

"Hold still and keep silent," Mary said. "It was the crawfish that brought dirt in the beginning of the world and showed us how to use it. You are being protected. This dirt had a hunger for you and the sickness is running away."

Using a pointed stone, Mary began to scratch the dirt between us. My eyes were stinging. Tears welled, and this caused everything to blur. I tried to focus on the elongated stone as Mary used it, but it rippled in my watery vision. I felt as though I was tilted sideways, and this had a dizzying effect. From sitting in an awkward position, I was beginning to ache. Yet, watching her mesmerized me. Her extravagant movements were lulling me into a trance. I soon realized she was etching something. With the slicing stone, she was creating a human form with a long neck. The dirt picture made me feel strange, and I shut my eyes.

"No, look at it," she ordered.

I opened my eyes. The incision looked like the stick figure of a woman, yet there was something wrong with it. It brought a dark presence, a dim area just above the top of my head. And this was being sucked down into the ground and into the thing. Mary began blowing her breath strongly over the figure. I watched it cover over and disappear. This affected the polarity of my body. I was being pulled toward it as it vanished. I tried to squirm backward but couldn't move.

"It's trying to suck me inside," I managed to whisper.

"Yes, don't be afraid," said Mary. "Dirts are alive. No dead thing can give birth to a living being. See the green stalks all around us? This soil swells with the miracle of life. Now I will tell you a story to illustrate this. Be silent. Don't move. Listen, because I have an important tale. A teaching story can help you forget your aches and pains. I did exactly as you are doing once. This is the way it was told to me."

Despite Mary's instructions to stay put, I shifted my weight a little to get more comfortable. Mary continued, "They say Yellow Tobacco Boy went to many holy places and got many kinds of dirts. He collected twenty-two big pouches. He dug a big hole in the ground and mixed the dirts up, using a sunpole with a big yellow feather sticking out from the top. He sang a mystery song, a many-kinds-of-dirts song, a song no longer known. Next, he used a hollow cane tube and blew many-kinds-of-dirts breaths. He molded and shaped and blew dust, and sang some more. He made Many-Kinds-of-Dirts Girl. And he immediately fell in love with her.

"She wasn't like other girls. He painted her with red ocher. He put vermilion flowers in her mud hair. He striped her body with yellow and black painted bands. Her arms and legs were decorated with shells, pretty stones, and colored beads. No wonder he loved her. She was very special.

"Of course, there were a few problems. She ate fifty pounds of rotten leaves and wood each day. She washed it down with gallons of muddy water. Yellow Tobacco Boy liked home cooking. He liked regular food and clear spring water. She couldn't stand his food, and he couldn't stand hers.

"Next, he realized he had put her feet on backward. No matter how he tried, he couldn't make Many-Kinds-of-Dirts Girl's feet face in the right direction. Finally, he shrugged it off. If she wanted to walk around backward, why should he worry about it? She was his mud girl, that was the important thing.

"Then there was the question of her hair. It was a real rat's nest. It hung down in a jumble of mud-mossy tendrils. Why wouldn't she just comb it?

"'Comb your filthy hair, Dirts Girl,' Yellow Tobacco Boy ordered.

"She shook it, slinging mud in all directions. 'I like my hair,' is all she would say in reply.

"To further complicate matters, Yellow Tobacco Boy discovered a mouth in the back of her neck. Maybe he had put it there. He couldn't remember. It made him feel queasy.

"She noticed his scornful look. 'Yeah, well, I don't like you smoking cigarettes all the time,' she complained. 'It makes me want to throw up.'

"Dirts Girl wouldn't stand for smoking, that was for sure. She went around waving her mud arms in the presence of smoke, chasing it away.

"Naturally enough, Yellow Tobacco Boy soon wanted to procreate. Dirts Girl thought it was a good idea. Imagine Yellow Tobacco Boy's shock when he discovered he was pregnant. He knew something was seriously wrong.

"When the dirts baby came, it was slimy and deformed and came out the wrong way. Yellow Tobacco Boy held it up to look at it. The repulsive, filthy, mucky baby shrieked and twisted away from him. He tried to grab at it but it ran off into the forest, still shrieking. 'Let him go and find another place,' Many-Kinds-of-Dirts Girl said in a fury. She stood there with her hands on her hips, staring after the baby. And then she softened. 'Dirts Baby wouldn't fit in around here anyway. I think maybe we should slip away too. I like it better in the forest, don't you?' Yellow Tobacco Boy didn't chase after the dirts baby. He just stood there and hung his head in frustration and shame, listening to the be-numbing child's wail in the distance.

"And for awhile, life returned to normal — as normal as it could be under the circumstances. True, Many-Kinds-of-Dirts Girl and Yellow Tobacco Boy still had their differences. But a man in love with dirts medicine will do practically anything to get along. He tried to keep her favor, but he often wanted to call her Many-Kinds-of-Troubles Girl.

"'I think I'll make another dirts girl, a better one,' Yellow Tobacco Boy said one day. 'Many-Kinds-of-Dirts Girl and I aren't very compatible. I think I want a more conventional woman.'

"This time Yellow Tobacco Boy traveled far away to the flat

land, an old sea bed. The dirts were pure white there. He used this dirt. He dug a big hole and did a mixup, again using his sunpole with the big yellow feather on top. He sang a mystery song, stirring and stirring. He sang a pretty girl song. He blew some pretty girl breaths through his hollow cane tube. He molded and shaped and blew white powders. He sang some more. He made Salt Girl. And he immediately fell in love with her.

"She was beautiful. He was careful to make her the right clothes. He brushed her hair thoroughly and braided it carefully in the customary manner. He sewed her up some pretty moccasins. He gave her the right feathers and beads. He tattooed her blue around the lips. When she was nearly perfect, he taught her to have good manners and to do things the way everyone else did. He instructed her how to cook and sew. He gave her some shy-medicine so she would be modest. He made sure she had the right parts in the right places.

"Salt Girl fit in perfectly, and the people all admired her. She was a picture of perfect grace. The food she prepared and served with elaborate care was good. Yellow Tobacco Boy smoked many cigars and cigarettes, and Salt Girl encouraged him to do so.

"He spent his days happily. Neither Many-Kinds-of-Dirts Girl nor Salt Girl paid any attention to one another. However, Many-Kinds-of-Dirts Girl often ran off in tears whenever she was offended, and she was offended most of the time. 'Let her cry. She should learn to live by our customs,' Salt Girl scolded. 'I will teach her.'

"Then he noticed Salt Girl was becoming critical of him. She was controlling him, telling him just how to act, telling him he must be like everyone else. She would get exasperated over his slightest impropriety.

"Many-Kinds-of-Dirts Girl was around less and less. He hardly saw her, and he was beginning to wonder if she would leave him altogether. He began to miss the rather shameful things they had done together so often. He loved her, but he also loved Salt Girl. He found himself in a dilemma. Salt Girl was uninteresting, and Many-Kinds-of-Dirts Girl was unendurable. What was he to do?"

Mary paused. She looked at me expectantly, cocking her head and waiting for my answer. I didn't have one. She studied me with quiet amusement and chuckled rather unkindly. I suddenly became aware of my ungainly posture, and my neck hurt and my arms seemed paralyzed. I was filthy.

"That's all? That's the end?" I asked in a puzzled voice. "What did Yellow Tobacco Boy do, Mary?"

"Obviously, he was husband to both of them. But what does this mean? I guess I will have to explain the teaching of this story when you are better able to understand it." She stood up, did an about-face, and walked quickly away.

"Wait, Mary. What do you want me to do with the dirt in my hands?"

Mary turned and looked back at me. "What dirt?"

I unclamped both of my hands, which until now had been tightly holding the dirt Mary had put into them. I looked at my palms. Both were completely empty.

"It's gone!" I gasped. I felt dizzy, experiencing another of what I was beginning to think of as my "reality blurs."

"There are many kinds of dirts," Mary replied. "Maybe it was the disappearing kind." She chuckled a bit unkindly again, so it seemed, and walked away without waiting for me. I got up and dusted myself off, feeling as contorted as a piece of bent wire. I tried to catch up. Finally, I found her sitting under the chinaberry tree near her cabin. She had a bundle in her lap. It looked to be a simple piece of canvas tied with rawhide. She stood up as I approached and tossed the bundle across her shoulder, carrying it like a slung rifle.

"Follow me," she said, motioning with her head in a different direction.

I followed behind her for ten or so minutes. We crossed a gully and then climbed upward on a narrow trail. It was very quiet, our way punctuated only by occasional bird chirps, the drone of locusts, and the soft sound of our own footsteps. We climbed to the top of the hill over some jutting boulders and turned obliquely to our right. Soon we were in a level spot in the rocky landscape.

Mary led me to a small place that was hidden from view. It was a squarish piece of grassless ground, but all around was vegetation of one kind and another. She swept the ground using a dead, leafy branch, evening and smoothing the earth.

Then she seemed satisfied. "This is the proper place," she said, glancing at the ground. She told me to remove my bracelet, watch, shoes, and socks, and all my other clothes except for my underwear. When I had done so, I folded my clothes up carefully and made a little neat pile. I felt embarrassed, knowing how comical I must have looked standing in front of her in my jockey shorts.

Mary told me to lie down on my back. She looked tall, towering over me in my supine position. I became more self-conscious. The more I tried to relax, the more ashamed and tiny I felt.

"What are you doing now?" I asked. The question was more addressed to the reddening sky above me than to Mary.

"I am going to place dirts on various parts of your body."

"But you already did that."

"Yes, but before it was only in a general way. Now we get to specifics. We will restore your bond with dirt. Since you are on the ground, the dirt power will be drawn up through you. You have lost touch with earth's chief emanations. Emotions come up from earth, so this will help you control them."

Mary knelt down next to me and unrolled her bundle. There were at least thirty bulging Bull Durham tobacco bags inside it. She began opening them up, undoing little yellow string ties and peering inside to examine the contents.

"What's in there?"

"Dirts. What else? A big assortment. I will use several. I collected some of them myself and traded for others. Some of them came from as far away as Africa. Stop worrying so much. I know exactly how to place dirts, and I promise you it won't hurt a bit."

"Yeah, that's what my dentist said, but it hurt anyway."

"This will be different. It won't be painful, although it can be dangerous, just as any medicine can be dangerous if it is in the wrong proportions. For instance, fire and water are both important helpers, but too much of either can be fatal. Of course, all these things you ask about relate to energy, deep rivers and pockets of energy. So does dirts medicine, *kallo* power."

"I don't get it," I replied.

"David, dirts medicine is simple and direct. There is a deep hunger within you. Dirts will feed it. Dirts will get to the center of your craving and fill it in. Dirts will give you a rush of power, a medicine of renewal. Now lie still and try not to speak. Let me work."

She gazed up my body, cocking her head. She took my ankles and shook them, pulling on each of my legs at the same time. She moved up behind my head. She took my two wrists and pulled my arms back, stretching me once more. It was a strong pull she gave me, but it didn't hurt. Then she placed my arms back at my sides, palms up.

After that, she set to work. I couldn't see what she was doing very well, but the dirts were of several colors — jet black, gray-green, ocher, and so on. She used a little horn spoon with a cone-shaped bowl to remove the dirts from the Bull Durham sacks.

Then she placed little mounds of each on different places on my body, taking care to be precise.

"Your head is called a planet," she said, placing a little mound above and between my eyebrows. "We are building dirt structures — little temples. There are river temples, fire temples, breath temples, and both female and male temples to honor central principles of life.

"First, I am mounding your brow and chin. We will pick up magnetized life force here, which will become excited and draw from your entire body. Shut your eyes and see what you might see."

It was suddenly as if I was dreaming, but with startling clarity. I saw relatives. My uncle was puttering around in his backyard with garden tools, and I saw two of my female cousins calling to a family horse named Knothead. Knothead shook his head at them, his mane flying.

Mary placed a small mound of dirt on my chin, and the scene abruptly disappeared. Now it was as though I was sitting on my own chest, looking down at my head and shoulders. I could see myself perfectly well. I could also see Mary bending over me with the horn spoon full of dirts. I watched as she placed two mounds near my collarbone, to the right and left of my shoulder. Next she did a series of dirts placements on my chest, and then down my arms to my hands.

"We have stopped your wobbling planet," Mary announced. "Now we are building four atmospheres. This second one relates to the star bringing you luck."

I had no idea what she meant, but now she was mounding the creases at both my elbows. Then she moved down to the center of both wrists. "In olden times, these placements were called the encircling hoof. Think of the horseshoe, which today is a symbol of luck. If you have both your arms at your sides and make a path across the top of your chest connecting them, this arch of energy is in the shape of a horseshoe. If it is out of whack, as yours is, you will not be lucky, not in love or marriage, not in business or commercial doings, and certainly not in gambling. I'm fixing it.

"It is a good practice to hoop your arms above you in the early morning and put the rising sun within their circle. Then bring your arms down straight in front of you with your fingers still touching. Think of this circle as a medicine basket, or bowl, containing the sun. Draw it into your heart, folding your arms over your chest. Be prayerful at this time. Thank Maker of Life for sending sunshine to us all. Remember, sunshine and earth are a great influence. They are at the very source of being. Honoring them is a good way to begin each day."

My thoughts, which seemed to be hovering about in the air above me, plunged back down inside my body. Mary made three more mounds, placing the first in the center of my chest and then two to either side of my solar plexus. When she was done, she said, "This third placement relates to inner sun. It may be emotionally painful to you, as the next one may also be."

She was right. At first so many images flickered by that I couldn't grasp the meaning of them. There was my father, my mother, and then I was a little child, frightened because I had lost them for a time. I saw painful incidents with my brothers and sister teasing me and telling me I was too little to play with them. I saw angry nuns, priests, and teachers and remembered being beaten with a rubber hose by a school principal. I relived a fistfight I'd had in the showers when I was in the marines.

I recalled, or rather relived, a barroom incident in a foreign country. I had been the ugly American, surrounded by antagonists. To escape, I had broken a beer bottle and charged the man guarding the door, aiming the bottle at his face. He tripped me and I went sprawling into the street. My right index finger was gashed and pouring blood. I got up and ran as fast as I could, chased by a bunch of angry drunks. I saw myself again cowering behind a fence, trying to stanch the flowing blood. My pursuers ran past without seeing me. I laughed out loud at their stupidity, because all they had needed to do was follow my trail of splattered blood.

"Let these things go, David," Mary murmured. "All of them. They are useless to you now. Let them pass through you. Send them packing. We have to finish our work. We must go to the fourth atmosphere, related to earth-moon."

Mary made two mounds of dirt on each side of my navel and just a little below it. I was smashed down so hard I gasped for breath. All the tragedies I had been reexperiencing were immediately forgotten. I was moaning for air, my chest heaving frantically. Mary completely ignored my struggling and went about placing more dirt above and below my knees, then at both feet.

"Listen," she said. "These are bearing placements, and connect with the moon. The moon always knows where the good road is located. Bear toward the good road, the spiritual road. This road is always of earth, married with the moon."

As Mary worked on, I felt as if my body contained a series of strings connected to each other like a net or web. Each time Mary placed a new mound of dirts, it set the web to vibrating. The effect of these gently placed mounds was to cause a cascading, harmonic ripple throughout my body. Each new dirts placement raised the vibration an octave in pitch. I had never felt remotely similar sensations as were reverberating through me, pleasurable but so unfamiliar they frightened me.

I tried to concentrate on the sensations. I noticed I was beginning to feel slightly numb, especially my left leg. The numbness percolated upward to my jaws, and I realized I was gritting my teeth tightly. My mind began playing irrational tricks. I suspected that Mary had deceived me. She was a spoiled child making mud pies, and soon she would splat one right in my face and laugh. That's all she ever wanted to do: make me appear ridiculous. I felt full of rage, first at Mary and then at other unpleasant thoughts and memories that had come to mind. Mary's dirt juggling was digging up things I had worked hard for many years to bury.

I was breathing heavily, and I could feel my skin turning red to match the evening sunset. I started to writhe, arching my neck backward and straining my body into a tense bow with most of my weight on my head.

I was overcome with self-pity and -hatred. I had done nothing worthwhile with my life. I was a big zero in the estimation of the people I knew. I felt my body dispersing, disappearing. Life had poisoned me, and now I was coming apart. Then somewhere far away I heard a wailing cry. I realized with a shock that it was me, screaming at the top of my lungs. I sat up suddenly, dashing all the careful mounds of dirts to the ground. I was wracked with paroxysms of sorrow, and feeling naked and exposed.

"It's okay," I heard Mary say. Then I felt her arms around me. "Your earth is being made clean. Flow. It takes a river of tears to do it." She held me pressed to her breast for a long time while I cried like a big baby. By the time I calmed down enough to put on my clothes, darkness had engulfed us.

Eleven

I SLEPT SOUNDLY and awoke early the next morning. Up before me, Mary had fixed some coffee and fry bread. We sat and ate our breakfast together on her porch in the predawn light. The sky was a smear of pastel, and the limbs of the big chinaberry tree dipped into the reddened light like curved fingers, leaves shimmering. The morning air was sweet, the night's stillness beginning to break into a medley of chirps and tweets. As I stared into Mary's shadowed face, I saw only a gleam from her eyes.

I felt tongue-tied and couldn't bring myself to ask Mary in plain terms the question that was still haunting me. I mumbled, "Could you explain . . . I mean how do you . . . about Salt Girl . . . Dirts Girl?" It was the best I could do. I took a quick gulp of coffee to cover my embarrassment.

"I can tell this," Mary said. "Dirts Girl and Salt Girl are the messengers. A conjure marries Dirts Girl on the left, and Salt Girl on the right. The conjure rightfully comes closer to Dirts Girl than Salt Girl. However, without the two of them together, he can do no healing. Only if he is married to both will he be complete and friendly with power. Only then will spirit helpers be able to recognize the married man and assist him. With spirit help, he can doctor dead-on."

I still wasn't sure I understood, but after that we sat around drinking our coffee and not saying much. Mary told me she was busy for the day, and for me to go away and go easy. I headed for my car before she could change her mind and drove over to

Nanih Waiya Lake, near Tuskahoma, to fish. I stopped at the bridge, where the lake narrowed. Dead brush stuck out of the water on both sides of the road. It looked like a good place to fish for crappie, so I sat down with my pole on a concrete abutment just off the asphalt.

My line snapped taut almost the instant it hit the water. My pole twitched, danced, and then dipped violently. I kept as much tension on the line as I dared, trying hard to maneuver whatever was on the other end away from the brush that jutted up so close by. Finally, a huge, greenish-brown hump came frothing to the surface. I had hooked a big turtle.

I knew instantly I would never be able to land this washtub of a turtle. It was just too heavy. Then its head broke from underneath the brownish water, and two glittering red eyes sent me an angry, arrogant look asking what manner of fool I was. We studied each other for a long moment. I could see it wasn't the first time the old turtle had been momentarily nabbed. Its scowling jaw was full of rusty hooks, tangled lines, and leaders. This was clearly an old warrior turtle, with many battle decorations to prove it. "Go ahead and pull me up if you can," the turtle seemed to say. "I've never been in the soup bowl yet, and I don't intend to be now. You might as well cut me loose, because you can't do it."

"I hear you, old one," I said, using my old marine-issue K-bar knife to cut the line. "Good medicine and good day to you, and may you win all future contests."

The turtle sank back down, turned, and kicked off toward the center of the lake, soon disappearing beneath the surface like a submarine.

Turtle is a great benefiting medicine. Island Girl, as turtle is sometimes called because she carries Turtle Island, enhances life force. She has incredible energy. The venerable I Ching, the ancient Chinese divination system, began by studying Turtle's back and realizing that it expressed much about the ongoing struggles of life.

I didn't feel like fishing anymore, so I set my pole aside. A sharp wind gusted from the south, blowing moist, cool air over me. Two white swans emerged from a stand of tall cattails and glided away toward some cozier spot, their twin reflections accompanying them. In time my eyes wandered upward to see a golden eagle flying south and east across the lake, and then circling slowly above the Choctaw Council House on the far side. Eagles have great vision. They are aware of any human presence long before our eyes can find them, and to see one is always a blessing and honor.

Watching the eagle, I remembered a story I had heard about this sacred bird. I must have been around twelve or thirteen years old, and Mama Opal and I had been watching two eagles hunt along a stream in the Arbuckles, a beautiful but small mountain range in southern Oklahoma.

The story was about a woman wounded by the hard life of being an Indian. This woman saw a beautiful eagle. It glided over her and circled around and around. It flew toward the sun. The woman, in her curiosity, had forgotten her sorrow. Without thinking, she stood up and climbed into the sky in pursuit. Arm over arm, she followed. As she climbed, she looked down at the earth. Far across the horizon stood regal mountains she had not known existed. She had been sitting by an icy stream only moments before, and now it seemed a mere trickle. She could reach with her hand and touch the clouds.

Directly below lay her *tamaha*, her town. It was so small. Higher up, the land became gray and brown. Then yellow, silver, and blue. There was an unutterable beauty to the world below.

"I must tell my people about this at once." When the people

saw their sister, their daughter, climb down from the sky, their eyes grew wide and their sorrows, too, were soon forgotten.

Ever since I had been old enough to put two and two together, Mama Opal had told me stories that touched me deeply. She was as battled-scarred from life as the old turtle I had just met. She had been hooked often, but no one had ever been able to reel Mama Opal in.

Mama Opal was fiercely proud of her Indian heritage. I often reflected on why Life's Maker had chosen her to be my mother. In the end I decided it was because I was supposed to learn her history from her, and then, from within it, to find my own. History meant more to me than superficial facts. It meant the myths that surrounded us, myths with hidden meanings and a deep touching of the soul.

I sat beside the lake feeling uncertain about what to do with the rest of the day. It was still early, so I stashed my angling gear back in the trunk and drove the short distance over to Tuskahoma.

Tuskahoma wasn't really much of a town — just a few houses, an ancient post office, and a bridge over the Kiamichi River. There were remains of an old sawmill. And there had once been a school for Indian women there. My grandmother had attended it, but it had long gone to ruin. Mama Opal told me the school had been practical, with a home economics curriculum featuring courses like cooking, sewing, and canning. The authorities didn't think there was much point in teaching Native women anything more intellectual than that, I suppose.

I parked near the crumbling school building and went for a walk. I imagined my grandmother once walking these same paths along the river. Soon I discovered an abandoned home site with a lush raspberry patch behind it. I got a large paper grocery sack from the car and filled it with at least two gallons of berries.

When I was done picking, I discovered stalks of garlic in an over-grown, long-abandoned garden. I pulled it up and ate a clove. Very potent. I would certainly be safe from vampires.

When I got back to the cabin, Mary took my gifts and put them away. Then she came out carrying an old tin can. She got into my car and pointed south. We drove south for about a half an hour, until Mary said to pull off the road. We got out and walked into an overgrown field. She came to a spot and stopped.

"We come for this," she said, kneeling down in front of a plant. It had an unpleasantly pungent smell and a short, weedy-looking stalk with fernlike leaves and drooping plumes of non-descript flowers. If Mary had ever described this plant to me before, it hadn't registered in my memory. It looked like loco weed.

"What is this?" I asked.

"We call it a word that means equilibrium. That's how it is used, as a restorative. We have come here to ask this plant to help you. We have done some good work on you up to now, but it will soon be shot. Without this plant's help, you would be afflicted all over again.

"And it's not simply the plant that we need," Mary ex-plained. "The entire spirit must be used."

Mary told me how to remove it. It was not easy, but I did as I was instructed. First, I trenched up all around it with my ma-rine K-bar knife. Then I shoved the blade underneath the roots and pulled everything out — dirt and all. I put it in the rusty can Mary was holding. She handed it back to me. I waited for her to tell me what to do next.

"You know," Mary said.

I realized my mistake. Taking out some tobacco, I made an offering to the plant I was holding, the dirt, and all the insects scurrying around inside the can.

"Take it home with you to the city. Put it in a big pot and

boil it up. Make about a gallon and let it settle. Drink about a pint a day, an hour before breakfast. After you have finished it, scatter the leavings on a red ant hill. That shouldn't be hard for you to find, since they're all over."

"Wait. I'm not sure I'm clear about this. You want me to boil up this plant, along with all the dirt, bugs, and grub worms — all this? And then you want me to drink a pint a day before breakfast?"

"Do it."

"I can't."

"Of course you can."

"Okay. You're right, I can. You want me to get rid of what's left in the bottom of the pot?"

"On a red ant hill, yes."

As if getting bombarded and crudded over wasn't enough, now this. I stood there holding the canned plant, probably looking as bewildered as I felt. It smelled bad. Besides its accompanying soil, I could see a sizable colony of agitated lower life-forms milling around. I watched as several small black and red bugs crawled over the rim and dropped to the ground, mentally congratulating them for escaping the soup. Other doomed grubs and earthworms were trying to sink back into the soil to escape. Little did they know what fate awaited them. And me.

We walked back to my car and drove to Mary's place. For dinner, we had fry bread with farmer's butter and honey from a nearby bee tree. And we had a mound of fresh Tuskahoma raspberries, eaten with our fingers.

Twelve

*I*T WAS TIME to get reacquainted with my job in Oklahoma City. After I packed up and was ready to go, I mentioned to Mary the date and time when I would return. It was a mistake.

She scolded me. "Look, time as you conceive it is nothing but a big mistake, a lie. Hours, minutes, seconds, they all sever you from truth and rob you of the very thing they purport to give you. That's why conjures are always saying we do things when it's right. We know when it's right, and we don't know that by looking smugly at the sweeping and swooping squat hand of a watch. We know it because we read more accurately those signs that are not yet charted. We know that time does not exist except at the boundary, the fringes. It holds all possibility and is dangerous beyond measure.

"Never again tell time by your watch. Don't refer to days and months. Go on olden time. Don't separate yourself from yourself."

She requested some paper. I gave her my notebook and ball-point pen, and she began to draw — and draw, and draw. Half an hour later, she had made a sketch that took up an entire 8½-by-11 page. When she began her drawing, it looked like a zodiac. As it progressed, it looked like a cross between a zodiac and a maze. Spaced around the outer rim, she had drawn perhaps fifty or sixty tiny symbols: snakes, deer, men and women, turtles, clouds, eagles, and so on. The inside of the circle was filled with converging lines and indecipherable characters.

She handed me the page. I held it out in front of me, examining it from various distances and angles. I hoped I didn't register how I felt — silly. I shook my head in bewilderment.

Mary smiled at my discomfort. "Yes, it's a calendar. Think of it as a gate to a corral," she said, "but it's not locked up and impossible to open. Inside this corral are gigantic horses called time. I want you to ride one of them. You see, time can be ridden like horses can be ridden. It can be harnessed. Right now, I see you standing around by the gate waiting for a horse to bust out. If you aren't careful, you'll get trampled. I am trying to show you how to catch it and get to your mount. The rigid calendar you use forbids you to look in the corral to see which horse is breaking free."

I made some lame reply, and then Mary began to tell me how to use what she had drawn. In spite of its strangeness, I did my best to listen.

"I'm not sure I understand, Mary," I interjected. "You want me to use your calendar from now on?" I pointed to the sketch. "You don't want me to use the regular calendar that begins in January and ends in December?" The idea of switching over from my familiar calendar to this hieroglyph was downright crazy.

"I insist you do this. There's no need to put up a fuss. It's not a burden. This calendar is true to your life's cycles as well as those of others around you. It's less complicated than it appears. It simplifies life. Your date way makes a devouring beast of time."

"I suppose you want me to throw my watch away too?"

"Ditch it."

"But how will I get to work on time?"

"On time," she repeated, shaking her head negatively. "Even the way you say time means you are cursed by it. You will get to work when you need to by learning a different way. Once you learn it, it won't fail you.

"The calendar I have given you is alive. Yours is dead. It

designates events of the past and tells you when to work and when not to. That's about all it's good for. It's dehumanizing — a master-slave calendar. Until it's changed, you can't expect human consciousness to improve.

"Your calendar is fixed on one dancer, but out on the celestial dance grounds there are numberless dancers in infinite regalia, whooping and shouting for attention. Your calendar cares not at all for these others. You can't expect people to be happy or healthy in their relationships with one another when they have no understanding of the celestial vault." She shook her head. "Prisoners — and they will remain so."

"I get the point, Mary," I said. "You don't like my calendar."

"It has not only robbed Indians, it has robbed everyone with its mean spirit."

"Well, I can't argue that with you," I said. "I only know the calendar I live by."

Mary cocked her head. "Live by? But you don't, you see."

"I don't?"

"No, you don't. Wake up, David. A true calendar is capable of tracking in many directions. It's not on a single road leading nowhere with no bearings. It pays attention to indicators, stars and planet guides. The calendar I have shown you does this. Because it doesn't lie, it leads you within as well as without. It leads to realization.

"I can tell you right now that before many generations have passed, we'll pay dearly for this neglect of truth. Believe me, without a proper calendar, new temples won't be built in their rightful place. Never. This tragedy is unfolding. Ancestors are forgotten. One day, all the nice steel-and-concrete towers and government buildings will crumble. Watery places will dry up. It's beginning to happen. Docks, seas, rivers, wells, beaches, will be cursed. There will be no more honors to be won. How can there be honors when people no longer honor themselves?

"This particular time of the world is called the time of whirling trees, because the people are out of harmony with practically all powers. Now the trees are whirling. You see floating tree sickness all about you. People are not rooted, living too much in the head and having no body, no roots."

We fell silent for a moment. Mary leaned back in her chair, waiting for me to respond. I did. "This calendar of yours, Mary," I said, pointing again to the page she had drawn. "How can it really change anything?"

"It has atmospheres like corn husks. Time itself is flayed, but your male calendar does not recognize this. You must shuck to get corn. Shuck yourself and get to your innermost essence. Follow that. Go deep into your nature."

"Flayed? Atmospheres?" I was becoming even more confused.

"Yes. You are flayed. Earth is flayed. It has an atmosphere. So do you. A power doctor peels off these layers and goes within. Anyway, go home now. I will tell you more about it another time. When I do, it's best if you learn it."

"Yeah, well, I'll be back to see you soon."

She smiled sadly at me. "David, my friend, I fear that one day you will head off to seek the whirling tree. This tree can be beautiful, like a Christmas tree with its gorgeous spinning lights. It can seem as if all beauty shines forth from its limbs. But you will be foolish if you let yourself be deceived by it. It grows in a dead place."

Thirteen

*I*RETURNED TO OKLAHOMA CITY to encounter technical problems at work. The days dragged by while we struggled to get a water-gathering system functioning properly. I was also having relationship problems. My girlfriend was giving me a hard time, or maybe it was the reverse. She came from a prominent Oklahoma oil family and had gone to a prestigious out-of-state college. Both facts I found unsettling, and I realized much later that while we were together she had been a kind of Salt Girl for me.

I hadn't told her much about my background, and even less about what I was doing with Mary. She would have thought I was insane. Maybe I was, a little. At the very least, I was getting off balance. I had one foot planted in Mary's tilted world while the other foot was on a workaday treadmill. My girlfriend sensed the conflict I was going through and tried to comfort me, but my misbehavior was poisoning the waters. At the same time, she resented my absences, and was jealous of what she didn't understand. I knew our love would soon belly up and die, which of course it did.

The Kiamichis had been pulling insistently on me, not only by day but also in a series of vivid but enigmatic dreams. I decided the dreams meant that I should return as soon as possible, and I arranged to take a few extra days off from work so I could stay there a bit longer.

I looked forward to a nice leisurely drive to the mountains. But right away, it was one of those days. First, I lost my wallet. After searching nearly an hour, I found it sitting prominently on the front seat of my car. Then, when I got in and turned the key, the engine wouldn't catch. Pretty soon the battery died, so I had to unclamp it and carry it four blocks to a filling station to have it charged. Big splotches of rain started falling on the way, and I was thoroughly soaked by the time I got there. After waiting around for what seemed like forever, sneezing and coughing, I had to carry the battery back in the rain and reinstall it. Mercifully, the car started.

Driving south, I thought my luck had changed when the sun came out. But soon I ran into several long traffic snarls due to road construction. I realized with a sinking feeling that the distraction of the dead battery had made me forget to fill up with gas. The reason I became aware of this was that the engine hiccuped once or twice and then stalled out completely outside of McAlester. I tried to hitchhike into town but no one stopped, probably because I was right in front of the state prison. I had to walk about three miles carrying my gas can, with the inmates working in the fields waving at me like I was their long-lost brother. I kept my head down and walked on.

A young guy at the filling station gave me a lift. When we got back to where my car was pulled over, a highway patrolman was parked right behind it, eyeing it and me with equal distaste.

"Having trouble?" he asked.

"Oh, I just ran out of gas," I replied as nonchalantly as possible, unscrewing my gas cap. For some reason the highway patrol always made me nervous, even when I didn't think I'd done anything wrong. I inserted the end of the gooseneck and drained the can. "No problem."

"Well, you've got at least a little problem. You have a flat, too," he pointed out, walking over to me.

Sure enough, my right front tire had pancaked all the way to the rim. "Oh, what a fool I am," I thought to myself.

The officer wanted to see my driver's license. When I dug it out and showed it to him, he asked where I worked and what I was doing so far from the city. I told him I had relatives who lived not far away, which in fact I did, and that I often came to see them. "I guess this isn't my day," I added. I began telling him my troubles, but he cut me off.

"Count your blessings, boy," he said. "Your plate's expired too. What are you going to do about it?"

"I'll get it taken care of soon as I get back."

"See that you do that." He gave me a two-fingered salute, touching his shiny visor, and headed for the patrol car.

"Thanks, sir," I said, turning back to my immediate problem.

I changed the tire, put the jack and the flat inside the trunk, slammed it, and took off — wondering what new ton of bricks was going to hit me.

Fortunately, the rest of the drive was uneventful. I stopped in Talihina for groceries, had the flat fixed, and soon arrived at Mary's cabin. A rust-colored pickup I hadn't seen before was parked off to the side in the grass. As I pulled up next to it, I noticed a large and very muscular young Indian sitting on the porch. He had long ropes of braided black hair falling down the front of his black cowboy shirt. The tips of the braids were tied with black ribbon, and he wore an old-style bone choker around his neck. All this was unusual in that day and time.

He was staring at me with an unmistakably hostile look. The instant I cut my engine and got out, he rose and marched resolutely toward me. He stood directly in front of me, blocking my way to the cabin.

"What do you want around here, city boy?" he asked. "Whatever it is, we ain't buying any of it."

"I . . . I came to see Mary," I stammered uncertainly.

"Mary who? She doesn't want to see you, and you better get your ass out of here fast."

His arrogant tone spiked my adrenaline, and I started to see red. I stared angrily back at him, with the nervous feeling that I was in a major eye-lock with a mountain.

"Why don't we just ask Mary if she wants to see me or not?" I replied with as much belligerence as I could muster.

"You know what?" the mountain replied. "You look just like that great big plastic man with red-checkered pants and a bib who stands out in front of all those Big Boy restaurants."

He seemed nearly twice my size, and the muscles in his neck were beginning to bulge impressively, but I was mad enough now to throw caution to the wind.

"Well, you know what yourself?" I countered. "You look like one of those silly wooden Indians they put out in front of cigar stores."

He didn't seem to have expected a comeback, and he looked off to one side for a moment, considering. Then he ran his finger around inside his bone choker, in the same movement a harried businessman might make fidgeting with his too-tight tie. Apparently I had thrown him off stride a hair or two, because finally he just barked, "Oh yeah?"

I didn't do much better myself. "Yeah," I replied.

His shiny black eyes ripped into mine, the time for talking clearly over. I was sure an avalanche of angry Indian was just about ready to crash down on me. It heightened my attention, and I became keenly aware of him. Despite my anger, I was still detached enough to admit that, all in all, he looked ruggedly handsome.

I clenched my hands into fists and was about to throw my most devastating haymaker, wondering if it would do any damage at all to this red granite wall, when Mary's voice yelled, "It's okay, Tub. Let him by."

Saved by the teacher. Tub looked me slowly up and down. Then he snorted and laughed nonchalantly, as if to say I was of no importance to him whatsoever. He turned on his heel and walked back toward Mary, who was standing in front of the cabin. I breathed a sigh of relief and then cursed him under my breath as I followed.

"I imagine you probably had some trouble getting here," Mary said to me. "That's because it wasn't time for you to come. If you would have remembered your dreams and paid proper attention, you would know I wasn't going to be here. Tub and I are going to a powwowing near Lawton. You have to learn to be awake at night so you'll know what's going on."

"I knew you didn't belong here," Tub said. "Dreams are Mary's telegrams, but you didn't get her wire."

Mary's comment about my dreams provoked a queasy sensation in the pit of my stomach, because I knew instantly what she meant. I had felt they were attempting to communicate a message, but all I had been able to remember when I woke was that Mary was in them, explaining something. I realized now she had been warning me not to come. Somehow her messages had exactly the opposite effect and had made me crave the mountains of southeastern Oklahoma all the more.

"Well, you're here now," she said. "Keep an eye on the cabin. Chop some wood and clear the brush around back. We'll return in a few days. We were headed out the door, but I had a feeling you were going to show up."

"We're going to powwow ten people — help them with their sickness," Tub said. "I'm her apprentice. I help Mary out," he added possessively.

"Well, I'm her apprentice, too," I replied stiffly.

Mary smiled. I walked with them to Tub's pickup truck and watched them drive away. It all seemed rather abrupt.

Well, I comforted myself that it really wasn't so bad being alone. I had some good books in the car and had brought plenty of good things to eat. I figured I might just as well enjoy myself, so I went fishing for awhile and then read several chapters of *Of Human Bondage*, a book about a crippled-up man in love.

Before dawn the next morning I cooked breakfast, crouched over the dew-wet ground by a small fire near my tent. I boiled some condensed milk and made a large tin cup of cocoa. Then I coated a small, pan-sized catfish with cornmeal and fried it up. After that, using the same iron skillet, I cooked some potatoes and an onion.

The first light began to streak across the horizon as I ate. The twinkling stars died out one by one as the dark overhead slid gradually into day. A band of deep purple mist lay low over the brow of the mountains, flowing into strangely shaped strands, changing shade subtly with the passing moments.

Fall in the Kiamichis can be breathtaking. The hills become awash in golden, fiery-colored leaves before they are stripped away by the wind. For me, it was particularly easy at this time of year to feel an intimate connection with each dogwood tree, each slate-gray boulder, each burbling stream, each animal. There was more than enough reason to get up early and spend the day knocking about in the mountains.

Before full sunrise, the mist began to weep a fine spray of rain. I fastened the buttons of my army surplus jacket all the way up to my neck to keep dry as I set out. Before long the drizzle let up, but the low mist still didn't lift. Thin purple smoke hung over the ground, veiling it. Only the taller patches of grass and brush and the upper parts of bushes protruded above it. The soil was soft and muddy, deadening the sound of my footsteps. I climbed to a high ridge, heading vaguely for an area known to the locals as the "Catclaws." Its name came from deeply incised rock formations that appeared to have been made by a monster cat scraping its claws into the hillside. I found a place where bulldozers had cut a rough dirt road, and I followed it.

Until then, I had been wandering absentmindedly, absorbed by the quiet scenery. Rounding a bend in the road, my attention became sharply focused. With a slight shock, I saw an unmistakable human form obscured in mist. I stopped dead in my tracks and drew in a sharp breath. A woman it was — a gaunt old woman was standing in the smoky vapors ahead of me. She was stooped and motionless. Her clothes were weirdly old-fashioned. Her dress was black, as were her long leather gloves, and her boots were buttoned up over her ankles. Most disturbingly, her face was covered with a veil. My first thought was that she was dressed for a funeral.

The woman held something red in each of her hands. I recognized the objects as vermilion-colored rattles. She lifted her left hand upward and dropped her right hand downward. She began to shake the rattles toward me, pointing one and then the other at me. I bristled. The sound had the unpleasant buzz of an X-ray when the medical technician hits the button and you sense that radiation is passing through you.

The old woman moved her arms and brought the two rattles together in front of her stomach. When they touched, the two rattles made a figure eight, or the shape of a red hourglass.

She shook them again in an ominous whir. She then appeared to levitate several inches above the earth. Her black-buttoned shoes were pointed toe-down. As far as I could tell, they weren't touching anything. Suddenly, she made a gravity-defying leap that propelled her the entire distance between us. I jumped instinctively backward as she landed exactly where I had been standing. I was absolutely terrified. My legs started pumping uncontrollably in reverse. Then they went out from under me, and I fell down flat on my back.

I rebounded immediately into a sitting position only to find that my numb legs wouldn't support me. I began scrabbling backward as fast as I could with the palms of my hands and my heels. I was too stricken with unearthly terror to make a sound.

The woman looked at me. I could vaguely make out her face behind her veil. It was chalky white, and the red slash of her lips seemed to be grinning at me like the mouth of a corpse. "You're Mary's," she said flatly.

"I belong to no one," I stammered back. "I'm not in any kind of human bondage."

"You think not. Well, it doesn't matter. You're in the wrong place at the wrong time."

I wasn't going to argue the point. I managed to scramble shakily to my feet. Without a word, I turned and ran as fast as my two legs would carry me. I heard the woman's demented laughter behind me as I fled. I ran and ran. I hit a tree limb and fell, but bounced back up and was running again without even noticing if I'd done any damage. Then I turned my foot on a round rock, did a crazy rigadoon, skipped once, spun around, and went straight down on my butt. Once more I shot up and was off again like a jackrabbit. When I finally reached Mary's place, I fell to the ground in front of my tent, heaving and gasping for air.

After my breathing returned to normal, I ate something and went to work splitting wood and chopping it into stove lengths to calm myself down. The day was warming up, and I began to sweat. My strange encounter continually replayed in my mind like a needle stuck in the groove of an old record, repeating the same sequence over and over. I worked furiously, but despite my efforts, the power of the old woman's image remained unabated. I set my ax aside.

A couple of hunting hawks flapped by overhead, but the old woman had completely stripped away the peace I'd expected to find in the mountains. The rain had stopped, though. The sun was becoming brighter and stronger, burning off some of the day's mystery. The warmth brought out the perfume of damp earth as the pools of water scattered over the ground began to dry up.

Thirsty from exertion, I went over to the well for a drink. As I lowered the bucket into the hole I saw myself reflected in the water below. Then the bucket splashed into the image of my face, sending out rings of ripples. I swung the rope back and forth to get the lopsided bucket to sink. While I hauled it back up, the surface of the water smoothed again and an image formed. Big as life, I saw the old woman's face staring up at me from the bottom of the well.

I dropped the bucket and staggered backward. I heard it splash when it hit. "Damn!" I yelled. "Leave me alone, you damned witch."

I went back to the woodpile and chopped feverishly until nightfall. I gulped down a hasty dinner. Great streamers of deep burgundy were stretched across the western horizon. The eight bright stars that formed the Drinking Gourd hovered over the mountains in the northwest. The sapphire-studded Dragon soon twinkled its tail in the deepening darkness. Mary called the constellations "our treaty belt with the universe." I had the feeling from her that the alignment of the constellations made some nights nourishing and others not. I hoped tonight's configuration was one of the more benevolent ones.

My sleep that night was no more than a blink and wink. I tossed and turned, and was glad to crawl sleepily out of my tent as soon as the rays of new sunlight fell across the mountains. Not bothering to cook breakfast, I just poured some evaporated milk over a bowl of dry cereal. As I ate, I noticed with an unpleasant start that the mysterious stump had moved several feet toward my tent. Between that and my too-strong memory of the old witch, I wondered if I might not be edging into madness.

After anxiously moving my tent once again, I worked for

most of the day clearing the brush behind Mary's cabin. Whatever I cut that was big enough to use, I dragged to the woodpile and snapped into kindling. Many of the pieces were rotten, so I just burned them. I didn't know how large an area Mary wanted cleared. I worked back and forth in a semicircle, going farther and farther from the cabin each time.

When it was about noon, I began to realize I must have gotten pretty heavily into some poison ivy. The vine was rampant there. I was covered with itchy welts and commenced to relieve my misery by clawing at them. I walked off toward the creek, thinking a bath might help. Mary's beat-up old claw-footed iron bathtub sat on pebbly ground a few steps away. It could be filled with buckets from the creek, then heated by burning wood in a fire pit underneath. The tub was also Mary's cauldron, in which she brewed medicine, and her washing machine, since she often put in a scrub board to wash her clothes. It was a kind of Kiamichi hot tub.

For awhile, it was beautiful there with the sound of the creek gurgling by, but I was soon uncomfortable again. The steaming water made my poison ivy itch even more. The rest of the day was a big dose of hell.

Somehow I got through it until Mary and Tub returned that evening. Before I could even begin to tell her about my frightening experience with the old woman, Mary took one look at me and had me strip down to my underwear. She told me not to wear my clothes again until they'd had a good washing. Tub found this enormously amusing and roared with laughter as I removed my clothes.

When I was done, Mary handed me a big jar of water with tiny pieces of something floating around in it. She told me to drink all of it.

"I know where there's some medicine for this," she said.

She went outside and was soon back with some plants that

she bruised in her hands and had me rub over my itchy skin. They smelled awful but gave immediate relief. When she was finished, she told me to go put myself into some new clothes.

When I came back, she put a jar of oily green gunk on the table and told me to smear it on my itchy places, as needed. Tub laughed and slid the jar of medicine toward me with a smirk. I snatched at it angrily.

"What's eating on you?" Tub asked.

I told Mary and Tub about the encounter I'd had with the old witch while they were gone, omitting of course my cowardly reaction.

"You met a grandmother," Mary said. "You survived. You must be too old for her, I think. We're friends, she and I, but you'd better keep away from her. She would as soon kill you as not."

Mary's words confirmed the sense of peril I'd felt. "Who was she?" I blurted out.

"She's an old grandmother of these mountains. I often call her twice great grandmother. Some call her the woman in black. She's been around a long time. Forever, it seems. She has trained many apprentices from infancy and then sent them out to other hills and mountains. She weaves a balance between life and death. It is said that if you meet her, you will either have a quick date with the cemetery or enjoy life as never before. What's it going to be with you?"

"How should I know? I hope I don't die."

"Well, you made it this far," Tub said. "These mountains are full of people who have disappeared without going off in a flying saucer — if you catch my drift."

"I think I've got the picture," I answered, not sure that I did. I wondered if he intended it as some sort of threat.

I turned to Mary and asked if she knew how the old woman had made her gravity-defying, fifteen-foot leap.

"Yes, I know exactly how it was done. You didn't really see an old woman dressed in black. You only thought you did. What you actually came upon was a small black widow spider. The red hourglass shape is her sign. She moved only a few inches toward you, but you saw it as a giant leap."

I laughed. "I know what I saw, Mary, and it wasn't a spider. I saw an old woman, and she was as real as you or me."

"You don't know a damned thing. You actually saw a spider, a spider with great power."

"Are you saying that my mind was just playing tricks on me?"

"No, you saw what grandmother wanted you to see. Don't think you are the only one to have seen this woman in black and been threatened by her. Thousands have had this same experience. I have seen her myself. The difference is that I have a true perception of her and know she is a tiny spider with enormous presence. Since your mind couldn't accept this as a possibility, it protected you. You experienced her in a form you were comfortable with — that of an old woman. You were wise to turn tail and run away."

"I didn't turn tail and run away," I lied in embarrassment. "Oh okay, I'll admit it. I was a tiny bit scared. I thought she was an old witch laying for me."

"No, only a seductive spider," Mary said softly. "Continue to use the sacred tobacco, David. One day you will see what is really going on. For now, live with your delusions."

"My delusions. Well, you've often told me about witches and wizards. Do they really exist, or are they delusions too?"

"Plenty of them around here," Tub said a little too loudly, giving me another of his stabbing looks. "I can tell you that much."

"Witches and wizards exist," said Mary. "They cause me no end of problems. There is nothing worse than a bad one. The old ones are the worst — the ones who have acquired power and know how to use it. They have nothing else to do but sit around and indulge in their evil arts, sending out bad spirits to do injury. They ought to have their heads knocked off."

Her statement startled me. "Mary," I said in shock. "I can't believe you said that. You told me always to respect elders."

"I mean both things. It is a sign of our times that old people are no longer revered, and so they are justifiably wrathful. Today, the world wants youth and believes that old people have outlived their usefulness. The elderly should be the most beloved of all, yet they are often despised. When they find themselves in this situation, many turn off onto dark roads in anger. They have had long lives and know where power is located, and they grab off some. They use it against people who have insulted them. They know how to keep close to the ground and strike like a rattle-snake. Don't think it isn't so. An old wizard is more capable than a young one. They have learned more about completion, so they can easily finish the story for others with their time-polished arrows, believe me. Always respect elders, whatever else you do.

"I'm getting old myself," she continued, "so I guess I ought to know. At night I go up in the air with my dream medicines. You can tell I've been up there by these streaks of white." Mary held out a braid of her salt-and-pepper hair. "See, I brought some of the white clouds back with me." She laughed.

"Well, I see I'd better be more careful how I treat you," I said. "I'm going to be much more respectful from now on."

Mary laughed heartily. "You ought to be careful always with me," she warned.

Tub matched Mary's prolonged laugh, but where hers was full of good humor, I felt his was still poking fun — targeting me. "Strange things do happen around here," he said. "Folks from the city have no idea. Maybe that's why they avoid us, Mary?"

"Maybe people avoid this area because of the likes of you, Tub," I said.

Tub turned and looked at me for a minute with impassive eyes. Then he replied evenly, "Why don't you stay away too?"

"Boys, boys, I don't need it," Mary interjected. "Quit riding each other, or leave."

Tub and I were both embarrassed. We sat silently at first, and then made small talk until Tub yawned and stretched. "I'm hitting the sack," he said. "I'm sleeping out in my truck tonight."

Mary told me to get some sleep too. As I left, I noticed with relief that the gnarly old stump had moved back toward its original place, farther away from my tent. I hoped it had given up whatever it had been intending to do.

Tub's cowboy boots were sticking out his truck window as I passed, and I heard his snoring from inside. He had fallen asleep immediately. I wasn't as lucky. I got in my tent and lay awake in my blankets a long time. I felt agitated and restless. The poison ivy no longer itched. My mental state was now the vexing problem.

When I finally slept, it felt as if a silvery gray curtain had fallen over me. It was creased with lines and folds, like trails that could be followed. I found myself walking in an unknown forest, where I came upon four black-coated fiddlers playing wild gypsy music in a rapid tempo. Spellbound, I followed them. They led me deeper and deeper into the forest. It was dark underneath the tall trees, but golden rays of sunlight shafted down through the leaves. The fiddlers came to a halt, and their music ended. They went off in four separate directions.

Suddenly, I was confronted by the woman in black. She was standing within a ring of trees. A mosaic of silken lines led away from her in all directions, glinting where they intersected the beams of bright sunshine. The lines were attached to the trunks of the trees circling her, as though she stood in the middle of a huge silken web. A faint breeze waved the strands softly. The woman was silent. I realized at once that her web was a time hatch, and that, passing through, one emerged into different dimensions. I knew the woman in black held within herself an accumulation of days, months, and years that added up to an untold number of lifetimes. She was able to play with time.

"I almost walked into your web," I said to her. "That would have been a mess."

"That is my lesson to you," said the woman in black. "Whenever you are blocked, remember my beautiful spinnerets. Check for damage to your web and repair it. Always return to your center."

"How do you know so much?" I asked her.

"I am the mistress of webs," she answered. "I am the principal spider spirit. All the spiders of the earth come from me. All spiders are connected to me. We are as one.

"If you had touched my web, I'd have eaten you," she said, eyeing me. "I think you'd probably be delicious." She began spinning a new thread, pulling at it with her teeth.

"Naw. I would taste bad," I said, feeling a little thrill of terror.

"I don't care for frivolous conversations," the woman in black said, not pausing in her activities. She sprang suddenly forward and pulled herself closer to me along a thread. "If you once begin a task, finish it."

"What is the silver strand you are weaving?" I asked.

"That is the moon strand, my child. The moon strand is the fabric of night. Night is the warp thread. It is made with a left-hand twist."

"And the gold strand?"

"That is the sun strand. The sun strand is the fabric of day. Day is the weft thread, and it is made with a right-hand twist. You see, I am very busy making both night and day. If I were ever to drop a stitch, it would be most confusing to practically everyone."

"It certainly would," I agreed.

"Come with me," said the woman in black, taking me into her arms before I could move. I was amazed at her great strength. A long strand of her web suddenly detached itself at one end and carried us aloft. Soon, we floated out over a great, wide river. The river rushed along below us, its water sparkling bright as sequins.

"Look down and see beneath the water," the woman in black instructed. "That is real gold you see shimmering, not glitter. To get it, pan for it."

Before I could reply I woke up to the sound of what I thought was rain beating down. It turned out to be Tub kicking dirt on my tent. He said that Mary wanted us to come to breakfast.

While we ate, I told Mary the details of my strange dream. I waited patiently for her to interpret it for me, but she remained silent.

"Well, what did it mean?" I finally blurted out.

After a few moments, Tub replied, "It's real simple. It means you're mentally warped and twisted."

Despite Tub's rudeness, Mary remained silent.

"Please, Mary," I pleaded. "Tub can joke all he wants, but I really am confused."

"The dream was a gift to you," she answered. "The more we learn of the living fire of dream the better off we are to face eternity. Magic lives where the two worlds meet and intersect. When you look for it, it's gone. Don't look. Accept."

"Okay, just tell me how to do that."

"Your dream is enough for you to know. I could tell you the four fiddlers were different aspects of time, that the river was life and the gold was spiritual understanding. I could say it means you must learn to live well and escape death. But that would do you and your dream a disservice.

"Dreams are sacred, and I won't go deeply into it. You may spend a lifetime entering your dream and you may find plenty of lessons there. If you're not careful, the dream web may catch and destroy you. What should be obvious to you, though, is that the spider woman has been teaching you about time. She isn't through with you yet. You can bet on it."

"Yeah," Tub seconded, not missing a beat. "Go dream some more."

As soon as we had eaten and the table was cleared, Mary told Tub and me she had some work for the two of us to attend to in Talihina. Tub drove us there in his pickup, making snide comments along the way.

Mary had instructed us to do some repair work for a woman whose house turned out to be little more than a shanty. The woman had three small children, and her husband had deserted her. She acted edgy and irritable, but Tub didn't seem to mind. We spent the day cleaning her house, taking pails of dirty diapers and other soiled clothes to the laundromat, picking up her yard, making small repairs, and generally lending a hand. We bought her two large sacks of groceries with money Mary had given us, mostly staples but also a few fancier things. The woman seemed ungrateful, even a bit antagonistic toward us. I wondered if maybe she hated men in general, and if she did I could see why. Her man had left her with a big job.

When we were finished, we went to a joint called Skinny's for burgers. Then we drove over to Tub's place on the outskirts of town. It had bare cement floors inside and was in even more of a shambles than the poor woman's had been. "Sit over here, why don't you?" he invited.

I parked on what served as Tub's couch, while he puttered

around. It was no more than a stack of boxes covered with a small mattress.

"Tub, this couch leaves something to be desired."

I began to get impatient, so I told him Mary would be expecting us and we'd best be getting back.

"Rein up. Hold on to your horses, buddy," Tub replied. "You can sure tell you're a city boy — always in a rush. Let's have a little drink first."

"Well, wait. What about Mary?"

"Stand up for yourself, man. Act like you've got some minerals down between your legs. A little drinky-pinky never hurt no one."

"Well, what did you have in mind?" I asked. "Do you want to go out to a club?"

Tub grinned at me mysteriously. "Naw. Those honky-tonks are too rowdy even for me. We don't need 'em. I've got something better."

"Yeah, what's that?"

"A gallon of smokestack lightning. You know, shine. Shinola. It's smooth as a baby's butt. It'll polish you right up. Want some?"

"Yeah, well, I guess a little taste couldn't hurt a body," I said. "Break it out. Guess we earned it today. We worked really hard. I could use a drink."

Tub got out the jug and set it on the table. He took a couple of old jelly jars that served as glasses, poured them full to the brim, and pushed one over to me.

"Swill on this, city boy," he said.

Agreeably, I grabbed the glass and tossed it back, letting about half of it slide down my throat. He was right — no store-shelf whiskey could have touched it, not even the high-dollar brands. It tasted as pure as wild mountain honey and turned me right into a honey bee.

"You weren't kidding, Tub. I swear, this Oklahoma corn has done been conjured," I said, smiling. "There ain't nothing else like it."

We spent the evening and about half the night drinking, swapping jokes, telling lies, having some good horse laughs, and singing Forty-Niner songs. We were drunk as a couple of old bullfrogs croaking at Granny Moon. I woke up on the concrete floor the next morning, feeling shaky. But then Tub offered me a little of the proverbial dog that bit me, and it seemed to put things right. Tub and I had become fast friends, and we remained that way then and forever.

Fourteen

WHEN WE FINALLY GOT BACK to Mary's, Tub pulled up a good distance from the cabin. "I'm not about to see Mary now. I'd never hear the end of it. She blames me for everything. Just tell her I'll be back in a couple of days."

"Okay," I said. "I'll make up some excuse why we were so late. I'll give her a load of bull. She won't know the difference."

"So long, buddy," Tub said as I got out. "Stay cool. It's the Indian way."

He drove off, and I walked up the road to Mary's. When I knocked on the door, she said, "Open it," and I went in. She didn't seem very welcoming.

She was sitting at her table decorating a piece of deerskin in the old way, with dyed porcupine quills.

"I will treat a man later this afternoon," she said. "I want you to drive me there. Since it will be your first time seeing a treatment, I want you to pay attention. But understand that this is not a formal powwowing, only a house call."

"Great," I said. "Maybe I'll finally learn something important."

"You may," she said. Then she paused. "How much did you two drink?" she asked. Her voice was even, and she didn't look up from her quill work.

"Who, me? Why, I've been sober as a judge, Mary," I replied. "Tub and I just worked late, so we stayed over at his place. That's all. We didn't have a drop."

"I can see lies, David. You and Tub were skunk drunk last

night, so don't waste your breath lying. You may be skillful enough to fool yourself, but you don't fool me. And for as long as I have my faculties, you never will."

"Okay, so we did get on a little harmless bender. So what? You're not my mother or Tub's."

"Alcohol and medicine don't mix, David. You shouldn't have trouble figuring that out. You grew up in Oklahoma, and you've seen what it can do to people."

"Are you forbidding me to drink?"

"Tobacco forbids it. Me, I don't care one way or the other. Go ahead and drink, and then I'll be rid of you." Mary swiveled slightly and looked at me for the first time. As she did so, she chuckled to herself. "Kill yourself, if that's what you want to do."

"What do you mean by that?"

"Too much drinking, which in your case is any drinking, leads to self-slaughter. It is a complete severing of oneself from this world. Drunks go over to the spirit world. They find happy old friends there. They don't know it, but that's why they drink.

"The problem is that when they sober up, they can't remember. Only drunks with power can do that. But the spirits remember perfectly well the good time they had. They hover around constantly, bidding the drunk to come join them once more. I can clearly see all your lonely spirit friends circling around you right now. You and Tub really tied one on — a pretty good one, judging by the number of spirits tagging around with you.

"You — you can't remember your spirit friends. 'Come on back,' they're calling. 'Have a little glass,' they say. 'Just one. Do it, and we will all be together again.'

"Admit it, David. Your throat is parched, and you feel their presence waiting for you. You want to have a nice cool one and then two, so you can be led back across. Oh, what fun you'll have with your treacherous little friends."

"I don't know what you're talking about."

"You don't? Then why do you look so frightened? I'll tell you why. Because the spirits call. You know it's true. Pretty soon your spirit friends will turn on you. Most probably they won't kill you quick because they like to have the solidness of flesh around. After all, they are spirits."

"You sound like a preacher, Mary. Maybe I made a mistake. What do you want me to do, confess or fall down on my knees and beg for forgiveness?"

"Neither. Be conscious, David. No man or woman can whip alcohol. Booze is tougher than any marine. It will put you down on the floor. The best you can do with it is don't." She shot me another one of her fierce, sideways glances. She added, "If you are going to drink, you must leave. The same goes for Tub."

I had been standing all this time, but I sat down heavily. The moments passed slowly and in silence. Finally, I went out to my tent.

Fifteen

*H*ALF AN HOUR LATER, Mary came out carrying a suitcase. She put it in the backseat of my car and then got in on the passenger side. Never once did she look at me. She just sat staring straight ahead with her arms folded across her chest. I figured this was her body language for "Get moving," so I took the cue and started the engine.

Following her directions, I drove for nearly two hours, crossing the state line into Arkansas. Mary sat impassively the entire time, simply pointing without speaking whenever she wanted me to turn in a particular direction.

We came to a little hill community of not more than ten dilapidated old houses. Mary then spoke for the first time, telling me to pull into a gravel driveway. We drew up to a particularly bedraggled house and parked.

If it hadn't been for an old flatbed truck with recent tire tracks behind it, I would have thought the place was totally deserted. There were large fruit trees, at least one apple and a peach, but they looked unattended and the yard was greatly overgrown. Dogs were yapping off in the distance.

I got Mary's doctoring outfit from the backseat, and we walked up the path to the front door. Mary knocked and went inside without waiting for an answer. She removed her fringed leather jacket and handed it to me. I hung it on a nail by the door, noticing the strong aroma of woodsmoke that clung to it.

The inside of the house was a shock: all in tatters and a total mess. The living room had become the main sleeping quarters, and an old man lay weakly on an iron bed. He was wearing grimy bib overalls but not much else. His cheeks were hollow. He looked as much frightened as he did sick. On the floor beside the bed were two unlaced, stained, and oily-looking boots draped with a pair of once-white socks, stiff with dirt. There was an odd smell of sweat mixed with other musty, undefinable odors. I hung back by the door while Mary went over to the bed. I stood a few feet behind her, holding her kit.

"Ned Henry, you're not feeling well?" Mary asked.

"No. I don't know what hit me, Mary," he replied slowly. Apparently noticing me for the first time, he added, "Who's this you've brought with you?"

Mary called me over and introduced us. I shook the old man's callused hand and then stepped back again.

Mary began to examine him, feeling the glands in his throat, looking at his tongue, taking his pulse, gazing deeply into his eyes. While she was at it, I regarded some ancient, wood-framed sepia photos on the wall. They seemed to be pictures of Ned Henry and his parents taken when he was a little boy. His parents were posed in their best Sunday-go-to-meeting clothes. Ned Henry was in short pants and he too looked all polished up. I wondered how he had gotten from his early life to his present circumstances. From his looks, his father was a so-called civilized full blood and appeared to be from one of the southeastern nations, while his mother might have belonged to a nomadic prairie tribe, possibly Lakota or Dakota.

Mary turned and instructed me to put her doctoring outfit on the table. I did as she said. Her outfit was just a regular-looking travel bag, indistinguishable from any other cheap suitcase.

"Find the fuse box and cut the electricity," she ordered. "I'll light some candles. I don't want any interference."

I went prowling for the fuse box. There were scraps of every conceivable thing lying about: rusty tools, dirty clothes, wadded-up bedsheets, and nearly anything else you could think of. The cluttered bathroom smelled of lye soap. The kitchen sink was full of iron utensils and grime-encrusted dishes. Mary lit some candles while I was still poking around. Finally I found what I was looking for and threw the switch, cutting off the power.

Mary was questioning old Ned Henry when I returned. "Are you still mixing up those cans of tomato sauce with water to make juice? Is that all you eat for breakfast?"

"Yeah. It's a lot cheaper that way than buying regular tomato juice, you know. I drink that along with a few cups of coffee."

"Well, I want you to quit that and drink my tea instead. I'll leave a sack for you before I go. Make it just like you would regular tea, and drink it every single morning. It would be good if you could also eat some ripe persimmons. Now, I don't want you to drink another cup of coffee, Ned Henry. You hear? But if you really can't stand it, and you just have to drink coffee, then at least cool it way down. No more drinking it hot. Understand?"

"Okay." He smiled weakly at her.

She turned to me. "David, you stay out of my way now. I have a lot to do."

I nodded and moved back a ways. First, Mary unfastened a long reed tube that had been tied to the side of her doctoring case. Then she pulled out a blanket and spread it lengthwise on the floor. Next she took out a bewildering assortment of items including bowls, gourds, small pieces of sharp flint, leather-wrapped medicine pouches, and other assorted objects, among them an ear of red corn decorated with feathers, which she called her "red teeth."

When she was ready, Mary took some leaves from an old fabric flour sack and scattered them on the floor around and on top of the blanket. I helped her lead the old man over to the blanket, and we laid him down on top of the leaves. I moved to one side again. Mary made Ned Henry comfortable and then sat down cross-legged just behind his head, holding a rattle. Next she prayed, smoked a cigarette, and blew some of the smoke on her hands as well as on the rattle. She placed a kind of wreath of what looked like dead brush on her head. Plucking one of the dried leaves, she gave it to the old man, telling him to chew it slowly. The leafy jumble on her head looked like a curious hat. Why she wore it was a mystery to me. She began to rattle and sing. I recognized power songs.

After an hour, she moved around to Ned Henry's right side. She undid his bib, pulled it down, and pressed hard with her index finger on his bare stomach, near his navel. She motioned for me to hand her a redtail hawk wingfan. She slowly drew the wing back over her right shoulder, as if she was going to throw it. Then she swept it over the old man's body. After several slow passes, she touched the side of his stomach gently with the feather tip and tapped several times.

She began to sing again, this time more like a chant. "Ah ah ah bah. Ah ah ah bah. Ah ———— bah. Ah ———— bah." Mary continued to fan and chant. Her trance-inducing vocables filled the room and made me feel dreamy, until she suddenly yelled "Feiah" with a great rush of breath. The unexpected shout was like a sobering splash of icy water in my face. I sat up, acutely conscious of my surroundings. Mary patted Ned Henry on the shoulder. "You have to get up now. I'm going to cut you."

He looked shaky, but he cooperated as Mary and I helped him to his feet. He shuffled a few steps, all stooped over, until he was where Mary wanted him. Mary told him to stand still and look at a point in the air just in front of him. "Let your eyes blur, or even cross," she said, by way of instructions. Ned Henry nodded his assent without speaking.

Mary used a lancet made from a sharp, black obsidian chip to cut an X about an inch long into Ned Henry's back. Then she used a buffalo-horn sucking cup to let his blood. Some of it ran down his back, so I got some towels and mopped him up. When the sucking cup was nearly full, Mary brought it around in front of him. Then she reached in and fished out an arrow-sharp piece of blood-dripping bone about three-quarters of an inch long. It looked as if it might possibly be human. She held it right in front of Ned Henry's eyes.

A big grin came over his face. "I knew that son of a bitch witched me. He shot me clean, didn't he, Mary?"

Mary nodded, returning his smile.

"How can I ever thank you, Mary?" he asked.

"Just get well and stay well, Ned Henry," she said. "Living here all alone like you do, I worry about you. I want you to start praying more and to take better care about yourself. If your mama were still alive, she'd tell you to clean up this place."

I helped Mary pack her stuff, and we said good-bye to the old man. Mary pressed a large paper sack full of tea into his hands. I was surprised that he didn't offer to pay her. He looked perfectly at peace and nearly well when we left.

We drove off in silence. I was angry at what I had just witnessed, and Mary knew it. I pushed down a little harder on the accelerator than I usually did, and we were soon back across the state line into Oklahoma, driving down the road back to Mary's cabin. I told her what was on my mind.

"I can't believe you did that to a nice old man."

"What do you mean?"

"You hoodwinked him. You didn't suck out that piece of bone. You slipped it into the horn yourself, didn't you?"

"I did. You're a good spotter. I can see I can't fool you."

"Don't be condescending with me, Mary. I don't think it was right to trick him like that."

"Well, did you want to take responsibility for his death instead? I didn't, not when I knew I could help him. Yes, I juggled him. The hand is quick. I'm a juggler. What did you think I was?

"Let me just put it another way. I spoke to Ned Henry in a language he understands. Ned Henry didn't go to high school like you, and he never bothered to teach himself. He can't read or write. He's not so sure of all those scientific laws as you are. But that doesn't mean he doesn't have mental power. Before I treated him, he had convinced himself he was dying, and indeed he was. Now he's convinced he's healed, and he is.

"And regardless of what you may think, there really are many old sly dog witches running about these mountains. There are some deadly shooters and throwers who can pitch with the best of them. The old man had insulted one of them, and he did take a dart in precisely the spot where I lanced him. With all your great book learning, you would be unable to heal in a similar predicament. Ned Henry is going to be fine now, but he was well on his way out the door, feet first."

I didn't answer. I often felt over my depth around Mary, especially when her logic eluded me.

When we got back inside her cabin, she told me she had a gift for my future doctoring outfit. After first washing it out thoroughly, she gave me the old buffalo cupping horn.

"I have a new one to use, but this little pump has assisted in many a cure," she said. "I want you to treat it with respect."

I told her I would. I was touched by her generosity, for I knew the horn meant a great deal to her. I went out to the tent and put her gift with my things, since I had to leave later that evening to get back to work.

Before I left, I told her rather forcefully, "I have a telephone, you know, Mary. We don't need to have any more confusion with your trying to send messages in dreams. You can just go into Tal-ihina and give me a ring collect anytime you want."

"I have nothing against telephones," she said, "even though they do rob you of many of your other senses. I hardly ever use them myself. But you never know. I just may give you a call." Her eyes crinkled at the corners as she smiled.

Sixteen

WHEN I GOT BACK to my apartment, I carried my things upstairs and unpacked them. I put the cupping horn on a bookshelf and quickly forgot about it. There was a lot I needed to do before returning to work the next day. First I went to a nearby store called the Milk Bottle and stocked up on groceries. Then I went to an all-night laundromat and did my wash.

When I got home again, the phone was ringing as I opened the door. I set my basket of laundry down and picked up the handset. "Hello?"

There was only a dial tone. "Hello? Hello?" There was still only a dial tone, so I hung up.

A little later, I was lying on my bed feeling slightly exasperated when it rang again. I let it ring several times before answering and noticed that it didn't seem to be ringing quite as loud as usual. Again there was no one there. I hung up and immediately called a friend, asking her to call me right back to see if my phone was working. When she did, it worked perfectly well.

Then it rang again. This time, I picked it up with a mixture of nervousness and growing irritation. No one there. It rang several more times that night, and then again and again at odd hours for the next few days. I decided someone was playing a joke on me, and enough was enough. I quit answering it, even though it meant missing calls from friends. Still, it kept ringing. Then I thought perhaps the sound was coming from downstairs, or even from another apartment house, brought to my overly sensitive ears by some acoustical quirk. I began searching for the direction of the sound, but each time I was about to get a fix on it, the ring-ing would quit.

Four frustrating days later, I stumbled on the source of the ringing. To my astonishment, it was Mary's buffalo cupping horn. I got to it while it was still ringing and picked it up in my hand. I didn't know what to do. Feeling stupid, I said, "Hello?"

I heard the unmistakable sound of Mary's laughter coming from inside the horn. I was terrified. I dropped the horn to the floor, and I'm sure my face must have drained of all color. I couldn't make myself pick the horn up again, even though it had stopped laughing at me. I just left it on the floor and went slowly off to bed. I had to be up early the next morning, but I didn't get much sleep.

Seventeen

ETURNING TO THE KIAMICHIS, I was surprised to find several people sitting around on the porch of Mary's cabin. Evangeline was there, and I was happy to see her. Tub was back. I was happy to see him again, too. I said hello to both and then met two other people who looked to be full bloods. Their names were Patricio and Javier. They both wore highly starched linen shirts that had hummingbirds embroidered on them. At that time gala dress like this appeared slightly effeminate. They spoke with Spanish accents but apparently knew English well, and both seemed warm and glad to meet me.

Javier was the smaller of the two men. He was quick and witty but perhaps a little distrustful. His eyes didn't miss a trick. Patricio, on the other hand, was jovial and fun. His smile went to both corners of his mouth.

"We're glad you're here," Evangeline said. "We're having a story fire tomorrow night."

"What's that?" I asked her.

"Oh," said Evangeline, "I thought you knew. Long ago, after a hard day the storytellers would assemble the people at a special fire. They told stories, mostly traditional tales. Thinking of the story fire helped the people during work and created a kind of excitement. The fire gave these stories warmth."

"Okay," I said. "I get it: entertainment like sitting around at night and telling ghost stories when we were kids."

"Well, something like that, I guess," Evangeline said.

"Yes, something like that," Mary said. "And we've been

waiting for you, David. We want to hear a tale from you." She was sitting on an old crate, a wooden packing case of some sort. She asked sweetly, "By the way, did you get my call?"

"Yeah, but I don't think it's funny. I thought I was crazy."

"You are crazy, and don't you forget it," Mary replied, laughing, causing the other men and Evangeline to join in with their own chortles. They were an exuberant bunch — truly, while I stood there embarrassed and blushing like a bleeding beetroot. "Crazy is the only way to be sane these days, David. You just couldn't resist our pack of crazy dogs, now could you?"

I took good bit of ribbing from Tub and Evangeline. Even Patricio and Javier put in their two or three cents' worth. Mercifully, Mary ended the roast by ordering Patricio and Javier to town for some items and setting Tub and me to work on the roof of her cabin.

A little later, Tub and Evangeline left for town to meet Patricio and Javier for lunch. Having just arrived, I didn't want to go with them. Mary found me attempting to build a little fire in a circle of rocks near my tent. I was squirting some small sticks of wood with lighter fluid. Golden sunlight slanted across Mary's face, but she wasn't smiling. She stood right there and didn't say anything, but I could tell I had done something to offend her.

"Okay, what have I done now?"

"David, I've seen people over at the picnic grounds douse their wood with kerosene to get it going. It disgusted me. I never expected to see you do it. That's a spoiled fire, a sign of impatience and arrogance. I never want to see this again, understand? I never want to see you use paper or any other quick starts, those flammable liquids. If you are in such a rush that you can't do up the fire properly, forget about it and do something else instead. If you start the fire disrespectfully, it won't like you anyway. It might warm your bones but never your spirit."

"Mary, hell. I just wanted —"

Abruptly, Mary said, "You are disrespectful. Fire centers the camp. It holds the world together. In the old days, fire was the heart of the nation. Fire renewed life's circle. A ceremonial fire was built every fifty-two years. This was always a time of great mourning and also of great celebration, because it meant the death of the old cycle and the birth of a new one. Fifty-two years is the age of an adult. Inner fires burn most brightly until this age. Life has four thirteen-year intervals until the age of fifty-two is reached. And so these years are called fire years. The years after those fifty-two winters, preceding death, are shadow years. The fires of life are gone to embers, but that doesn't mean they can't flare up ever so often."

"I'd say not, where you're concerned, Mary."

"There's many a kind of fire," she went on. "Lightning is a spirit-knife fire. Trees cut by lightning make a very useful fire for treating toad sickness and sorcery.

"It used to be that upon conception, the mother would plant a tree. When the child was born, the tree was fed the placenta. If the tree was strong, then the child was strong. If the tree died, so too would the child. If lightning struck the tree, the child would become a power doctor. If lightning were to strike the tree four times in one night, then the child would know everything.

"The sky, the universe, holds us in a great cooking pot, an inverted kettle. Master of Breath blows into it and stirs us up. We are all food being cooked within this pot, and it is important that we learn just what manner of food we are. When something is cooked it changes in different ways, according to its nature and just how it's cooked. Change is the rule. We are always being changed.

"Learn that traditional cooking fires are female fires. They have three stones representing Spark Girl, Fiery Girl, and Ash Old Woman. These stone beings support a flat stone used as a grill to help in the job of cooking.

"You are my apprentice. I am cooking you. I am grilling you. I am changing you. Right now, you are roasting in a blue hummingbird fire."

"What's that?"

"Blue hummingbird fire is a complete fire, a fire of love. Without love, we are incomplete. Whether you know it or not, right now you are being cooked in the flames of love. When you are finished, your clothing will be succulent flowers. By that I mean that you will one day understand the plant world, and you will not allow yourself to be separated from it. You will be given a long healing knife of obsidian. You will get doctor powers. You will know how to use your knife to remove witches' arrows."

"Are witches also cooked?"

"They are. Wizards and sorcerers are prepared on the blue jaguar spit, sobbing and weeping while they're being roasted. The smoke of the dark fires surrounds them. This is the smoke of dead and departed spirits. The apprenticeship of wizards and sorcerers is a long and painful one. They are taught hatred and instructed in evil arts. That's why a witch is so happy causing trouble. They like to make you suffer. It's what they know, and they have plenty of sorrow stored away for you and ready to dish out."

"If we are food, and if we are being cooked, then do we get eaten?"

"Of course. It is best to be wet food, full of moisture. Wet food is full of power. Dry food is not so good. And a lot of food gets spoiled."

"How about me?" I asked.

Mary laughed. "David, you're the dessert."

"Are there many fire sicknesses?" I asked.

"Yes, but they are generally called campfire disease. Fire sleeps in every being, and it is her dance that is the greatest dance of all. Fire can give such pain and linger so long. Direct burns can be difficult to cure, and often even time and distance will not heal them. The scald is carried in flesh's memory and won't easily go away. The curer must reach this memory and soothe it, in order to get results. Even then, it may not work.

"Mother of mothers was born of fire — our earth, our planet. An old story tells of a man who was sitting on a rock near his campfire, idly poking a stick into it — Yellow Tobacco Boy, his name was. You've heard of him, haven't you?"

She winked at me, and I nodded and smiled.

"Anyway, Yellow Tobacco Boy was gazing absently into the flames one time and not paying much attention, I think. He was so careless that a spray of fire walked right up the stick and caught him by the hand. It was Living Fire, reaching up from within the flame. He pulled Yellow Tobacco Boy to his bosom and into the land of fire.

"Living Fire said, 'No lazy man will be a good hunter. In hunting, it brings bad luck not to kill your game. It is also bad luck to build a bad fire. A lazy man builds a lazy fire, a fire that goes out, a disrespectful fire. Never use living wood or rotten wood. The good man builds a good fire, a fire that cooks, a fire that protects, a fire that heats tired bones. Build a good fire, one that is properly banked away from the wind. Use good wood. A man who builds a proper fire will have his arrows sharp and ready. He will be successful in hunting.'

"Yellow Tobacco Boy asked to dwell in the land of fire for four years, so he could learn how to cure campfire sickness. Living Fire agreed and faithfully instructed him. At the end of that time he visited Yellow Tobacco Boy.

"Living Fire said, 'Yellow Tobacco Boy, you have apprenticed well. You have listened and learned much. You have dried and neatly piled your firewood. You have learned that smoke from the hunting fire blesses the heart of the hunter. You have learned to smoke yourself with a bough of cedar in a sacred way.

You have learned harmony with the spirit of the game. Go now in my name and treat campfire sickness.'"

Mary lit a match and held it upright, so the flame danced on the tip of it. She waved it in front of my face. "You know what you're looking at when you watch TV, don't you? You're watching an electronic fire. Me, I'd rather see this."

Following her example, I lit a sulfur match. I studied it, trying to see it in a new way, as Mary did. "Ouch, hot damn!" I yelped, shaking it out. "I burnt my finger."

"See, fire has power. It was the first magic."

I blew on my finger. "Getting burned must be a campfire sickness."

"Yes. But most everyone learned how to avoid that. Anger is a kind of campfire within. It can cause a terrible disease. Most cancer is an imbalance with fire or some form of unseen heats. Of course, the old curers don't call cancer by that name. Every campfire sickness has a different cause. One kind is black bass, and another is horse. These are campfire sickness. Campfire-on-a-cold-morning is another disease. Scorched brains is one that drives you crazy. There's snow woman sickness and fires-of-many-colors disease. Green, brown, and yellow fire sicknesses are caused by the improper lighting of tobacco. There are many others.

"There are hundreds of unlucky cooking fires, and other fires of unknown character that few people understand. There are ghost fires and strange light fires, which are called swamp jacks and jack fires. These cause spells and frights. There is talk of upside-down and backward fires. Some say there are even nitwits and sacred clowns who have the ability to reverse the power of fire. I don't know about this.

"Pretty soon I'll show you how campfire sicknesses are treated. These diseases often sneak around in their milder forms.

You need to know how to protect yourself, if nothing else. I hope you can see to use fire properly."

I nodded in agreement.

Mary showed me the right kind of tinder and kindling, and its proper placement. When we were done, the stacked logs were surrounded by a circle of round rocks. I was proud of our work.

"Spark it," she said.

This was done by taking a flat piece of fool's gold and a sharp flint, and striking the two together to cause a shower of sparks to fall on the tinder. I blew carefully for it to catch and create a small flame. We must have constructed the fire properly, for it took right off and was soon going good and strong. I fed it some more wood and then sat down next to it.

Mary nodded toward it as it was building. "This is a good fire. You can do this tomorrow, build a story fire. You will be nourished by it."

Eighteen

*E*ARLY THE NEXT MORNING, Mary sent me to pick up a box of roots and herbs from a healer who lived in Antlers. A dark woman answered the door.

"Where's Mary?" she asked.

"She didn't come," I said. "Do you have a package for me?"

She disappeared inside and returned shortly, carrying a box overflowing with various kinds of plants. I recognized a large tied-up bundle of what Mary called the little white man, otherwise known as native ginseng.

"I dug all these fresh," the woman said. "The cuttings are less than a week old. Mary will know."

I wasn't clear on the arrangements, so I asked, "How much do I owe you?"

"Nothing. Mary's money could never be spent with me. Mary has taught me more about plants in one day than I learned by myself in twenty years. She's a magician when it comes to making remedies."

"Well, thanks," I said. "I'll get this to her right away." I left with the box.

Driving back up the road to Mary's cabin, I was surprised to see a station wagon leaving her place. The driver wore a white shirt and had a graying beard. I eased off the road into the weeds to let him pass. He nodded at me and I waved back, but I didn't recognize him.

"Who was the guy?" I asked Mary, as I carried the box of roots and plant cuttings into her cabin.

Mary told me he was "Doctor so-and-so," an anthropologist from some big eastern university. He was writing a book and had come to ask Mary some questions. "I didn't tell him much," she said. "He baffles me. He wanted to pin me down like some dead, dried-up bug. He wants Indians to remain the same so it will fit his notions. Yet things die if they don't change." She cocked her head in a way that meant she was glad to be rid of him. Eyeing the box, she said, "Look at that. You brought home half the neighborhood. I see some old friends in there."

She started rummaging around, sorting. She took out several tied-up bundles of stripped bark, smelled them, and put them in a box on a high shelf. She hung one sheaf of dark green leaves from a nail in a ceiling joist. Examining the ginseng, she broke off a small piece and handed it to me, saying, "Chew on this."

As I watched Mary sort through the box, I decided to ask her more about Javier and Patricio. Of the two, Javier seemed to have the more dominant personality, while Patricio was louder, more forward, and more active in general. Javier didn't seem as accepting as Patricio, who was open and secure. They were so close, they often appeared to communicate with each other by telepathy.

"They are on a different road than yours, David," she said. "Their tracks will follow the old traditional paths with care and precision. They have difficult responsibilities. Javier and Patricio will have to carry the medicine root, if they can, and never let go of it, never be able to diverge from it.

"You walk an easier road," she said. "You will live on the everyday highway of life, or so you think. You will hide behind the scenery, like a fox. But you are fox's cousin. You are the blood of coyote. Coyote is always smelling the kill before eating, to determine whether it belongs to another or has been contaminated by man. When you dig yourself out of your coyote ruts, you will be an old, smart coyote then — a tired but undefeated old yo-deler — a howling moon dog. I wish you well. You used to think you came to me by choice, to drink of my medicine teachings as you will. But, as you have probably guessed by now, it was really your spirit relations who desired this for you. I have taken you on as a favor to them. I have divined you, and the old one, the to-bacco spirit, has told me it has tasks for you. But first, you must open your eyes and see this.

"You must come to this realization on your own. That is why I allow you the freedom to pretty much come and go as you please. I am not going to chase after you to keep you, so I realize you might just wander off. I was young once myself. But what-ever you decide to do, I don't believe you will be any the worse off for your experiences with me."

I protested that I had no intention of ever leaving. She replied that I was like an oak leaf torn from the branch and blow-ing in the wind. She said I had lost the memory of being oak, and that because of this, I was without purpose. Of course, I dis-agreed sharply with her.

She laughed and said, "Prepare the fire just as I have shown you, for there is many a tale to be told."

Nineteen

A CRESCENT MOON WAS UP, creating a diffused light through the thin cloud layers of the deepening night. We were sitting around a little story fire I'd built. We had been making small talk, cracking jokes, and rolling on the ground in laughter. Just now we were discussing millipede sickness. Mary told us how to recognize and treat it. Then she asked me for a cigarette. I shook a Lucky out of my pack. She lit it and took several breaths.

She stared at the fire for a long time and began praying. She raised both hands up as though to grasp the veiled moon between them. "Creator," she prayed. "Hear my voice. It is the voice of a conjure woman. Listen to us here, amidst the upheavals of our changing times. Listen to the prayers of your conjure daughter. Don't forget us. We are your children.

"Protect us outwardly and inwardly. May our blood and shadow keep its strength and all power and strength aligned against us disappear. Give knowledge to our left hands and strength to our right hands. When we come as strangers to a strange place, let no enemy or bad magician be able to harm or disturb us. Protect us from bad conspiracies or other bad powers, from whatever direction or some dimension or direction unknown to us. Save us from bad magic.

"Creator, help us to observe and understand so that we may walk our walk in a manner that is pleasing to you." And she switched to Choctaw and prayed for a few more minutes. When she finished her smoke, she sat down on the ground and took up her drum.

Using her drum, she began to sing in a soft chant with the beat. She later translated for me. "Ho kay yo. Ho kay yo. I am of the people. Ho kay yo.

"This I have spoken. You who are making the fire dance as I am dancing here by the fireside. Ho kay yo.

"My conjure eyes are turning right side up as you have instructed. Cast me on the inside. Cast me on the outside. Ho kay yo. There is no other. Ho kay yo.

"These are my words. Ho kay yo. Ho kay yo."

When she was finished, she carefully placed her drum out on the ground in front of her along with the drumstick. She turned her head, looking at each of us for a moment. "Now, I want to tell you. Here is a millipede story, and it's about a beautiful maiden," she said. "Can you see her? How pretty she looks and what a lovely smile. It happened that this maiden walked far away from her fire, her village. She got lost. She walked and walked, trying to find her way back. But the farther she walked, the more confused and lost she became.

"'My legs are so tired, I believe they are wearing away,' she said. 'I can't take another step.'

"She sat down with her back to a tree and went to sleep. When she woke up, her legs wouldn't budge.

"'Oh me, oh my,' she said. 'What is to become of me? I fear I am far away from my fire and no one will find me. I will surely die.'

"Hearing her, Millipede Girl poked her head and a few wiggling legs out from underneath a rock. 'You are in a fix,' she said. 'May I offer a suggestion?'

"'What's that?' asked the maiden.

"'As you can see, I have more legs than I know what to do with. I think so many legs make some people very confused. I think I make most people who watch me get dizzy. I think I can cause them to trip up — to become uncoordinated and addled.

So if you want to trade me some of my good legs for your useless ones, it wouldn't make any difference to me.'

"'Let's swap then,' said the beautiful maiden.

"And so Millipede Girl traded a bunch of her legs to the beautiful maiden. The number was about forty, fifty, sixty-eleven — you know, give or take a leg or two.

"'Now we are sisters, half sisters anyway,' said Millipede Girl. 'I will teach you about my powers and how to cure millipede sickness.'

Mary sat silently a long moment, then said, "Millipede sickness begins with aches in one or both legs. Then the legs fail to respond correctly, which causes a great deal of confusion and inner struggle, resulting in fatigue. First the patient has difficulty walking, but eventually he can't walk at all. It's not life-threatening, but it can be crippling or incurable."

"Brings you right down to the ground, huh, Mary?" I said, smiling. "Time to get to whittling some crutches."

"Depends," Mary said. "Often it can be treated successfully. You can try foot rubs and hot dirt rubs. Tight herbal wraps about the calves might give some relief. If there is a good deal of pinching, lightning-root water helps. Of course, the millipede might come to you in a dream or even in person and tell you the treatment needed, just as animals often show up with the cure."

We made more small talk, and by and by Tub said, "Here's one I learned up in Montana. It's about a moose sickness, I guess. They say there was a time when Moose was tiny, tiny, tiny — even smaller than a mouse. Moose didn't like this arrangement very well. All the larger animals were picking on her, and some were eating up on her. Moose decided to puff herself up with some importance in order to grow. She threw her head back and puffed and puffed. Soon she was as big as a dog.

"'Oh, that's much better,' she said. Then a bobcat pounced on her and had her for lunch.

"Moose threw her head back and puffed and puffed once more. Soon she was as big as a bear.

" 'I'd like to see you attack me now,' she said to a bunch of bobcats. 'I'm beautiful. I do big things. I will go places, so that you can see me. No one will dare harm me now. I'm a true big chief. I'm the biggest chief of them all — Chief Moose.'

"Hunters sent arrows to knock her down. Moose was certainly surprised.

" 'That was a mean trick,' she said. 'I'm going to get so big I'll squash those hunters like bugs.'

"Sure enough — puff puff — she grew even more. Up, up into the sky she grew, until she towered over the treetops.

" 'Ha, look at me now,' she called. 'I'm prettier than rainbows. I'm bigger than big Chief Mountain. If that doesn't impress you, what will?'

"An eagle was soaring around her head. 'Just what do you think you are going to eat, Chief?' asked the eagle.

" 'Why, I'll eat the forest, drink the lakes and rivers. See? Watch.' She pulled up a tree and swallowed it whole, but this did little to stem her growing hunger. She traveled up and down the land eating the forests and drinking the lakes dry.

"Soon, there was nothing left to eat or to drink. She cried and cried. 'What will happen to me now?' She cried herself to sleep. In a dream she saw Creator.

" 'Have you learned humility?' Creator asked.

" 'Yes,' she answered. 'I just want to fit in.'

" 'And so it shall be,' said Creator."

"Good story, Tub," I said. "Are you talking about yourself?"

"No, it's really about a city boy that gets busted up here in the mountains."

Javier, who had been sitting quietly, gave a slight groan. He looked gaunt in the shadowed firelight. "How can you tell when someone is getting moose sickness?" he asked Mary.

"Moose is a charger bashing your defenses, allowing pain to flourish. One sign is the smoking of lots of commercial cigarettes, smoking them way down. Overeating, or destroying relationships for no good reason, may forewarn moose sickness. It may come as self-hatred. Self-punishment follows right behind self-hate, nipping right at its heels. Self catches self, and all selves tumble. Eventually, down you go with this sickness."

Patricio asked, "How do you treat it?"

"In its beginning stages, it can be cured by prayer alone. Later, the early shoots and roots of blue flag might help. It comforts the moose spirit. And there are many other remedies. Moose is a curer you want at your side."

I poked at the fire with a stick. Mary reached over and took the pack of cigarettes from my shirt pocket. Shaking them out, she gave one to each of us. We lit them by passing around the smoldering stick I had been using.

Mary told us some more about the moose. We talked awhile longer, often laughing giddily at scant scraps and snippets of humor. Evangeline, who had laughed a lot but hadn't said much, spoke up. "Tomorrow night, me."

Everyone said good night. Evangeline, Tub, Javier, and Patricio headed off in different directions to get some sleep. Mary was in no hurry to leave, so I stayed put. When the others had trailed off, I said, "Mary, I really love these old occult teachings. Thank you."

"David, these are not occult teachings. Where did you get such a dumb idea? These are common, ordinary things. I am teaching all of you so that you may share with others and be of service. Of course, I am not teaching you everything. There are some medicines best kept concealed for now. Maybe a better word would be shielded, or kept out of reach, the way we used to hang meat high in the treetops so that bears, lions, and other animals couldn't get at it. The meat was for all the people.

"I have no respect for those who believe they are wiser and better than ordinary people. They try to take the meat and share it with no one. There are more and more people who do this. That's why I live out here, in a place few people would be interested in.

"Ordinary. That's all I am. And that's all any of you are."

I stared at her. "Do you really think you are such an ordinary person, Mary?"

"Yes, no worse and no better. My world is more ordinary than you know. The ordinary world is filled with wonder. That's my only secret."

"But Mary, you just said yourself that you don't share everything. You are the most secretive and hidden person I've ever met."

"No. I will tell you everything, David, as long as you can understand it. That's the real problem. Often you don't get it, so my work is always going back down the steps, taking you by the hand and leading you up again. You will climb the steps at your own speed, and there's nothing I can do about that except to get behind you and push, and maybe kick your butt every so often.

"If I push you too hard, you will trip and fall. If I kick you too sharply, you will become angry and refuse to budge. You act so much like a black tortoise while I am trying to lead you to places where the wild geese cry.

"At least, lift up your eyes to their honking."

Twenty

THE NEXT NIGHT the moon was even bigger and brighter. The fire was toasty. I sat next to Tub. Patricio and Javier were tinged in red as the flames licked upward. Mary and Evangeline were next to them. Evangeline stood. "This one is a tale about Yellow Tobacco Girl," Evangeline said. "The moon is up full, so let's talk about her. She often gets neglected, you know. She has a love story to tell."

As we looked up at the moon, a bank of white clouds drifted over it and obscured our view.

"Look," Evangeline said. "Tonight she covers herself and runs to hide.

"It is told that Yellow Tobacco Girl had turned her back on all the young men of the fire, the village. 'None are good enough,' she explained to her conjure mother.

"And true. She was indeed lovely. And she was as kind and gentle as she was beautiful.

"The young men continued to pester her. She shook her head, no. She was not inspired by any of their pleas or antics.

"'Are you never to be married, my daughter?' asked the mother over supper. 'Perhaps you should take pity on one of the men of our village. It is long past the time for you to have a husband.'

"'Must I weep?' the girl said. 'All these young men leave me cold, Mother. Surely I will die if I am forced to keep a blanket with one of them.'

"Her daughter's words made the mother sad. She went out

and conjured the sun. She told the sun of her daughter's predicament, and the sun listened with interest. 'I have no wife,' said he. 'I have seen your daughter many times, unbeknownst to her. She is beyond earthly beauty. I will marry her if you have no objections.'

"And so it was arranged.

"Day came. A beautiful golden warrior appeared before the young woman. He was dazzling and lit the world around about. 'I have come to take you home with me so that we may live together and be married forever.'

"'You are the one I have waited for,' she said. 'My heart is full of joy.'

"When the warrior touched her hand and held it, she floated in the air — higher and higher. With his true love at his side, they hurried to the world above our many campgrounds.

"'Where is my daughter?' the father inquired.

"'Our daughter has left us to live in the sky. But there is no reason to sorrow. You can see her in all her majesty most any night. The people will refer to her with each change of season. She will tug at the bellies of women like the tides, so that women will continue to know her. Coyotes and wolves will sing her praises and call for her to return. Maybe one day she will.'

"Now I will speak of the secret meaning of this tale. It tells us to pay attention to the moon. Some nights in the autumn, she is golden like tobacco. If you look carefully and gaze deeply, you will see beautiful Yellow Tobacco Girl as she walks across the night sky. She is there in the sacred hoop, and she will smile that you have seen her. She will embrace you.

"They say when she appears before you, a little more love will visit your life as well as a new sense of being connected."

We sat in silence for awhile. Mary passed around medicine cigarettes, taking a handful from her shirt pocket and handing us each one. She told us to smoke them and quietly reflect on the powers of the moon. We each lit the cigarettes, passing a smoldering stick from the fire. They were tightly rolled in a prepared corn shuck. The flavor of the mix suggested it contained a good deal of Indian tobacco, an herb often used by women. It was a pleasant smoke.

Evangeline still stood silhouetted against the immense full moon and chalky night sky. She was beginning to show her pregnancy considerably, her belly rounding out. Orange from the fire lapped over her — a beautiful Madonna. This was indeed a moment of the caring heart.

Twenty-one

S INCE THESE STORY FIRES to this day are sharp in my memory, I will relate a few of them. In the beginning of his narration, Javier looked scared. But as the story progressed, he warmed to it. It affected me as a sort of maze that I was drawn into — perhaps going deeper into levels of my own being. His English was probably better and more correct than mine.

He stood by the fire and seemed to be reaching into a hidden store within his memory. He began after a long pause. "Yes, I know well enough how to tell it. But I have to twist it in words from a foreign language. Some stories have powerful guardians. For a story is a gateway, and once inside you will find yourself on a new road. There may be many dangerous and mysterious beings awaiting you. You may walk through heaps of fallen leaves or through a meadow dappled with bright flowers. You may find yourself in a thicket. You may visit an encampment of animals or even lost tribes of forgotten worlds.

"But that is not the kind of story I will tell. I am simply going to tell you what happened in our village. As you know, I live in the east coastal area of central Mexico. My life is a simple one. It turns with the pathway of stars just as the earth turns. Like life everywhere, there are days of want and days of plenty. There is love and laughter in our village. There is happiness.

"A mysterious man came our village one day. His name was Jose Crow, the raven. He wore city clothes with sunglasses and a straw hat with the brim turned down. He was tall, elegant in his movements, and even before he revealed himself he caused a great sensation because of his self-assurance and manner.

"A few days after his arrival, he came to the market and people gathered around him. He began doing tricks, if indeed that's what they were. They defied all logic. Birds would appear in his hands and then disappear right before our eyes. He would pull silver coins from the ears of little children. Balls would float in the air in front of him. Flowers would grow from the ground he walked on. He could read minds and reveal your secrets before everyone.

"As you can imagine, this raven held everyone's attention like a vise. Our lives, which had been drab, became filled with wonder as he would perform these and other feats each week in the marketplace. Each week, everyone hurried to see each new miracle the great magician Jose Crow would perform. 'Marvelous.' 'Unbelievable.' 'Fantastic.' 'What earthly powers does not this man possess?' These were some of the things the people said.

"Jose Crow knew secrets lost to the ages that were whispered to him from the leaves from an old gramoir. He could walk invisibly upon the Earth. He could traverse the dimensions. He could pass unnoticed in crowds and glide upon currents of air. By this sorcery, he earned his livelihood. Each time he did a trick, Jose Crow, the great magician, became more and more enamored of himself.

"Far away, there was a mysterious and sacred lake at the top of a mountain, guarded by a huge dragonfly. Some said it was silver, others turquoise. Still others argued the dragonfly was burnished gold. Many mentioned a naked fire that burst from the dragonfly's green eyes, while others said its eyes were spinning rainbows. There were rumors that this dragonfly could make mountains appear, but no one knew for sure. Debates began among the people as to who was more powerful, the dragonfly or Jose Crow.

"The magician heard this talk and became jealous. When he could take it no longer, he stalked into the mountains, vowing to prove himself the greatest of all magicians. Higher and higher he climbed, until he came to the sacred lake where he sighted the enormous dragonfly. He had to admit that it was a beautiful creature. The magician stalked closer and closer. Then, quickly, he cut off one of the dragonfly's wings.

"'I'll use this for my fan, to show the people how great I am,' he said in triumph.

"Walking down the mountain, it seemed as though he saw his life pass before him upon the delicate glassy surface of the wing-fan. He saw scenes of wondrous beauty and scenes of hideous ugliness. He saw many other realms, jewel-like cities with jade walls and obsidian turrets.

"In the village he immediately went to the marketplace. The people assembled, and he walked about, strutting. 'Look at me,' he said, holding up his fan. 'Now can there be any doubt that I am the greatest magician of them all? I have made the dragonfly's wing my own.'

"The village people shuffled, embarrassed. Finally a man stepped forward. 'Jose, you are deluded. We don't see anything.'

"Now I ask you, what are you deluded about?"

After Javier's story, the entire group laughingly professed to see the world clearly and to be free from all delusion

I might as well give one of the stories I told. The rules to the story fires seemed pretty flexible. You could make up a story. However, if you told a traditional story, it had to be told as accurately as possible. Otherwise, it was thought to be an insult to its spirit. I began, "Okay, here goes. Listen up, everyone. It's like this. You see, Toad Woman invited Yellow Tobacco Boy to dinner. Old toad that she was, she used a love medicine potion on him. She put a big dose right in his soup. Got it? A potion."

"'This tastes bad.' Yellow Tobacco Boy spit. 'What's in it?'

"'Oh, that's one of the good old recipes,' cackled Toad Woman. 'I learned it from old Grandmother Toad. I can tell you this, she had plenty of handsome beaux who came a-courting back in her day.'

"'She did, did she? Well, I hope she was better-looking than —' Yellow Tobacco Boy suddenly stopped. He seemed to be in a daze. Chalk it up to toad love potion number nine. 'You know, you have some nice warts,' Yellow Tobacco Boy cooed. 'I hadn't noticed until now. There's some real attractive qualities about you.'

"Church bells ring-a-ling-ding. And Yellow Tobacco Boy was very happy with his toady bride. They went on a little honeymoon, to Bermuda I think. They settled down in a little white cottage. Rose bushes. Picket fence. All that stuff.

"They went about the usual business of married couples. Toad Woman kept house. And Yellow Tobacco Boy went out and provided.

"One morning Yellow Tobacco Boy kissed his wife's bloated face. Saying good-bye, he headed for the grocery store, or to be more accurate, the forest.

"Coyote fell in with him. 'I've been meaning to talk to you. I wanted to ask you, that wife of yours — what exactly do you see in her?'

"'Why, everything,' answered Yellow Tobacco Boy. 'She's the sugar in my coffee. Cream too. She's the grass I walk on, so sweet and fair. She's the bloom on my sweet rose bush. She's the —'

"Coyote cut him off. 'Well, if I may be allowed to speculate, it seems to me like she's real ugly. Why, I bet you could throw her in the river and skim off ugly for a month. She ain't going to die. That woman's going to ugly away.'

"'You take that back,' said Yellow Tobacco Boy.

"'Why should I? It's the truth. Listen, I'm a coyote, right? They say we coyotes will go to town with old grandmothers or even gopher holes. I tell you. I wouldn't touch your plug-ugly woman. She's repulsive, ugh.'

" 'Take it back. I can lick you.'

" 'Oh yeah?' said coyote, growling. 'I'm rough and tumble. I'm fresh out of the jungle, and I don't back down from man nor beast. I'm one hundred proof chained lightning, and I'm spoiling for a fight. I can lick you on one of my bad days. I guess you want to die.'

"Yellow Tobacco Boy soon commenced to fighting with that coyote. There were fist flingings and teeth chompings. The coyote bit him right up one leg and down the other. But true to his word, Yellow Tobacco Boy grabbed hold of coyote's tail and went around and around, kicking him all over — kicking him in the side, kicking him on the shoulder, kicking him in the head — but mostly kicking his butt, just like he said he would. The poor coyote yelped and pleaded and begged, but Yellow Tobacco Boy kicked even harder. Coyote was feeling run-over, shanked, cannonballed, half drowned, and hung out with the wash. 'Besides seeing stars, I see what you mean,' panted poor coyote. 'You plumb wupped the ugly right off of that woman. She's cute as a ladybug, I'd say.'

"That's it." I closed with a bow, expecting approval.

Instead, there was silence all around. "Good story, huh?"

No one said anything. I looked at very impassive faces, the firelight playing over them. Mary seemed to be scowling.

"What's the point of that story?" Tub finally asked. "Don't mess with Yellow Tobacco Boy?"

"Yeah, I guess so. What's the matter with that?"

"You are supposed to tell a story that has medicine in it," Mary said, "not just insult animals. Toad might put you away for that. You owe her an apology."

"Okay, I'm sorry. I was just trying to have a good time and spin a good yarn."

The firelight in Mary's eyes seemed to flame toward me. "No 'sorry.' Apologize."

I heard Tub snicker.

"Okay. My sincere apologies, Toad Woman. Okay?" I felt embarrassed at having to make amends to some abstract quality of thin air. Maybe I was just a cynic. But if indeed such a thing as a toad spirit existed, did it even understand English?

As if to answer my question, Mary said, "Toad Woman knows your heart. Otherwise, I would be greatly angry at you. Your heart beats true most of the time, so I don't take a big offense." Then Mary smiled and even chuckled a bit. That seemed to give everyone else permission to laugh with her.

Here's another of Tub's stories. "One day Skunk Man was walking along. He wasn't real happy either.

"Skunk Man said, 'I have teeth but Lion's teeth are sharper. I have a cloak, but mine doesn't compare with Bear's. I can't fly. I can't climb very well. I'm neither large nor small.' On and on. And on and on. Skunk Man had many such complaints, but the animals soon wearied of listening to them.

"Skunk Man was nosing around one day, when he bumped into Rabbit Man.

"Rabbit Man said, 'Skunk Man, we all know you are displeased with yourself. Why don't you ask Creator if you can't be changed?'

"Huffing, Skunk Man turned his back. Rabbit Man shrugged and hopped away.

"'It's plain to see that Rabbit Man doesn't like me,' Skunk Man said, his voice full of self-pity. 'That bunny thinks he's so smart, cavorting around all the time. Telling me what to do. I had the same idea myself. I've been thinking about it for a long time now. If I want to see Creator, I will. And if I do, it will have to be a short visit. After all, I am very busy most of the time.'

"Skunk Man followed a narrow path and winding trail through the forest. Creator's house was big and shiny. Skunk Man abruptly walked in. 'Creator, I want a change,' he said. 'I am unhappy with the garment you have given me.'

" 'What do you want?' asked Creator.

" 'I want to be black.'

"Suddenly, Skunk Man found himself outside of Creator's house clad in a luxurious black cloak. Surprised and triumphant, he went home. Everywhere was covered in snow. Many of the other animals had shed their dark coats for white garments. Skunk Man was very conspicuous.

"Rabbit Man laughed at Skunk Man. 'Creator has played a joke on you,' Rabbit Man said, still laughing. 'You stick out like a regular carrot on wheels.'

"Indignant, Skunk Man returned to Creator. He barged in. 'Creator, that no-good Mr. Rabbit said I look like a dumb vegetable on wheels, and he blamed it on You. I want to be white,' he demanded.

"Again — he didn't quite know how — he found himself outside.

" 'Hey, check this out,' he said. 'Creator has given me a dazzling white cloak.' He danced around and sang a little tune, very much admiring himself.

"This time, when he got home, flowers were blooming. Butterflies were skipping from blossom to blossom. Spring was in the air. And Skunk Man heard some birds quarreling. Sparrow Woman, Blackbird Woman, and Blue Jay Woman — dressed up in colorful garments — were arguing.

" 'I'm the prettiest,' said Sparrow Woman. 'I'm so darling and petite.'

" 'No, I'm the prettiest,' said Blackbird Woman. 'My beautiful coat shimmers like the silver night.'

"'Not a chance,' said Blue Jay Woman. 'In my beautiful coat, I am as deep as the bluest sky.'

"'No, I'm the prettiest,' said Skunk Man, startling everyone.

"All the birds immediately stopped fussing.

"'Look at Skunk Man,' said Blue Jay Woman, her beak hanging open in surprise.

"'He looks like a snowman,' said Sparrow Woman.

"'I wonder if he'll melt soon,' said Blackbird Woman

"'Yeah, stick a carrot in his nose,' said Rabbit Man, who had recently joined the group without an invitation. 'We could use some prunes for buttons.'

"Blackbird Woman hopped up and down on a limb, fluffing out her wings. 'Get snow-blind around here just looking at Skunk Man,' she said.

"Skunk Man was crestfallen. He felt pretty ridiculous.

"The birds all laughed derisively. Then they flew away to further insult him.

"'Creator isn't doing you any favors, old man,' Rabbit Man said. He hopped away, his little cotton tail quivering considerably.

"Skunk Man returned to Creator. He entered. 'Creator,' he said. 'I've been black. They laughed at me. I've been white. They laughed at me. Now I want to be black and white. And by the way, give me some sharp claws to dig with, will you? And now that we're talking about it, I can't get any respect. Can't you do something about that?'

"'Done,' said Creator. 'But get out of here. Can't you see all the work I have to do just keeping up appearances for you? Now, don't bother me no more.'

"Again, Skunk Man found he had gotten just what he had asked for. 'Good day,' he called out once he had returned home. But all the animals ran away very quickly. No one wanted much to do with the little stinker.

"'Well, at least now,' reflected Skunk Man, 'I may not be popular, but still I'm getting a little respect.' Whether he earned it or not, I'll leave you to judge," Tub finished.

Mary explained at length the traditional conjure teachings about skunk sickness. Basically, skunk was responsible for a wide array of related diseases, the most memorable being leprosy. Skunk diseases were treated with powdered herbs and roots. After her explanation, we sang some songs and drummed until late in the night.

"Now," Mary said, afterward, "I'm going to show you how to call skunks. You use this root, and you bruise it." She held up something that looked like a rutabaga, then beat it with a stone and waved it around. "Here, skunks. Here, skunks," she called. "Come, skunks."

It didn't take long. Several polecats came prancing right in amongst us. They were sniffing the ground, holding their tails elegantly extended on high. The story fire was over. We immediately ran for cover and called it a night. Mary didn't budge.

Twenty-two

ON A LATE AFTERNOON during this time, Mary and I sat watching a sunset. The cool air was scented with cottonwood leaf and spike grass, and the sunlight was flattening out in layers of magenta, orange, and pink. We sat silently taking pleasure in this delicious splendor.

After a time, I asked, "Mary, is there such a thing as sunset sickness?"

"Oh yes. It is a form of sun sickness. Sunsets can pull you too far. You don't ever want to be on bad terms with the night sun or the day sun."

"Are there many conjure stories about the sun?"

"I will tell you an important one. Long ago, the sun had his wife boil the first people in a big kettle. They turned red. These were Indians. The sun said, 'Throw some sunflower petals in there, and boil some more people and see what happens.' These were the yellow people. The sun threw ashes on some of the people. These were black people. He bleached the rest of the people in his rays, and they turned white. These were white people. We are all children of the sun. Race is important because different races are prone to different diseases. You must always first ask the sun what is going on.

"If you aren't tired of hearing stories, I have another."

"No. I'm not. Not in the least. Not conjure stories anyway."

"You see, one day the sun walked across the sky with dazzling mirrored moccasins. Yellow Tobacco Boy's paddle blade sliced into the river water with an even pressure in a wide-sweeping

J-stroke. The canoe shot forward and then fell back in an even drift. The blade hit again and again, thrusting the bow ahead. Yellow Tobacco Boy maneuvered the paddle in the exact and proper way.

"The canoe then shot into the sky. And it is told that Yellow Tobacco Boy walked about in Sky World until he met the sun.

"'Great Father of Life,' Yellow Tobacco Boy said. 'My desire is to be a mighty conjure. Only with your help will I be able to accomplish this intent. Will you teach me?'

"The sun said, 'Yes, I will be your father. Each day, leave tobacco offerings to me. Your apprenticeship will be for eight years. You must remain with me for four years, and I will teach you about sun disease and how to cure it. Then you must return for four years, and I will teach you how to always find me and other important things.'

"Yellow Tobacco Boy gained much of benefit from the sun. The sun showed him what to do in every case.

"'Sacred Instructor,' Yellow Tobacco Boy said. 'It is now time for me to leave you. I will do as you have said. I will return to my land, the land below. I will pray to you. I will sing your praises and honor you each day in order to gain more knowledge of your holy nature.'

"'My son, these are my last instructions. Each morning, go to the top of the hill that bends. Four times cut a small piece of your flesh, your sacred tobacco flesh, and leave it for me. Sing the songs that I have taught you. Hold up your two fingers to my light. I will put a sun feather there. This sun feather will be called painted with light.

"'Each evening, go in the direction of six fires. Come to my sacred ground and my sacred altar. Make offerings and remember me. When you see me over six fires, mark it well. When I reach the farthest point on the right hand, again mark it well. I will be teaching you the proper times to hold ceremony in my honor.'

"Saying good-bye, Yellow Tobacco Boy got in his canoe and went home.

"Each year, he observed the sun closely. His marks were off by an early thirteen days the first year. The next year he was early by twenty days. And the next, only two days late. The fourth year he was able to forecast the turning exactly. He also learned to do nighttime star checks. Sun ceremonies were held in both winter and summer. Does that answer any of your questions?"

I nodded my head that it did. "Is sunburn sun sickness?"

"Yes. But the nature of sun sickness varies. It is almost always due to too much sun. The sun nourished by the sweeper, the planet Venus, has devastating power. There is heat in the crown and general malaise. The heat builds to an intense headache. It can affect the eyes and nose. Nosebleeds are often a sign of sun disease. The sufferer may even lose consciousness.

"Treatment consists of various washes of sun water poured on the top of the head and allowed to run off into a bowl. Sun water is easy to make, mostly from the petals and the root of a sunflower. This conjure water is usually kept on hand during summer months. Remind me. I'll give you some to take home with you."

The story fires were not lit again for awhile. I suppose Mary was giving us time to digest what we had already heard. One evening, we all gathered near her cabin. Tub had carefully built a small fire inside a new circle of stones. Seven people huddled around it at close quarters. Besides me, there was Tub and Evangeline, Javier and Patricio, Mary, and Betty. Betty was there to pick up Evangeline. They were leaving in the early morning for New Orleans.

Betty sang a beautiful Caddo stirrup song, which was a

quick-tempoed horse-honoring song. Her voice was wonderfully engaging, and she shook her head from side to side while singing. I had moved back away from the fire and sat on a rock outcropping, but all the others were close to it. It crackled and spewed every so often, sending a blizzard of glowing sparks into the air.

After Betty's song, we began spontaneously asking Mary to explain various conjure teachings.

"For every disease there is a medicine," Mary said. "If this were not so, we would not be here. How can a thing be born without its unraveling? It is the same with disease."

"What is otter disease?" Evangeline asked.

"It is told that Yellow Tobacco Boy sat down all by himself. He began to cry. The tears escaped his eyes slowly, and the land and distant lakes in front of him were smeared in monstrous shapes. The tears were soon rushing down his cheeks in a steady stream. In about four hours — maybe it was five — his tears made a little river. By and by Yellow Tobacco Boy was sitting on the bank. An otter came swimming up to him. They say she taught him the cures of otter sickness.

"Otter illness is a serious problem. In men, it is the inability to honor women. In women, it can be menstruation problems. Dark self surfacing to the milk of the moon. And it can be related to moon sickness. Remember that moon sickness may take the form of fear of the moon, stars, or other planets. Other otter ailments may manifest in the beginning as distracted thinking and a loss of the mystery of life. That and fragmented energy are the first clues. Can be devastating. Don't think otter problems only happen in women. I think all of you men have a form of it most of the time."

I inquired about lynx sickness.

"I will tell you a story to illustrate the powers of lynx," Mary said. "A long time ago, lynx walked off the world and into the great Pebbly River, the Milky Way. Up and up through wondrous fields of stars and newborn galaxies. She saw sunbows, moonbows, and comets. She passed through cosmic mists and celestial thunders. Past a million suns.

"Only then did she see the house of the Maker of Life, the house of many-gathered-spirit smokes. She crept silently through the door.

"'This must be the most beautiful place in the whole universe,' she said.

"She heard the Maker of Life, the Master of Breath, coming. She did not turn and run but waited. When their eyes met, she was struck with a blinding light. It seared through eternity. That's why the lynx squints to this day. She entered the spinning whirlpools of the galaxies of forever.

"'You have seen my designs,' the Maker of Life said. 'You have understood the silence. Now your eyes will squint, for you have seen me. You will carry a celestial map on your body, your fur — to show others the way here. Keep silent and let others learn from your silence.'

"'My eyes have observed everything,' the great smoking lynx cat said, sitting on a rock ledge under the moonlight. 'I have seen what humans will do in all their futures of destructiveness. For this reason, I will confound them with my powers. I will hide the answers to many riddles from them until they are willing to learn from me.'

"To insult the lynx power is a grave mistake. There are several poignant illnesses caused by lynx. The lynx can entrap you in a false self, where your every premise is a lie and you have been imprisoned in it. You will wear a false face that you dare not look at. To do so would be to admit you are lost forever — that there is nothing genuine about you, and your road has been paved to hell. You best ask forgiveness from this great power and don't stop asking. One way or another, the lynx will have satisfaction and the last laugh.

"Lynx claws in the stomach is another malady. Another difficult-to-cure lynx sickness is claw-marked-tree sickness. It is a deep illness and takes some time to remedy. It strikes at your personal tree. It can kill."

I moved in closer to the group. I asked, "How do you recognize dog sickness?"

"Easy. You'll see it immediately — fever and delirium, growling and biting and going about on all fours."

"What about coyote?" Tub asked.

"Coyote can cause shivers, fits, and even howling at the moon. When people start acting goofy, this is a sign. Obsessiveness. Addiction is a sign of coyote sickness — drug or alcohol problems or sexual obsessions. People who are unduly dependent on one another have coyote sickness. They often want this lesson for spiritual growth. If a hunter disrespectfully kills or even chides a coyote, it is said that the hunter's child will get it. Always be extremely careful with coyote, because a coyote can only coyote you. Whipping a dog or other relative can cause sickness. The master shooter shoots coyote arrows through his eyes. You better always show your respect by an offering of tobacco."

Evangeline asked, "Will you tell us about beaver sickness?"

"If you kill a beaver disrespectfully, believe me, your whole life will fall apart. Everything that you once believed will come crashing down on your head. Old Dame Beaver, Grandmother Two Teeth, can gnaw you in your dreams, so that when you wake up, you are broken. Of course, I am speaking in the extreme. There are many minor beaver problems. Beaver sickness can cause you to get dammed up. I'm sure you know what that means."

There were guffaws. Tub was grinning as though he was quite familiar with this last beaver problem

Javier wanted to know about catfish and other fish.

"You might catch fish sickness by building a dam or fishing improperly. Some signs of catfish or other fish sickness are running sores around the mouth," she said, finishing by making her mouth into an O, opening and closing it like a fish. She laughed almost imperceptibly and continued. "There may be swelling of the feet and stomach. Clammy skin and ulcers may indicate this sickness. Catfish phlegm can cause diseases of the lungs.

"There's finny tribe sickness, black bass sickness, perch sickness, and many others that can cause harm. We could discuss it all night, but we won't."

"What about turtle sickness?" I asked.

"Turtles do not die from disease, and their meat and bones are good medicine," Mary answered. "Turtle meat is strength-giving. Living turtle hearts are eaten for power. Turtle oil is used for fever and for aches and sore joints. It's also a good gun oil.

"Watch out for turtle sickness. There can be bladder problems. Also, turtle fever. People who get turtle sickness can go into their shell and never come out. Turtle sickness walks hand in hand with unbalanced earth — earth in the wrong place, either spiritually or geographically, maybe both."

I asked about spider.

"Ah, spider," said Mary, light dancing in her eyes. "Knit one and purl two. Keep things separated. Don't try to eat while you're knitting. Spider teaches us this. Spider is a benefactor and does service to us all. Spiders are our elders, one of the oldest beings we may communicate with. They make good kills and teach us how to do likewise. Never kill a spider, no matter how it frightens you. You may find yourself in a snare for a lifetime if you do. Don't spit on a web or the humiliated spider spirit may slowly crush you in her spiritual web. Don't play around with them either. And don't tease them, whatever you do. Spiders have the ability to tease back in ways you can't yet imagine.

"The first spider disease is bite. Most bites are harmless, but a few can be extremely dangerous. Untreated, certain bites can kill you. There are many other sicknesses spider is able to weave. Most of the time she doesn't bother. She teaches us industry and about various forms of entrapment. She keeps many love medicines. There is much to learn from her, from spider.

"What about buffalo?" Tub asked. "Are there many buffalo diseases?"

"Yes, many. Butchering and skinning out disrespectfully can cause them. Any kind of religious bigotry brings them on. These are diseases of society that involve a spiritual intolerance. Spirit buffalo gores and slashes the victim's spirit. This can lead to overwhelming depression, feelings of isolation, and various distortions or projections. Buffalo or bison sickness can manifest in a lack of appreciation for life and its gifts. Many suicides are caused by it."

"How about bear sickness?" Tub said. His voice sounded unusually gruff.

"You are a bear, Tub," Mary said. "At heart anyway. Bear taught the human how to foretell future events, make war medicine, and the use of certain roots such as bear root and herbs such as bearberry. Bear also taught the secrets of the left hand. Bears are left-handed, and the left hand, they say, has a heart. The right hand only has a brain.

"Disrespect to the bear may cause one of two most usual illnesses, bear sickness or bleeding bear sickness. Defiling a tree can cause it. Bear sickness first strikes with an extreme thirst. The lips will be cracked. The patient will flounder around on the bed. There will be a high fever. Bleeding bear sickness is even more serious. It causes the victim to vomit blood. It is treated with a certain bark tea and with conjure waters, as well as cupping and singing to the bear spirit. I have managed to heal this sickness a few times, but I've lost just as many."

Patricio managed somehow to get everyone's attention by not doing anything but smiling forlornly. He said, "Several years ago my sister Corina was struck by lightning. This hit was in the neck, and it tore her body in half. There were only charred and blackened remains."

Mary looked at Patricio a long moment and said, "In the old days when lightning struck a person, it used to be an extremely grave tribal matter. If they lived through the experience, they became knowers, great medicine keepers of power and ability. No matter what, life or death, ceremonies were held. Did any of your medicine men do them?"

Patricio hung his head and shook it, no. "Corina was buried in the church. No one any longer remembered the proper rituals."

Mary said, "From now on, it is your responsibility. I will show you how. Remember that the flesh of a lightning-struck animal is never eaten. The head should be faced to the west and corn pollen or meal placed on the tongue. Lightning is a kind of spirit knife. Naturally, the toad, the keeper of knife and spear points, is called upon. He is asked to go up in the sky and send back dream messages from the great ones. Toad will return with instructions and a revelation about why this has happened. Much curing knowledge is revealed in this way. Patricio, you need to do a ceremony immediately for your sister. We will do it privately."

Patricio looked at Mary sadly, nodding his head to show he understood.

"The most common form of lightning disease is called little-man-shooting-his-silver-darts-from-above-and-causing-sickness. It is often caused by improper bathing. It can lead to serious deterioration." Mary had some difficulty explaining the difference between lightning sickness and other disorders. When she felt we all understood, she told us several remedies.

From somewhere in the treeline, an owl called out in its "woooo" vibrato. Then there was silence. No one spoke for a long time.

Evangeline interrupted the mood. "Mary, you once told me about a strange water disease called little-animals-frolicking-around-in-the-water sickness. Will you tell me again?"

"Evangeline, you have a good memory. I told you that several years ago. In its most apparent form, the victim will have a great thirst. When the invaders came with their great gifts to our people, cholera was one of them. Cholera was placed in this category of disease. It became untreatable. Many conjures died in battle against it. Later, a few had some success. Imbalance with water and the little frolicking animals may manifest in a mental breakdown, the mind flowing off in the wrong direction."

"I don't remember the treatment," Evangeline said. "What did you say about it?"

"Depends on the form of the disease. One form that can be cleared up almost immediately is a stomach disease that causes vomiting. It is treated with clear whirlpool water collected at a waterfall. It is administered in sips to the patient. This water is rubbed vigorously over the body, and especially kneaded into the stomach. The patient is steamed and wrapped in blankets. Other treatments are boiled waters."

"Didn't you tell me there was snail sickness?" Tub asked.

"Of course there is. But don't get the wrong impression of snail. It can be very dangerous. It can make even the strongest conjure slip and go down. It is the continuous mother, continually giving birth to itself. Snail carries the great emptiness, the zero. It can reduce you to that. Snail is the androgynous lady of whirlwinds, and she can take your mind and whirl it around. Snail disease begins with a phlegmed-up cough. Fasting is one of the best ways to cure it, if caught early. It can snail along until it's got you plenty good. Then it is very serious."

"How about crow sickness?" I asked.

"There are immutable natural laws, and if you break them, you will get this sickness," Mary answered. "Any big conflict with the world around us may indicate this imbalance. Believe me when I tell you, there are other crimes than the crow scratchings of the white man's law books. There are serious crimes against the land. Earthly and spiritual laws are being broken every minute. This always comes back to the people. You will see a lot of crow sickness in times to come. There are ten or more traditional conjures for crow sicknesses. Perhaps the most virulent strain is called gleaming black feather. It will happen. There will be hell to pay. People will become sick from unjust laws administered by a den of self-serving, avaricious thieves. Another crow sickness is caused by intentionally harming bird's nests or eggs."

Tub asked, "How's about turkey sickness?"

Mary walked toward him, her head bobbing slightly. Then suddenly she sprang forward and ran about like a scolding turkey. She went "gobble gobble" — a perfect imitation — right in all of our faces. We were roaring with laughter and possibly a little afraid at this performance, it happened so unexpectedly. There was another ripple of laughter. We remained in this state of merriment while Mary explained. "Turkey sickness usually begins with repressed anger. The human puffs up with false pride like a turkey. Normally, it strikes in the fall of the year and leads to many turkey-related sicknesses, from swollen glands to cancers. It strikes the kidney. It is as though the flame of the heart has been turned up too high, causing disturbances throughout the body. The holy turkey was venerated. Turkeys were seers who could lend you their eyes and advise you on any conjure matter."

I was still sitting behind the group, away from the warmth of the fire. I was cold, so cold in fact, I was shaking a little. Not only that, I was uncomfortable. I stamped my feet to get the circulation going. My physical body was rebelling. More importantly, my mind was starting to wander around in a kind of mental zoo, where great and small beasts were at odds with us poor, miserable human beings. Through no fault of our own, the outraged creatures were doing their level best to destroy us. Men and beasts were split into hostile camps attacking each other in a kind of everlasting war. There was carnage on both sides. And what did we conjures have for protection against this virulent onslaught? Why, a few roots and powders, a little bit of smoke, flashes of insight, a few songs and dances, and powwowing — a ceremony to give a little hope. It seemed to me that life was precarious and dangerous enough already. Our job as conjures was to bring peace onto these ageless killing fields, where there is such hostility and no peace can ever exist.

Mary continued, "Occasionally, children will get turkey sickness, but this is rare. They have a way of comforting the wounded turkey spirit."

"I'll bet there's a big Thanksgiving Day turkey sickness," I interrupted, trying to introduce a little humor. "Why not? Drumstick sickness. Stuffing sickness. Giblet sickness."

Mary said sarcastically, "Yes, you're right. Turkey reminds us of indigestion as well as cranberry sauce."

"And do all these sicknesses have traditional remedies like Tums for the tummy?" I asked.

"Yes, smart boy. Every one of them. There is some form of traditional treatment. Mostly, but not always, the plants give the cure along with doctoring."

"You know what?" I said. "I'd really like to hear a little science with your teachings, Mary. All this stuff is getting pretty far-fetched."

Mary snorted. "Well, you know what? Science can kiss my ass."

Betty, who had listened impassively, tried to change the subject and said, "Tell us about butterfly sickness, Mary."

"Betty, I know this is an important medicine for you. You want to remember the old happy times and cycles of power. Certain trees are your allies. You like to continually travel in this quest for spiritual understanding and beauty. Butterfly is strong and healthy inside of you. To understand butterfly sickness, you must first understand butterfly in all her cycles of being. A story the old ones told to illustrate this concerns the caterpillar."

Mary's voice was suddenly raspy in order to play the part of a caterpillar. " 'I'm trying to get comfortable under these circumstances and under the shade of this great leaf,' the caterpillar said. She swiveled slowly, reaching toward the surface of a leaf below. She almost lost her balance and fell.

"Directly above, there was a whisper of wings. A butterfly landed on the lip of a white flower petal. Her wings hesitated, folded and unfolded.

"The caterpillar had to catch her breath. 'There cannot be another such as you in the entire world,' she said. 'You are so very beautiful.'

Mary projected a different voice. It was sweet as mountain honey. " 'You will be a beauty like me one day soon,' said the butterfly. 'You will be as breathtaking as me. And you will be able to fly about and see the woodland meadows. The red and blue flowers there are wonderful to explore. I can tell you, the world is a most amazing place.'

"The caterpillar blinked and lifted her head. She chewed and swallowed. 'Nonsense, beautiful lady. I must crawl along and cannot think such rubbish.'

"The butterfly beat her wings and skipped down closer. 'It's not rubbish. It's the truth.'

"'Sure it is,' the caterpillar said, drawing back.

"The butterfly, with her delicate orange-and-black wings outstretched and motionless, pushed them shut and then open again. Suddenly, she swooped away.

"That night, enfolded in her chrysalis, the caterpillar reflected on the meeting. 'The nerve of that beautiful lady. She made fun of me. I'm so ugly. Just look at me. I don't appreciate that beautiful woman making such sport of me. Why, the very idea that I could be as magical and exquisite as her.'

"The little caterpillar soon fell into deep sleep to dream wondrous visions of a sweet life set free and open to the warm sunlight. Her veil of ignorance vanished, and her beauty surpassed her wildest fancy.

"Think what this story means: we don't trust the natural order of the Creator. When we refute it, disease follows. A form of epilepsy is the most serious butterfly sickness. It is known as flickering-white-butterfly sickness and makes your brain flicker. Butterfly can flutter by and cause other serious problems. Walk away without acknowledging her, you may be struck. Lack of momentum, fear, repetitious action with no release — these are the indications of lack of harmony with butterflies. They are often conjured for their elusiveness. They have powerful warrior medicine."

Patricio said, "Squirrel?"

With all eyes on her, Mary mimicked a squirrel eating a nut. It was a grand performance, and everyone howled with laughter. She looked like some sort of escaped lunatic. She stopped her act. "Just look. I see squirrelly tendencies in all of you," she began. "If you steal from a squirrel, take only half. Always leave a token of respect. Squirrel causes you to eat too much or too little. You will know this sickness. You will know when you are acting unwisely or turning into a shriveled-up turnip. Your cupboards are bare because you're too lazy to do something about it. Call up squirrel on the spirit telephone.

"As to sickness, the major squirrel problem is the loosening of teeth due to deteriorating and sore gums. It is serious, for, untreated, the resulting loss of teeth inhibits eating. There is an unconscious impact on mental health. It is a symbolic threat to life and an obvious great loss of power. We want to keep a sharp bite for as long as possible. A mouth rinse of boiled toothache root is used to treat it. This is followed by an even-pressured gum rubbing with the right mix of tooth dirts.

"There are several other squirrely sicknesses. I will show you what they are and how to treat them."

Evangeline said, "Didn't you tell me there is a birdsnake sickness?"

"Again, good memory, Eve. This sickness caused by birdsnake is often called knifewing or flintwing sickness. Laceration of the skin by flint. According to the old beliefs, knifewing can cause you to have an accident resulting in abrasions. Poor relations with birdsnake can be disastrous and a greatly painful experience. This creature is a being born of wind and lightning and cannot be seen with ordinary eyes. Birdsnake is eternally present in the eastern skies.

"Birdsnake disease causes spirit drain or even complete spirit loss. To treat the disease use a boil of bullbriar stems. Remember you must sing to the spirit, asking to be forgiven for the affront. The afflicted person is allowed to have a few sips of birdsnake conjure water as needed. The body must be steamed using a loose blanket sweat with a pour of the same brew over hot stones. The treatment lasts a couple of hours and is done each day for four days."

Mary looked toward the eastern horizon and chuckled. Personally, I didn't see anything that looked like a birdsnake. I couldn't even imagine one. I don't know what the other people saw, but I certainly wasn't going to discount the possibility of this extradimensional creature being out there, not with all my strange experiences. I waved weakly out of acknowledgment and respect, just in case.

"You told me the other day to watch out for strong-man sickness," Tub said. "Could you tell us more?"

"Yes. Disregard for limitations is the cause of this sickness. It's unwise to make physical efforts of which one is incapable. It can be incapacitating.

"Strong-man sickness begins with sharp shooting pains at the base of the cord. It is caused by heavy lifting and can feel like several arrows have entered the center of your back. Other animals interact differently with gravity than the human. Pressures are well met. Strong-man sickness stabs the upright human with pain and paralysis.

"The best treatment is rubbing with conjure snake oil, which I will show you how to make. It's not difficult to learn."

"Will you speak of snake?" Patricio asked.

Mary stared for a long moment at all of us. "Yes, snake is an old friend. The snake tribes have scattered just as we indigenous peoples have been scattered. They are just as confused as we are and don't know what hit them. What great pain and great sorrow lie over our nations. How could it happen? The ancestors speak of the temples and how they were built with prayers for fertility. They descended the underground steps to the raised dais of the snake. They speak of the temple python, and of its great head and fanged and open mouth, how it would bend forward and blow its breath over the body.

"The ancestors speak of the sacred brown stone kept atop the black lava corn grinding bowl. These first corn magicians were women. They used their menstrual blood, mixed it with white cornmeal. They made dolls and broke them on the temple floor. They spread the orange meal before the snake. Art and magic were aligned. This took the place of human sacrifice.

"No one remembers this — our great priestess, her breasts plumed. It was she who put light on the ground. Now there is only darkness. Our gods are angry gods. Jaguar soldiers standing before the temple with their lances ready to strike and draw blood. The ocelot soldiers are in revolt. There will be many wars. The corn magic bowl is empty. The principle of the snake which flays itself is forgotten. I want you to think and re-member."

Mary hesitated a long moment. She looked tired. She continued bitterly, at least it seemed that way to me. "One of the things I most despise about white people is their treatment of snakes. Not all whites, but many. I simply cannot understand this murdering instinct. The snake is within us as surely as I am speaking to you. From the dreams of snakes came our first world, the world upon which all other worlds would be built. Snake is the greatest of all conjure beings.

"We conjures are noted for our use of various kinds of snake oil. There are directional snake oils and oils of many uses. Usually, four snakes are hung over a pot and heated in a dwelling constructed for this purpose. The oil drips down and is collected. Combined with the proper roots, snake conjure oil aids the conjure in many ways. Snake oil is a bewitching oil. It is a shooting oil to be used on the fingers. With the smoke and the night and the oil, you can crush anyone. Your arrows rubbed with this oil will never miss the mark, and they will always kill. Snake oil on the tongue is used in snake conjure breath. This is one of the most potent of animal breaths and can accomplish almost any healing. Rub this medicine on the eyelids, and you will be able to see in the dark. You can use your eyes to see sickness and its cause. You can see far down into the earth. If you desire precious jewels, gold, or other treasure, you can see it. You can see underwater, deep down in marshes and rivers. You can see what's hidden there. You can always see your enemy in this manner, and you can enchant anyone.

"Killing snakes and insulting them causes snake sickness. There can be spirit snakebites, where fang marks will appear, infusing the body with spiritual poison. Impulses are frozen, causing you to be stopped in your tracks. You won't be able to lift your arms or even nod your head. The neck will be limp and the head droop. This is one form of snake tribe sickness.

"Another way to be out balance with snake is to be bitten. Most bites are frightening but harmless. Even if dangerous, you can use snake root to heal a venomous bite. I would much rather be bitten than have other forms of the disease.

"Snake spirit sickness will often take a long time to manifest but can strike with a vengeance at just over fifty years of age. It will be felt for many years as a slight tightening of the chest, no more. When the sleeping snake spirit wakes up, it becomes a constricting band. Snake disease sometimes launches in the neck and affects the lungs and chest. The victim will feel as though his heart is being ripped out. The snake spirit may be a weight, pressing on the shoulders and down along the rib wings and cord. It may collapse the upper body and affect breathing. There may be an S-curve in the cord. The shifting skeletal connections can damage the heart. If the eyes don't blink and there is a slither movement to the gait, it is an indication of snake-spirit presence and resulting sickness. The pulse is likewise slithery. The patient may weave continually like a serpent ready to strike. Snake will have taken the person over."

Javier spoke up. "You told me my face had ant sickness," he said, referring to his shotgun scatter of pockmarks. "You said ant had done this to me. Will you say more?"

"Yes, you have one form, but there are many others. Ant can teach you how to use flint and crystal. Ant certainly knows the rituals of cutting and surgery and scalping the enemy dead. With flint, it is easy to cut the thread of life. Ant has such hidden knowledge.

"The conjure has many responsibilities to the ant world. At night, the conjure dreams to the ant people, who aided humans greatly. They shared their food with us, and that's why they have such tiny waists. We help the ant people with our dream power, so they can remember their once-great civilization. Ants ran the world. It was a civilization much like our own. They worshipped machines, and they put everything on autopilot. This lasted for eons. Every possible need of the ant people was met by this mighty machine. But over time, their brains atrophied because they no longer had to use them. One day, the machine broke down. They couldn't remember how to fix things. Now the ant people go from day to day, doing and doing, and trying to re-member what happened. That's why we conjures help them, so the ant nations will return to their former greatness. All in good time. If humans make the same mistake as the ant people, it is said ants will once again inherit the earth. See, the circle goes around and around.

"Remember, too, that bear is a big enemy of ants. Bear loves to eat them, will go to the ant house and rip it apart to get at them. Javier, where you come from there are anteaters who also devour ants. Ants have many predators, more than people think. Ants are our close relative. We should respect them. Stings can be serious, especially to children, but are easily treated. Ants know never to go far from their tribal boundaries. There are di-gestive diseases brought by ants, the inability to process sugars. There are many remedies for this also, and some are harsh. Ant bites are often administered on purpose to help in cases of vari-ous manifestations of deer disease."

It was getting along toward midnight. The wind was whis-pering down the hills, and our little fire was burning to embers.

Leaves stiffened, and tree limbs scraped and knocked. There were ominous hootings of an owl, flutterings, and other animal sounds.

"What about toad sickness?" I asked.

"David, you are obsessed by toad. Witches and wizards are masters of toad medicine."

"Hey, who are you calling a witch?"

"Not you. You haven't learned anything from toad, her various potions and the powers of lightning. Toad sickness first comes in the form of an accident. Then, strange sores appear on the body that no medicine will cure. The body bloats up. There are often strange lacerations. Toad is flint keeper and knows how to throw knives, arrow tips, and spear points.

"Toads are master shooters and throwers. They are bean shooters, corn shooters, feather shooters, bead and glass shooters. Here the conjure must use the smoke to see the disease, then suck the intrusion out, and take it at least nine miles from the conjure house. It must be buried very deep in the earth. The word *yulluhbuhshuh* should be said four times, and once addressed to the actual intrusion. The witch or wizard who shot the dart will soon die.

"Now I will speak of spirit-of-the-dead sickness," Mary said quietly. We drew in closer. "Any dead animal or dead body can cause spirit-of-the-dead disease. Bowls of vinegar are often placed under coffins to prevent this sickness. The cut half of an onion is said to work well for this purpose, although I've never tried it.

"There is haint sickness, blistering ghost sickness, boiling and burning ghost sickness. Avoid eating in the dark. It attracts spirits who are hungry. Your nose may bleed. You may have nightmares about your ancestors. This is a bad sign. In burning ghost sickness, blisters cover the bottom of the feet just as though they had been burned in a fire. A metallic smell in the air is a dead giveaway. Depression and a desire to commit suicide may overcome the victim.

"If a friend or relative dies, take food to the grave site and eat. Leave a portion for the spirits, for you must feed those who have passed. Do this with reverence and respect. The smoking of conjure cigarettes helps the conjure to know what's going on. Conjured dirt is used in cases of burning ghost sickness. Many conjure waters can be used, and a good house-sweeping with fir branches must be done.

"Graveyards and burial grounds are dangerous places, where spirits congregate. A child is left overnight near the scaffold of a dead relative. The child waits and meditates on death. Very late, a mist stirs and ghosts rise up and surround the child. If the child is willing, they lead her off into a faraway ghost land, where she is taught many things, many powerful ghost remedies. The ghosts teach her how to use herbs and other doctor medicines in order to cure spirit-of-the-dead sickness. They teach her how to do soul stomps and soul dances to search for and recapture a soul that has wandered off, following the pathway of the dead. There are so many stories and teachings about spirit-of-the-dead sickness."

By now, I realized Mary was speaking from her own childhood experience.

"Who could help you with death in a big city?" I asked.

"No one. You won't find any conjure houses in cities. You must come down here to me. You have never seen me turn anyone away. This was my agreement with the ghosts. If I can be of service or help to anyone, I will be. You will never see me refuse anyone as long as they are respectful."

I sat in the dark for a long moment. Overhead, a white dusty stream of stars was shimmering in waves. I thought I might as well take advantage of the lull, so I said, "Mary, you know I've met several medicine men and a few medicine women."

"Yes."

"They call you a snakeskirt, a conjure, a powwower, right?"

"Yes, and other names."

"Well, what's the difference between a medicine man and a conjure?"

"A medicine man is tribal. Perhaps they are carrying a long familial responsibility. They might belong to a medicine society after a long apprenticeship. Others are informed by a dream or a vision. They may be powerful or not, but most of them are, as you should know. They have a certain way of doing things that they must do. They have to practice their tribal traditions. They may or may not treat foreign people different from their tribe, as they choose. There is a good chance they have experienced cruel assaults from others or seen brutality directed at their people and their beliefs. Many, therefore, use their power exclusively for their own.

"Conjures are born from many specific tribal traditions but they have stepped out of the ring — expanded it. Over thousands of years conjure borrowed. Why act so surprised? Why do you think it's called powwowing? The very word *powwow* means to confer with others, does it not? In the old days during powwowing, large crowds would gather nearby and pray to help and support the conjure. You see, the community once rallied around the conjure. Not so anymore.

"Here is another reason it is called powwowing. Many people would meet. Now, however, curing the sick is an illegal act so it is done in secret. When I'm powwowing, I always pray that the real spirit of the people is with me, for I feel this is the way it should be. Each conjure brings forward a different tribal foundation, you might say. For instance, I honor my family, my clan, and my tribal nation, and I don't feel estranged from them — not at all. My feet are firmly planted on the spiritual bedrock of my own people. Yet I believe the conjure is for everyone. I hope you believe this way too and embrace all who need you.

"I will tell you more about sickness and the proper treatments another time. Right now, I'm tired and calling the cord of this night cut."

Twenty-three

ALONG ABOUT THIS TIME, an unfortunate incident occurred. My marine K-bar disappeared. I kept it inside my tent, along with my other things. When I found it was missing, my heart sank. I didn't think Tub would take my knife. Neither would Evangeline. I was sure either Javier or Patricio had stolen it. I had seen Javier watch me as I whittled a stick, and he surely coveted it. Discreetly, I tried to find out if he had taken it and hidden it somewhere. He acted suspiciously, and I decided to confront him with the theft and do whatever necessary to get my knife back.

Mary asked me why I was behaving so oddly. I told her about the loss. "Javier took it," I said. "When I find it, there's going to be big trouble. He could have just asked, and I would have loaned it to him."

"This very thing almost destroyed the nation," Mary said.

"What very thing?"

"Talk like that without any reality."

"My knife is gone. That's a reality."

"I want to tell you about the black handkerchief conjure," Mary said.

"What's that?"

"A black handkerchief conjure is a tracer conjure."

"Tracer? You mean like finding something?"

"Yes, that which is lost or stolen."

"Like my knife, my K-bar?"

"Like anything. Sit down. Listen. Here is a story that will

help you out. One day Yellow Tobacco Boy was having a philosophical conversation about the nature of ownership with a coyote. The coyote was saying, 'Look, everything belongs to the Maker of Life. Among us animals, we don't hesitate to take what we want. If I can steal it, it's mine.'

"That night Yellow Tobacco Boy went over to his neighbors and stole two rabbits. He took them home and ate them. 'This is good,' he said, licking his fingers. Why haven't I discovered this before? Stealing is so good.'

"Following Yellow Tobacco Boy's example, people began to steal from one another. Innocent people were accused. Quarrels broke out. Family and clan feuds heated up. Then there was a murder. It didn't stop there. Wives and children were stolen. Sacred packs and power objects disappeared. There were many feuds and many deaths. Woe fell over the nation.

"'Why must I carry these great burdens?' the *minko* asked. He was full of melancholy because of such wicked acts. He went off to isolate himself in a sacred grove. A raccoon appeared before him and gave him his eyes. 'Use these eyes to bring stability and happiness,' the raccoon said. 'They are black-circle tracer eyes. My eyes are so shrewd, I am even able to trace lost souls. With them, you can find any missing article. There is no way to deceive my medicine. I myself am a bandit, so I have had to learn bandit ways. I've had to learn tracer ways. With my eyes, you will be able to see footprints shining as though wet, leading away from any theft. All you have to do is follow this glowing path until you find who is responsible. Practice my seeing art, and you won't be disappointed.'

"Back at the village, the crier called the people to the rainbow — the town square. When all were assembled, the *minko* said, 'You may never steal from one another again. It will be our tribal law. Raccoon has given us eyes to trace. If you steal, you will be caught and severely punished.'

"Afterward, a black handkerchief conjure was brought in to trace any theft. The culprit was quickly found and given twenty-five lashes with a dogwood switch. If it happened again, it was a hundred lashes with old hickory.

"Gradually, conditions returned to a peaceful state.

"'Well, if you think I'm going to quit stealing, you've got more thinks coming,' the coyote told Yellow Tobacco Boy. 'You may be able to trace me, but you can't catch me.'

"'Well, trickster man, I'll never steal again,' Yellow Tobacco Boy said, acutely aware of the burning switch stripes on his back. But Yellow Tobacco Boy added with a wink, 'Unless it's a good pony from another nation.'

"If your knife had been stolen, I would trace it for you. I would show you the use of the handkerchief to see. You learn to see through the silk. I would find the thief, and there would be hell to pay. But your knife wasn't stolen. You left it on my front porch, and I threw it on the front seat of your car."

"But Javier . . . Patricio . . . ?"

"Did I say that false accusations were punishable by twenty-five dogwood stripes? No apologies accepted. Just go get me the switch."

"Mary!"

She let out a scream of laughter, and shook with it, holding her stomach. Tears streamed down her face and she rolled, holding her stomach, over her porch floor where we had been sitting. "Ah, David," she said, after calming down and sitting up straight, "you look like a petulant child. What am I going to do with you?"

"Send me to bed with no supper?"

Twenty-four

NOW IT WAS BACK to the grindstone and city life for awhile. I had to earn a living. It was hard to get into the swing of things, even though my job often consisted of little real work, just pushing the right button and pulling the right lever at the right time. My duties at the water plant also required some figuring to determine exactly the right moment to cause a machine to activate and pump water from ninety miles away. This in turn caused a chain of other automated machines to activate all the way to the city. Either that, or I could set the controls of the console on autopilot and read a book, which is what I did most of the time. I was exercising my inalienable right to be lazy.

There was a fellow worker at my plant named Jim. I often exchanged banter with him in between his monitoring of water-gathering-system consoles. He had a high forehead and thinning brown hair and wore a khaki uniform, which was not a requirement of the job. Jim was a worrier and often overly conscientious. He had taken a couple of years of college engineering and had a kind of cynical wit that was both subtle and swift. I liked him very much.

For several weeks after my return, Jim's cynicism turned vehement and he was difficult to be around. When I chided him for his scornful comments, he went on and on about soldiering in the Korean War. He was a combat veteran with at least one war wound.

"How does war fit in the context of our plant? I don't want to hear it," I said. "We're supposed to be doing our job, not standing here and reliving old, stupid battles. There's a truce over there. War's not relevant here in Oklahoma anymore. The Texans aren't attacking us yet, are they?"

"Big joke," he said. "You could never understand."

"Probably not," I answered. "I've done my service, and I just want to move on. War is the pits." From that point, I stopped talking to him or at least reduced our exchanges to a bare minimum.

A few days later, Jim got into a violent argument with a coworker, but it was broken up before they could come to blows. Jim was becoming impossible. Then I heard in the lunchroom that he was abusing his wife and son. When I returned to Mary's, I explained about Jim and asked her if there was anything I could do about the situation.

"It's a most difficult illness," she said. "Jim appears to have the signs of spirit-of-war sickness. Sounds like this spirit has entered him."

"How does it happen? Is it war that causes it?"

"Not always. It can be caused by any senseless carnage or some other reason — fear, anger, revenge."

"Can you give me an example?"

"Many, but here's one that should suffice. This is a story about what happened to Yellow Tobacco Boy when he heard about a massacre. Some say this massacre happened a long time ago. Some say this massacre is still in living memory, but I have no direct knowledge of it. The way he heard it, hundreds of unarmed Indians were murdered. They say a full moon was glowing brightly. Yellow Tobacco Boy saw an Indian bow and bloody scalp on the moon's face.

"In his village, the people were listening to the *minko*'s oration. The *minko* was holding high a weapon as he spoke. 'The land that once joined us together is broken. Our people scatter like mice, scampering for safety. The old ones told it, how the diseased eaters of filth would arrive in their wind-driven canoes. They would become strong with stolen power and make our children serve unknown gods.

"'Now, my children, is a time for war. We will form together once more and become whole. Fallen corpses are dancing in the spirit world, summoning us to do a dance of war. They are calling for us to take scalps to avenge them. We have but to listen and to act. If we fall, we will be with our brothers and sisters once more.

"'This war is not a new war. The enemy believe themselves to be invincible, a people of plenty. They march always under a banner of self and selfishness, but they are deceived. They have no union with the Maker of Life.

"'Remember our fathers and mothers, our grandfathers and grandmothers, and touch the earth where they are sleeping. Lift your right hand to the east, toward the sacred sun, to the south for our children, to the west for our dreams which have been stolen, and to the north for honor, for courage, and for truth. Oh, noble combatants! Oh, warriors of the sun! We have faced the enemy many times. Let war be our answer. Once again it is the time to fight!'

"Yellow Tobacco Boy was aware of the intensity of the moment. His torment was great. His feelings of justice had been shattered. Peace and love were out of the question. What was left? Hatred. It was an exalted hatred, and that is all he was aware of. He felt it as waves of coldness rising up from the ground and surging through his body to his head.

"'Obviously! Obviously, the *minko* is right. War is the only solution!' he screamed, stumbling in rage. 'I'll take their hair and spit on the grave of their ancestors.'

"Don't believe everything you hear," Mary said. "The rumors were false. No one was killed. There was no massacre, but the spirit of war heard Yellow Tobacco Boy and entered him anyway. This spirit lurks near distraught people and sometimes forces them to do violent acts. Yellow Tobacco Boy's mind became filled with images of war day after day, a war that could never end. And it didn't end until he was cured. This happened only when he forgave his enemies."

I blurted, "And why should he forgive his damned enemies? I wouldn't. It seems like there's a big difference between the people and their enemies."

"No, there is no difference between friend and foe, but it takes an awakened heart to realize it."

"Well then, I'm not even close."

"You certainly aren't," Mary said.

"Okay, Mary, I admit it. I never said I was a saint. Is there any way I can help Jim?"

"You may not be able to. Spirit-of-war sickness begins with sudden emotional outbursts like the ones you told me about. There may be long discourses about weapons and wounds. There may be talk of persecution and reprisals. This strange and muddled thinking leads one ever further into delusion. Cussing and shouting are common. And other forceful statements may be made. Unaided by conjure, it leads to death. It sounds to me like Jim is on the way there."

"Can't it be treated?"

"The patient should be steamed at the onset and blanket-sweated with war water and bathed in it. He should be led back to the natural order of a peaceful life by spending a great deal of time out of doors. The word *coward* should never be used around him.

"Another way to treat this illness is to do prays and sings. I'll teach you some songs and send some medicine with you if you want to give it a try."

"Sure," I said. "I don't know how I can convince Jim, but I'd like to help him."

When I got back to my job, Jim was gone. My supervisor told me, "Yes, he completely wigged out. He attempted suicide. He was fighting a demon. He's in the nut wing at the hospital right now, and the doctors don't expect to let him out anytime soon. Tell you the truth, I think Jim's working days are over."

Twenty-five

A MONTH AND A HALF or so later, we were sitting over breakfast in a diner in Seminole, Oklahoma. Betty had dropped
off Evangeline again, and right now Evangeline and Tub were
sitting across from me in a booth. Tub ate every bite on his plate
and leaned back contentedly. He had wolfed down bacon, eggs,
and pancakes and was on his third cup of coffee. Evangeline and
I were just beginning to eat our French toast. Tub lit a cigarette,
took a couple of puffs, and set it down in the ashtray.

"Hey, guys," I said. "What is what's-inside-of-me sickness?
That's what I want to know."

"Come on in out of the fog, David," Evangeline said. "What's-
inside-of-me is what it is. Tub, you explain it to him."

Tub took his cigarette from the ashtray and blew a long
breath of smoke. "That woman who came to Mary's cabin was
sick with what's-inside-of-me. Mary fixed her up, that's all."

"What's-inside-of-you or -her?"

"Me," Tub said. "Does it matter? Me, her, you, it's a disease."

"Is there a story about it?" I asked.

"You bet," Tub said. "But let me think a minute. Oh, yeah.
One day Yellow Tobacco Boy was poking himself." Tub prod-
ded his shirt several times with a rigid finger to illustrate. "He
pushed here. He pushed there. He stuck his finger into his belly
button."

"You mean he was kind of like playing with himself or
what?" I interrupted.

"Listen to the story," Evangeline said, taking a drink of her chocolate milk.

"He wasn't playing with himself, you pervert. He was just curious, that's all."

"Curious about what?"

Tub ignored the question. "'I wonder what's inside of me?' Yellow Tobacco Boy asked. His insides didn't make any sense to him. They seemed dark and formless.

"'I'm sensitive,' said What's Inside of Me. 'Quit pushing so hard.'

"Yellow Tobacco Boy removed his finger from his navel. He listened and waited a moment. But soon he was poking again.

"'Don't, I said,' said What's Inside of Me.

"Yellow Tobacco Boy said quickly, 'I won't.'

"'I have contents inside of me,' said What's Inside of Me. 'You will find that I am made of every part of you.'

"'Inside of me?' Yellow Tobacco Boy asked.

"'Yes,' answered What's Inside of Me. 'I am waking and dreaming dreams inside of me. I have your thoughts and beliefs and abilities inside of me. I am countless red and blue tubes and blood. I am breath going in and out of me. I am skull, brain, tonsil, tongue, teeth. I am neck apple, ribs, hollow, lungs. I am liver, heart, pancreas, spleen, kidney, gallbladder, bladder, and bowel. I have bones, marrow bones of the arms and legs. I am sweat, spittle, urine, and semen in men. I am menstrual blood in women. I have animal bones and animal teeth inside of me. I have tears inside of me. I have what you eat inside of me. I have hair inside of me and a cord up my back.

"'I have eyeballs, ears, nose, mouth inside of me. See me inside of me. Smell me inside of me. Listen to me inside of me. Taste me inside of me. Eat me inside of me. You don't have to be stuck inside of me. Remember,' said What's Inside of Me. 'The whole durn universe is what's inside of me.' This story is about acceptance of disease."

I asked, "Are you saying a disease can be caused without an outside cause?"

Tub shook his head. "Yes."

"Look," Evangeline said. "A disease can only come from the inside or outside. What's inside of me is a decision of the body. If it comes from the inside of me, it's what's inside of me."

"Eva, what's inside of you is a big watermelon," I said.

Evangeline smiled but made no reply.

When we were finished talking, Tub said he would catch us in the evening at Mary's, that he had to be going. He took off, and Evangeline and I headed back toward the mountains. In the little town of Hartshorne, I had my gas tank filled up. I paid and got a couple of Cokes. As I was driving away, Evangeline yelled, "Look out!"

I hit the brakes, spilling my Coke. Evangeline flew forward and nearly hit her head on the dash. My car skidded to a halt. An old rust-colored hound dog was lying in the road. I honked the horn and yelled, turning to Evangeline. "Are you all right? You're not going to throw the kid or anything, are you?"

"No, I'm okay," she answered.

The lazy hound dog, greatly perturbed, stood up. He slowly walked to the side of the road.

"Damned dog," I said. "Next time, you're road toast. So sorry to inconvenience you, buddy." I honked the horn again for spite.

As soon as I could, I drove away. In my rearview mirror, I saw the old dog return and lie back down in the middle of the road.

"When a dog blocks your path, it is said to be a T in the road. You can go left or right but you can't go straight ahead. So we have to do something else before we can go back to Mary's."

I eased my car off to the side of the highway and cut the engine.

"You don't want to go back to Mary's?"

"Yes, I want to go to Mary's, but I want you to drive somewhere else first. Humor me. Do what a pregnant woman tells you."

"Like where?"

"Drive over there for awhile." She pointed.

"That's out of our way."

"Do it," she said emphatically.

We ended up going over to an old couple's land north of Wilburton. The couple were known to be keepers of a lake rumored to be the habitat of a sacred horned snake. Old people maintained that the horned snake was the purveyor of secret conjure medicines. I had visited the couple a few times. Mary introduced them to me.

The lake was a deep blue-green color and smelled of moss and water-rotted wood. It was set in a circle of steep hills. Jagged fingers of rock and clumps of cattail were scattered along the shoreline. There were snakes around, for sure — water moccasins, tie snakes, and other water snakes. I had seen plenty before and knew there were nests of cottonmouths. But on a cold day like today it was unlikely any reptiles would be out. Besides, I doubted very much if horned snakes even existed.

When we pulled up to the lake, the old couple's car was gone. I suggested to Evangeline that we take their canoe and paddle around for awhile, maybe fish.

"Too cold," she protested.

"I have field jackets and blankets in the trunk. And you can wear my leather jacket too." I finally persuaded her.

"I won't go fishing. I've had too much of that," Evangeline said. "But maybe we can go out for a little bit. I'm game."

I hoisted the canoe on my back, bent forward, and carried it over to the dock. I flipped it off, and it hit the water on its side with a big slap, then righted itself. I used a paddle to hold it next to the dock. "Get in," I said. "Don't sink it."

Evangeline sat down on the dock and then gingerly got in the canoe, sitting down and holding on to the aluminum sides. Then I got in. Evangeline sat forward, facing me, and I sat in the rear of the canoe in order to paddle.

"Show me around."

"Okay, I'll run you to a couple of good spots."

I stroked the paddle into the water, feathering the blade forward and cutting out toward the center. The sun was out but the air over the lake's surface was damp and cold. Evangeline was ducking her head and huddled down in my army jacket. I was stroking. Pretty soon we were out in the center of the lake.

Evangeline began to sing in French.

"What song is that?" I asked.

She smiled enigmatically.

"Okay, Mona Lisa, if you don't want to tell me."

"I come to you with a message," Evangeline said. "I will sing a little song for you and teach you what's-inside-the-sea illness, and if you listen, you will know how to cure it."

"Since I don't understand French, I doubt if I will know much of anything."

Evangeline sang for awhile. Behind her, I could see the tall trees on the hills facing the lake. We drifted. Water slapped and gurgled against the rocks near the shore.

When she was finished with her song, I said, "That was lovely."

"Here's the story," she said. "A tale told by mermaids. Mary says there's a sea in the human that communicates with the outside sea. And our inside seas speak to other humans, animals, and plants. I'll tell you what I heard about it."

"Shoot," I said.

"Well, one afternoon, Yellow Tobacco Boy was walking

along by the sea. He collected a basket of shells and other gifts the sea washed up. This was in the land of flora — or Florida as it is now called. Waves were crashing on the beach. Seagulls hung on the wind. Pipers ran along the water's edge.

"As he was reaching down for a lovely pink shell, he noticed two blue mermaids splashing not far away in the surf. He realized the mermaids were singing a magical song — a love song that had a decided pull on him. The glistening blue-skinned mermaids were truly beautiful. They had crimson eyes like polished rubies and long sea-green hair of kelp — and how captivating and wild like the sea itself, he thought.

"Yellow Tobacco Boy was afraid they would swim off, but they motioned for him to join them.

"'I'm a bit of a land lover,' Yellow Tobacco Boy called. 'Come join me on the beach.'

"'We can't cross the water line,' a mermaid answered in a sweet voice, still beckoning with delicate arms the color of wet lapis.

"'I'm not ready to die,' said the other. 'It's best if you come join us.'

"'Where are you going?' asked Yellow Tobacco Boy.

"'We are going down to the underneath place. Please come. We will hold your hand. You can go down between us. We will lead you to our magical grotto.'

"Yellow Tobacco Boy took his basket of sea-gifts and set them in the sand away from the tide and tide pools. He joined the mermaids. They took his hand and began going down, down beneath the sea.

"Sea-green and thick flowing hair — pulling him further down by the hands. They were soon on the bottom. That's when they met the old water man. He was all shriveled up and deformed, waiting near the magic grotto the mermaids had spoken of.

"The old water man pointed toward it. It looked like a monumental chamber of living shell and was half hidden by a tangle of sea brush.

"The old water man said, 'Here is the magical grotto, and the sea maids are its owners. They have waited patiently for you to come. Their magic grotto has many strange wonders. Now you have arrived to sample them. You may enter the grotto proudly, for not everyone gets the privilege. I suggest you make haste.'

"Without thinking too much about it one way or the other, Yellow Tobacco Boy slipped inside. He thought he stayed there for four days but he was actually there for four years. The grotto is where he learned what's inside the sea. He held council with the fish and eels and water snakes.

"These beings were angry with the humans. They told Yellow Tobacco Boy they would make terrible dreams and send fevers to haunt them. Then, they told him how to make cures by using sea weeds and mosses. They gave him the remedy for all the many what's-inside-the-sea illnesses. They told him which plants to conjure with.

"The adept conjure of the sea has hidden and unsurpassable powers," continued Evangeline. "So my song was about how Yellow Tobacco Boy became the holder of these various cures. I memorized it from Mary and put it in my native French. Better still, I know how to dose people up with conjure juice for that illness. There's a lot of this inside-the-sea sickness in Louisiana."

"It's a pretty ballad. You ought to go on the radio."

Evangeline laughed like I was making a joke, but I wasn't. She pulled herself straight and rocked the canoe a little. I paddled toward the far shore and then let it ride.

"Do you know catfish sickness?" I asked.

"Yes, I can cure it."

"Tell me what you know."

"You mean the conjure story?"

"Yeah, if you know it."

"I haven't been studying with Mary without learning her stories. She told me Yellow Tobacco Boy jumped off a cliff. No sooner had he hit the water than he found himself sinking down until he reached the very bottom of the lake. He tried with all his might to swim to the surface. Strange to say, he found himself going down rather than up. And stranger still, he found he had grown gills and could breathe perfectly well. He looked at his hands, and they were webbed and green and so were his feet.

"'First, I dropped down here like a stone,' bubbled Yellow Tobacco Boy. 'The next thing you know I'm a frog. What will happen to me next?'

"Yellow Tobacco Boy did not have long to find out, because he saw a beautiful maiden coming toward him in silhouette — and then even more brightly outlined as she drew near. She wore a dress fashioned of tiny turtle shells, and two larger shells covered her breasts. Her long jet hair flowed back smoothly with the waves.

"'I am Snapping Turtle Woman,' the woman said in a gurgly voice. 'And I have come at the request of your new father, catfish, who wants to formally adopt you as his son. Will you come with me?'

"'I don't see why not. After all, I'm rather out of my element, wouldn't you say?'

"'One element is good as the next,' Snapping Turtle Woman said, smiling. 'Come along now.'

"Yellow Tobacco Boy followed behind her, holding her hand. She pulled him through tangles of fluffy moss and weeds. Schools of minnows fled in needle streaks of silver.

"Yellow Tobacco Boy had to walk carefully, for there was a

region of skulls, bones, spear points, and pieces of broken toma-hawk. There were old rusty cannonballs and remnants of chain. One minute Yellow Tobacco Boy was sinking to his knees in silt. The next minute he was drifting like a sky-borne leaf in this curious water world.

"Then he saw them. They were far away, but that lasted only an instant. A circle of catfishmen with long whiskers quickly surrounded Yellow Tobacco Boy and Snapping Turtle Woman. The *minko* catfish — the king fish — came forward. He stopped in front of them. He was larger than the others. His features were more pronounced.

"'You are my new son,' he said. His voice was laughably harsh, and a clump of bubbles poured from his throat. 'There are no tears here below. I have called you so that you may learn the remedies and cures of catfish sickness. Once, long ago, the grub worm called a meeting of all the insects and finned ones. We agreed to attack the human in dreams and make them sick when we were abused. Are you willing to learn how to obtain our help?'

"Yellow Tobacco Boy answered, 'Yes, Grandfather. Many of my people are sick from the fish tribe. I want to be able to conjure your aid when necessary.' That's catfish story."

I asked, "What does Mary use to treat it — chicken blood and stink bait?"

"I will teach you whenever you like," Evangeline said.

I nodded gratefully. Then I stroked over to an inlet full of reeds and brush.

"This is a good place to fish for bass," I said. "I wish I had brought my tackle to get a line in."

As I was glancing down in the gray water, I happened to notice a stir of brown mud. Then there was a bubbling commotion, like a boiling cauldron. Evangeline and I looked on in terror.

What came to my mind was that I had suspended us over the dwelling place of the great snake. What else could it be? Then I saw it, just beneath the surface — a silvery snake longer than the canoe. As it glided by, I saw its horned head. Then it dipped back down deeper and was gone as quickly as it had appeared.

Both Evangeline and I must have sat there gazing unblinking and unbelieving at what we had just witnessed. Believe me, once I came to my senses, I got the hell out of there fast.

Later that night, sitting with Evangeline, Tub, and Mary, I spoke of the day's events. Mary thought it was hysterically funny. Tub seemed subdued and embarrassed by our tall tale telling.

"I wish I was there. You two probably saw an indigo snake," Tub said. "They get over ten feet long, and they have a red throat and chin. From a distance that could look like a horn."

"No, it was a real horn," I said.

"Yes, it was," Evangeline insisted.

Tub rubbed his forehead. "I still think it was an indigo. Magnified by the water, their blueblack color can make them appear twice as large as they are."

"I know what I saw," I said. "I saw a horned snake."

"Me too," Evangeline said. "I saw it too."

"Well, maybe you two did see something," Tub said thoughtfully. "I have heard of this snake all my life, lived in fear and awe of it. I've tried on many occasions to call it and took my chances. But the great horned one never answered. My uncle told me how to steal its medicine. He had some, I think, because he could do many things that seemed impossible."

"Don't ever mess around with it," Mary said. "That slim snake body with the hooked horn is dangerous. The slightest error is fatal. First it hooks you. Then it ties you. Then it has you for dinner. If you gaze at one of them, these snakes have the power to hypnotize you and compel you to come. It likes

Indians, but only those who have kept with the old ways. I think it heard your songs and stories and let you be."

"And this all happened because of that damned hound dog in the middle of the road," I said, shaking my head in wonder. "Thanks, dog."

Twenty-six

*A*LL MARY'S GUESTS had taken off for parts unknown except me. I spent the next morning working in Mary's garden. The sun was gaining when she called me in to eat. I was hungry, and it was a pleasant surprise to find that in place of our usual simple meals, she had fixed up a dish of fried squirrel and turnips. I dug in.

When I was finished eating, Mary asked me not to leave the table. Then she spent a great deal of time positioning my chair according to some configuration that only her unfathomable logic might explain. Just when I thought she was done, she told me to stand up. She moved my chair a few more inches to one side.

"Sit back down," she said. She tilted her head toward me in that familiar way of hers and asked, "Comfortable?"

"Yeah. I guess so," I answered uncertainly.

"You must commit what I say now to memory, every detail."

"Well then, I'd better write it down. You know me. I get distracted. My memory is iffy."

"That's because writing it down gives you permission to forget it. But I know this is your way. Go ahead, set it down by hand."

I went out to my tent and found my notebook and came back. When I sat back in the chair, my pencil was poised at the ready.

"Tea?" Mary asked.

"No, I'm fine. Maybe later."

"Does the light bother you?" she asked.

"No," I replied, feeling impatient. "I'm just fine, Mary. Quit making a fuss."

"I am making a fuss because this is the right time to reveal the teachings of *shilip*. Without this understanding, you will never know what you are doing. Without it, you will be lost.

"Many thousands of years ago, apprentices spent long years arduously studying and contemplating the shadow. In doing this, they began to see our manifestation on this earth as a fracturing of original light and to understand life as a struggle to return to it. First they studied shadow. By doing this, the *shilip* and its various distinctions slowly became apparent. Apprentices learned that shadows cast shadows.

"Understand me well. Here we are speaking of thousands of years of dedicated effort to gain knowledge, which was then passed along down the generations. Eventually it was discovered that by fasting, this process of learning and understanding could be accelerated.

"The problem with speeding things up is that, if you are not careful, it can eliminate the deeper understanding gained from experience. When you drive in your car and the scenery quickly flickers by, you don't really see it unless you make it a strong point to pay close attention. There is a great difference between going from here to Tulsa by car and walking there. If you walk to Tulsa, you'll never forget it. Maybe, seeing all the cars and big rigs zooming by, you would feel sorry for yourself because everyone else was getting to Tulsa so easily, long before you.

"I promise you this, David. You are going to Tulsa. You will not have to walk, but because of this you must be very careful to pay close attention to the scenery. You have bought a cheap ticket from the tobacco spirit. I am about to give you this ticket. The blood of tobacco must be respected, and now you will find out some reasons why. This spirit can get angry if you do not pay proper respect to it, and it can be a hard driver over bumpy roads. There will be a lot happening over the bumps. If you fool around, you are liable to fall out of the bus. Don't ever get smart with the driver. The tobacco spirit would just as soon boot you off on the side of the road. You'll never get to Tulsa that way, and your road back here to me will be paved with sorrow.

"Now, I will explain to you what Tulsa looks like, how it feels, and so on. You don't want to be afraid once you get there. You want to know how to line it out. You want to know the lay of the city, so you will feel at home there. I am speaking to you now of Tulsa, but what I am really talking about is the place of the *shilip*, our inner shadow. Listen carefully. When you go to Tulsa for the first time, go there with my words.

"The *shilip* is the spirit we are all contained within. The world itself is the shadow of the Maker of Life. Our material form is only a disguise, a mask. The shadow is an unfailing indicator of our true state. The shadow has color, and it has weight. As seen by the conjure, the qualities and attributes of the shadow are a direct measure of health and well-being.

"Consider for a moment this *shilip*, this inside shadow. Partly it is inside a sphere. It is the sphere or shell that envelops the human body, and also the so-called material body of an animal or plant. It is the being of the sphere. Inanimate objects can also have an inside shadow.

"This oblong sphere, or *shilip*, can be clearly seen around the fourth day of a tobacco fast. The feeling of awe that accompanies this experience cannot be overemphasized. The sphere is elastic and can expand and contract. Further, the nine flayed, the human body contained inside the expanding and contracting sphere, becomes transparent. The powwower is able to see mysterious objects floating or contained within this body.

"With vision or sight, the *shilip* may be seen in an inexhaustible variety of ways. It can appear as light surrounding the body. During powwowing, the shadow may change texture, color, or shape — even before the altering effects of the tobacco smoke. Sick or dead animals may be seen within the *shilip*. It may appear as a stylized animal such as a fetish. It may present itself as a buffalo head or an animal sprouting wings. It may even change into a large stone.

"The *shilip* may be seen as a fireball or a cloud. It may be seen as a burst of light like the petals of a flower, or as a series of intertwined snakes. I have seen it as a pale blue light with intricate forms floating above it. It can be egg-shaped with a little wind cave projecting an unearthly light. Often, it looks like a life-sized ball of cotton candy, or a pink sunburst. It may look like a glass container with a cracked and broken dish with flapping wings suspended within it. It may exist as a geometric design as complicated as a snowflake. Sometimes, it looks like latticed globes spun by spiders. I have seen inside shadows that look like great gingerbread cookies, or multicolored spinning tops. It might look like a squirming octopus. It may be an orange sphere, or a drifting, horned moon. It may look like a chambered nautilus or a filigreed egg sitting on bands of different colors. The variations are endless, and to the conjure, each is significant.

"The importance of the inside shadow is that it is enhanced identity. As you will see, it has many characteristics. Outside shadow, the area accompanying nine flayed, sometimes called the bordering shadow, may tell of the external condition.

"What I say next is crucially important. We humans are said to be an arrangement of twenty-two subtle rings or hoops. That is, we have twenty-two partitions in our state of being. Twenty-two circlets that comprise the complete *shilip*. The actual substantial body of the human, the physical body, is called nine flayed. It has nine gradations. Regardless of whether we are speaking of a man or woman, nine flayed is said to be female. The area surrounding nine flayed is called thirteen flayed. This is the immediate environment around the body. It is said to be male.

"Additionally, one aspect of the *shilip* is a radiance of myriad variety. It begins at one of nine flayed, and it is capable of piercing through all flayeds, and beyond. This light can indicate a realized being. Usually, however, it is locked into one place and stunted, indicating stagnation. The radiance can be trapped in many ways. Often the shrinkage of this brightness speaks of our preoccupation with the concerns of the world.

"If the light is carried too high within the *shilip*, it becomes a weight, a burden. People who carry their light about the head are those who are overly identified with the mind. Their thinking is always at war with life — constantly judging, and heartlessly nagging themselves to death. The more this happens, the higher their radiance moves toward its uppermost configuration. These people often need a good jolt, to make their radiance come unglued. It can happen when tragedy strikes.

"In healthy people, this radiance floats about in the area of the navel. When it is out of whack, either in ourselves or in others, our task as power doctors is to restore it and marry it to its proper place. It cannot be seen or measured without training and the aid of a teacher.

"The *shilip* lives on when our body dies. Death is a return to radiance — a time of no time and a self of no self. Our *shilip* is indestructible. It exists forever.

"As I have said, the complete *shilip* is called twenty-two flayed. *Shilip* is our sacred clothing, our true clothing. In this instance, our clothing is us."

"Just as I always thought, Mary," I had to cut in. "Clothes make the man."

"Hush, now. I'm doing the talking, and you're doing the listening — you better be. We remove this clothing only when we return to light. Only when you are capable of understanding the *shilip* will you learn your true identity. Only then will you know authentic essence.

"Flayed is also energy. The path of the power doctor leads first to the innermost core, or one flayed of nine flayed. This is where flayed is densest, where life pushes into being. Our bodies are so difficult to come by and so easily lost. Something more about it: this light keeps the heart beating. It carries the ritual and ceremony of life, and self inside life. It holds our dreams. It's at once everything we are. When it's gone, it's gone. It vanishes as quickly and as surprisingly as it came.

"One flayed of nine flayed is called the keeper. This aspect of *shilip* defines our limitations, our boundaries. It is the place of balance. It is our direct connection to the Life's Maker, but it must move through all twenty-two flayed to get there. One flayed is our site of holy heat, or inner sun, but surprisingly, it is ruled by the moon. Moon is our mother. And the moon has a great deal to do with our destiny.

"At your death, you will meet the guardian of nine flayed and the guardian of thirteen flayed. Your guardian spirits might appear as angels or part human and part animal, such as a man or woman with a bird's head. They might be seen as some other fantastic being. This meeting will cause a division, a great split as though you have been sliced into two parts. First you will hear distant thunder that becomes ten thousand choruses of celebration. The two guardians will block your path. When this happens, you won't worry much about your death. Death will become a small sideshow, the least of your concerns. The frightening guardians will be your biggest worry.

"Escaping the guardians, you will return to one flayed of nine flayed. You will see it as a tiny point of light. It will grow larger as your being is sucked toward it. You will realize this point of light contains everything. There is no use to struggle. You might as well relax. You will see celestial fireworks and phosphorescent worlds beyond imagination. That will be your return to one flayed—to a new birth and a new beginning.

"I'll tell you right now, David. There are many sounds you can't yet hear. There are many shadows you can't yet see. The power doctor both hears and sees all of this. To understand one flayed of nine flayed fully, at your limited stage of development, would greatly imbalance you. Delusion ends upon entering one flayed of nine flayed. One flayed is the strongest. One flayed of nine flayed is only a minute speck, but it forms the density that is the cause of causes. It ripples just as if you had thrown a stone in water. We are flayed in this manner. One flayed of nine flayed carries all the states of life from embryo to death and rebirth.

"The outside shadow, the world, is the deceiving shadow. It is the invincible illusion, the domain beyond the bearers and embracers. Earth's *shilip* has nine sky, thirteen sky, and it is the same with us humans. Nine flayed is often called first lord or lady. Thirteen flayed is similarly called two lord or two lady. Nine flayed is of night sky. Thirteen flayed is of day sky.

"Remember the ancient holy pipes with two bowls that represent nine flayed and thirteen flayed. One pipe bowl is a man smoking a pipe, and his pipe is also in the shape of a man smoking a pipe — the smoker smoking in two distinctive worlds of shadow.

"But understand this. It's all one *shilip* in the end.

"Now I will speak to you of the order of *shilip*. One flayed of nine flayed is called undulant movement.

"Two flayed of nine flayed is duality, not as a division, but as a continuum. It is called scissors and seeks elegance.

"Three flayed of nine flayed is called the diviner, because it mediates the force of two. Your debts are added and subtracted in this flayed.

"Four flayed of nine flayed is called the just. It is the meeting ground of the clans within the human being. Four and nine are caring numbers. Four is completeness, and nine is used in healing because the earth itself is flayed nine times. Four is the flayed of activity and intent. It is the flayed of accomplishment.

"Five flayed of nine flayed is called the upright, the first humans. It is the steps of the temple stairway. Five is mysterious. It speaks of vanished peoples and previous worlds. Perhaps that is why this flayed loves change so much. It is always seeking itself and has a great love of history.

"Six flayed of nine flayed is the bowl. It sits on the altar, and cedar is burned in it. It goes its own way, and can be disconcertingly original in all its aspects.

"Seven flayed of nine flayed is called the double skin. It carries the knowledge of sacrifice.

"Eight flayed of nine flayed is the victorious. It teaches humility.

"Nine of nine flayed is called precious skin. It represents our conscious connection with the world. It is the house of confinement.

"These nine of nine compose the human body. All are ruled by night benefactors who travel about in the sky below. We are constantly aware of nine of nine as we go about our day-to-day affairs.

"Understand thirteen flayed, the binding or accompanying shadow. Thirteen flayed is the carrier *shilip*. It is often compared with the fluid around a fetus, and truly so. It is sometimes called incubator.

"In thirteen flayed there is one beautiful monster, one stalker, one sweet medicine, one farmer, one minister or helper, one death, one sweeper, one water-comes-down-from-the-nose, one rabbit, one thunder, one flint, one arrested or inactive human, all ruled by thirteen.

"We encounter color at one flayed of thirteen flayed. For the purpose of medicine there are but five colors: red, white, yellow, black, and turquoise or blue. The first four are bearers, and they stand at the cardinal points of the indestructible mirror wheel. The fifth color, blue, is central. It is symbolic of the spirit to which all races must return. Blue is the dominant color of thirteen flayed. Blue acknowledges blue snake, the ascending and descending serpent that connects us all to earth.

"One flayed of thirteen flayed is echo. Here we seek perfect understanding.

"Two flayed of thirteen flayed is sibling. It is a flayed of magnetism — either pushing or pulling.

"Three flayed of thirteen flayed is enigma. It is imperfect and seeks order.

"Four flayed of thirteen flayed is spindle. A spindle is used for balance. It resolves paradoxes enabling one to act forcefully.

"Five flayed of thirteen flayed is the prudent, ruled by Salt Girl. Here is sacrifice in women and avoidance in men. The prudent love pageantry and beauty, especially in architecture.

"Six flayed of thirteen flayed is called the counselor. This is the domain of silence and intention.

"Seven flayed of thirteen flayed is the herald, the ability to lift up in order to see better. It brings and sends messages.

"Eight flayed of thirteen flayed is the obscuring leaf. The branch is pushed aside and we take on or reject illusion. This is the place of enchantment.

"Nine flayed of thirteen flayed is the watchtower. It is a far-seeing warrior.

"Ten flayed of thirteen flayed is the sacred arrow. It is held in eagle's talons day and night.

"Eleven flayed of thirteen flayed is red corn. The red is blood, and the blood is menses. This is a noble woman.

"Twelve flayed of thirteen flayed is the green woman. It is said to be a blossoming garden.

"Thirteen of thirteen flayed is called first flayed, because at the end there is always a beginning. It engages outwardly. It is a stalker. It seeks birth.

"Don't think that when you see it, the inside shadow will appear to your eyes exactly as I have described it. But be clear about this. Passing from one flayed to another is as literal as going from one city to another.

"I have spoken here of what has been told to us by our ancestors. We are not seeking exactness here, but a loose correspondence. I have pointed the direction. Twenty-two flayed will never manifest exactly in these sacred proportions. The actual inside shadow will appear in an infinite variety of forms and colors with endless symmetrical differences. Just as all human beings differ, so too does their *shilip*.

"Not only our deeds, words, and appearance affect people we encounter. Our flayeds can either energize or enervate. Flayeds contribute either dullness or clarity. We know when we are in the presence of holy people. We sense their *shilip*. We are drawn to some people while avoiding others. We sense their good and bad *shilip* states.

"The powwower learns that the *shilip* responds to thoughts. Desire can be a powerful thought. As an example, if a person enters a room and sees an object that interests them, a part of their inside shadow may attach to that object. That is why our attachments, our habits and desires, especially the strongest ones, are a spiritual bleeding that can weaken us.

"People may conceal attachments, or they may not even be consciously aware of them. Yet the powwower is thoroughly familiar with this plane of being. The powwower will not be deceived. The power doctor is always aware of how men and women or people of the same sex affect each other. *Shilip* tells it."

I had become so fascinated I quit scribbling notes.

Mary brought over tea. "Your task is to remember and understand these teachings. Keep them. For I will often ask for them back."

"I was wondering, what about animals? Is it the same?"

"Animals understand shadow well. Like us, they fight for their identity. Unlike us, they are at one."

Twenty-seven

*L*ATER THAT AFTERNOON, I decided to head back to Oklahoma City. Mary walked me to my car. She had never been very physically demonstrative, but this time she held my hand. I thought perhaps it was because she had shared so much of her knowledge with me, and she was sad to see me go. When we got to the car, she let go of my hand and put her hand on my shoulder. She was smiling, and her eyes were shining.

"Before you go, I have one more instruction for you," she said. And then, either purposefully or accidentally, I wasn't sure which, she moved the hand that had been resting on my shoulder and brushed it lightly across the nape of my neck. It caused a bewildering sensation that shot up from my toes to my head like a burst of electricity. My hair bristled. Mary continued forcefully, "Do me this service. Don't look at shadows."

The instant she said "shadow" my eyes blurred. When they focused again, it seemed as if my vision had been turned inside out. The world of substance had hidden itself. It had become of little or no importance. Instead, I was starkly aware of all the shadows around me. They had somehow increased in significance and leaped to the fore. My awareness transformed. Shadows danced, and the dark dancers held me transfixed.

"Mary, I think I'm seeing backward. I can't drive to the city like this."

"You'll do just fine," Mary replied calmly.

Yet I was unable to reverse the shift. It was like playing a very intense game of chess and being able to see only the black squares. These squares, the countless shadows around me, held infinite counterpossibilities. I got dizzy and clutched the side of my car to steady myself.

Through the dark latticework, I was faintly aware of Mary. She was off somewhere in a world beyond mine. She rubbed her hands together quickly, making them warm. She touched her palms to my eyes. They blurred again. When she moved her hands away, my perception just as quickly reverted to a normal state. It was as if a small searchlight in the back of my head had been turned on, removing all awareness of the intrusive shadows.

Mary smiled again, and the shiny quality in her eyes darted back in place. "Don't worry," she said. "There's nothing to worry about."

Twenty-eight

*T*IME PASSED QUICKLY in the city, and soon I was once again packing my car for the familiar drive to the mountains. The strange incident before leaving Mary's had stayed with me, but in a surprisingly positive way. I was sensitive to a new energy that seemed to flow through my face and pull back my shoulders. There was much on my mind, and I wanted plenty of time to talk to Mary about it.

As soon as I was seated comfortably in Mary's kitchen again, I told her about the strange new sensations I had been feeling and asked if she could explain them.

"I have told you that you are *shilip*, shadow. I altered it for a moment. This shocked your *shilip*. It caused changes in you, but that's good."

"Will you tell me some more about *shilip*?"

"Yes. Once you truly see it, you will become a lonely sentinel. You will have purity of sight. I have told you that the conjure works with shadow. The shadow has a direct influence on consciousness and health.

"You will see the *shilip* body in many ways. It may appear to you as a blue-gray feathery ball, or a ball of billowing smoke, or in other forms. Either way, it will seem to be smoke, but when there is sickness it will be an inward-turning smoke with no ascension. The smoke coils around its center but does not rise.

"The sick body is easily viewed. It is not receptive; that is to say, the sick body is locked up. The light inside its *shilip* is ashy. Perhaps it will contain intrusions of some kind, or it may look like a wheel whose spokes have been crushed. Either way, it will be damaged in such a way that there can be no elasticity. The person is shut down."

"What does my inner shadow look like?" I asked. "I mean, if a power doctor were looking at me?"

"A power doctor is looking at you, David. Your shadow is not abnormal. Its circumference and dimensions have improved at many points since you have been coming here. It has good symmetry, and I see no immediate health problems. It shows a potential for greater realization."

"Can you see your own inside shadow?"

"Of course. The ceremonial healer is contained within a similar smoke. The difference is that the powwower's inside shadow is more resilient. The experienced healer knows how to use the inside shadow to change form to that of an animal, or any other being. Additionally, the power doctor, as I have told you many times, is able to blow breath feathers and plumes. The powwower can blow different animal spirit breaths — deer, snake, bear, and other power breaths. These are seen as issuing not from the mouth but from deep within the inside shadow. It is breath that makes healing go straight to the mark. It is breath doctor conjure who keeps the ceremonial memory.

"Power doctors are often called masters of the animals, because they understand and maintain close contact with their helper spirits. The healer has the ability to ask questions and receive answers from the appropriate animals. A true conjure is qualified to ask for cooperation from most animals, either from the individual animal or from the collective animal spirit, the master spirit.

"Power doctors usually fast for four days before powwowing unless there is a great urgency to begin immediately. Also, no pork should be eaten for two weeks prior to powwowing. During the four-day fast, the conjure drinks only green tobacco water.

Other tobacco waters can be substituted if green tobacco water is unavailable.

"At the beginning of the fast, the garments to be worn during powwowing are placed in a tree. Later they are soaked in tobacco water and dried out again. The conjure bathes in a spring or creek and then puts on the medicine garments. The clothes now have power. Don't doubt it.

"Long ago we were able to cure any sickness. We had corn magicians and many other kinds. There were more kinds of ceremonial conjures than you can imagine, singing doctor conjure, dancing doctor conjure, rattle doctor conjure, drum doctor conjure, arrow doctor conjure, sucking and blowing doctor conjure. There were animal power doctors as well — bear, turtle, blackbird, and so on. Always remember that the animals are the true source of our healing powers.

"'Now, certain animals are leaving us. Our powwowing must be done without their assistance. Little by little, we are losing ability, power. It's draining away like a fading dream. And hardly anyone wants to learn it anymore. The price is too high, and the reward is too little."

I shrugged my shoulder. "I guess so, if you take the world's measure."

"David," she said with a mysterious smile, "you are becoming my son, my brother in spirit. I'll make a man of you yet, a real conjure. And by the way, I've washed your tent and conjured it. Before you go to sleep tonight, I want you to go bathe in the brook. Severe tests await you."

Twenty-nine

MONTHS AGO Mary had instructed me to cut my calories drastically — though these were not her words for it, but mine. It was a cleansing, a purification. She had given me a cloth flour sack full of wild rice and two cigar boxes full of powdery pale green herbs. I was to make tea or broth with them. One broth she called "hungry broth," and the other she called "stomach broth." The first was to drink anytime hunger pangs struck, and the other was for when my mind begged me to quit the whole deal. As Mary had undoubtedly foreseen, this happened continually. Luckily, the stomach broth had a noticeably calming effect that steadied my resolve. Besides the rice and broth, I could also eat any boiled greens I wished, especially turnip greens.

The most difficult aspect of this diet was the loss of coffee, which Mary had forbidden me to drink. She made me promise to quit smoking commercial cigarettes. Instead, she gave me several little cotton sacks of Indian tobacco, which was to be rolled in corn shucks. It was a pain. But eventually, cigarette making became a near ritual, a meditation that put me in touch with the tobacco and personalized it for me. No doubt, this was Mary's intent. I smoked the rolled corn-shuck cigarettes at work and the more peculiar leaf-rolled ones in the privacy of my apartment. I didn't want anyone getting the wrong idea about me.

Mary stuck her head into my tent the next morning. "Give me everything that's inside here," she ordered. "Your sleeping bag, even your clothes. You'll be staying in your tent for several days. Here's a blanket and towel. When you leave your tent, use them to cover yourself. And be brief. Go back inside at once."

Mary handed me the Pendleton blanket, a towel, and a stiff piece of leather with a large mound of cigarettes and matches on it.

"What's this all about, Mary?"

"This is a green tobacco water fast. It is the first drinking of tobacco water. When you make this fast, you are reaching for holiness and power. There can be no alienation from the divine in powwowing. The tobacco may or may not like you when you meet, but we will soon see. We will soon find out what kind of mischief you're capable of. Try to keep in balance with it."

"Now remove your clothes," she said. "Get everything else out of your tent except what I have just given you."

I reluctantly pulled off my pants, which I had been sleeping in. I wrapped myself in the old Pendleton, rolled up all my other things into a big wad, and shoved it out to her. I spread the towel at the back of the tent and set the stiff leather with the cigarettes on it. Mary passed in an enamel basin containing a greenish liquid that smelled of the pungent green tobacco. I put this next to the towel and cigarettes. The basin had a long-stemmed gourd cup to drink with.

For the next two or three hours, I listened while Mary drummed, rattled, and sang from various directions outside the tent. She left without saying a word to me. When I went outside to relieve myself, I noticed that the ground around the tent had been swept clean and scattered with bird plumage. Mary had tied hawk feathers to the two peaks over the tent's entrance and rear. Two effigy figures about a foot long, carved of red cedar, sat on the ground on each side of the tent. I knew better than to touch them.

There was also a staff made from cane leaning against the tent. An aged tobacco leaf and a raptor talon hung from it. The crown of the staff was a face fashioned from a coconut shell and black feathers. For some reason, the face made me feel a little giddy, and I went back into the tent and rested, smoking the cigarettes now and then. They were as strong as harsh, stinky cigars.

The first day was by far the hardest. The tobacco water didn't do much for my hunger. It tasted rather sweetish, like licorice, with a bite to the tongue. I had what might best be described as a continual low-key nausea. I swallowed a lot. I sipped often from the basin and dozed off to sleep now and again from sheer boredom. Having little to do made me acutely aware of my hunger, which soon became a raging in the pit of my stomach. Mercifully, this lessened as time passed. Once, when I had to leave the tent, it was drizzling rain outside and a beautiful rainbow spanned across the mountains.

Back inside, I tried to get comfortable. The tent walls began to light up and pulse for long moments, followed by low rolling thunder. The storm passed by, and it was quiet again. Once in a while I would hear a twig snapping nearby or the snarl of an unidentifiable animal.

Time became meaningless. I could no longer keep track of minutes or hours. I became so confused I couldn't even remember if it was the second or the third day of the fast. The level of the tobacco water gradually dropped, nearing the bottom of the basin. I was smoking a lot, one cigarette after another, so my cigarettes were dwindling at the same rate. My mind lost direction, and I was amazed at how it would fasten on some particular theme and then uncontrollably repeat and repeat it.

Finally, I became apathetic. I tried not to think at all. Thinking took more energy than it was worth. I didn't have the energy for it, for rationalizing or for justifying anything. There was no point. What difference did it make? I slept and slept again, in daylight and darkness indiscriminately.

Mary didn't show her face once during the entire fast. I often thought I heard her outside, but when I called out there was never a reply. Either she chose not to answer or she wasn't there.

When I did see her again, I was unprepared for it. I was half-dozing when I became aware of a dark form floating just above me. I recoiled in panic, shouting out in surprise and fear before realizing the mysterious object was my clothes, and that Mary was handing them to me from outside the tent.

"Get dressed," she said, "and make certain you put nothing on backward. I've prepared your clothes properly. Wearing them backward would spoil it."

I pulled on my clothes and tucked in my shirt as best I could in my cramped position. I laced up my boots and crawled outside. My legs were stiff, and I was dizzy and trembling. It was nearing sundown, and the soft light hurt my eyes. After such long isolation, it felt strange to be in the company of another person again. I fumbled for words, trying to tell Mary I needed a moment to get my bearings.

"Hush," she commanded. "Don't talk. Do as you are told. Now come with me. Be quick about it."

I followed Mary down an overgrown path that crooked off to the right. I discovered there was a cold wind from which the tent had sheltered me. Mary went faster and faster. We came out way down in the bottomland a long way from the cabin, although it seemed we had been walking a few minutes at the most. There were frames, spaces of time, that were lost to me. I even wondered if Mary had somehow shortened the trail.

"Over there," she said, motioning.

She was pointing at a strange little tipi. It blended completely into its surroundings. I had never seen anything like it. It was nothing more than a small cone woven like a basket. Strips of matted dark brown bark were entwined through the vertical saplings that supported it. There was a small entrance. I stood looking at it uncertainly.

"Well, get in," Mary ordered. "You will have to lower yourself and crawl in backward. Go ahead and wiggle inside. Hurry."

I sat down with my back to the thing. Mary had correctly predicted that my head was too high to fit through the doorway, so I had to lie down on my back and shimmy inside. The space was small, but I found it wasn't too uncomfortable. It wasn't completely dark — not yet, anyway. Around me, attached to the structure's interior surface, I could see glimmering strips of mica and some sort of milky glass. I wondered why Mary had wanted me to come to this strange place instead of just leaving me inside my own tent. It seemed to me that one place would have been as good as another.

She closed the small opening through which I had entered, using a flap woven of the same material as the walls. She fussed with it briefly. When she was done, I could no longer tell where the entrance had been. Although it was now much darker inside, the mica flared mysteriously like many starlit eyes. The ground felt cool and damp beneath me. I looked down and discovered it was gritty, black sand. When I reached my hand down into it, I couldn't find bottom. Around the sandy perimeter, lining the walls, a circle of fist-sized quartz crystals had been arranged.

"I am going to make some adjustments," Mary called to me. "Tell me if you feel anything unusual."

She seized the structure and seemed to be wrestling with it. I thought for a moment she might even be deliberately trying to collapse it. Perhaps destroying it might be some kind of enigmatic metaphor. But this wasn't the case. She was merely bending the entire dwelling to my right in order to suit some inscrutable purpose.

"Anything?" she called.

"Yeah, I feel trapped," I said, trying to joke.

Mary didn't answer. Again the little hut rotated slightly, twisting and bending back and forth.

"Now?" she asked.

"No. At least not that I know of."

She rotated the structure again. This time an electric current shot violently through my body. I yelped. "Ouch. It shocked me, Mary — like you hit me on my funny bone."

"Is it gone now?"

"What?"

"The feeling."

"If it wasn't gone, you'd see this whole place streaking off through the woods with a pair of feet sticking out the bottom, believe me."

"Be still," she answered curtly. I sensed she was adjusting it again, but I couldn't tell for certain. It sounded as if she might be running her hand over the hut, though to what end I couldn't imagine. I heard a sharp crack like a piece of wood breaking, and then Mary said, "I have to go now. I'll return in a few hours. Whatever you do, don't leave this lodge."

"Why not?"

"It will be dangerous outside. I won't be responsible for you if you come out. If you do, you might be destroyed."

"What are you talking about?"

"Never mind. But no matter what happens, it is important that you remain where you are. Do you understand? Give me your word and honor it."

"Yes. I think so."

"The only permissible answer is yes."

"Then yes. I'll stay put."

I heard Mary's footsteps die as she walked away. I was alone. The walls of my strange little lodge flared again, mysteriously illuminated by the glow of the mica flakes. For a moment they gave the impression of being little sparkling animal cutouts, but soon resumed their random shapes. I pushed down on the sand with my hands to move myself slightly forward into a more comfortable position. Looking at my hands in the odd light, I found they had a far-off, dreamy look. They were bluish and glowing, floating before my eyes as though they were unattached to me.

My tongue was dry, and I wished I had brought along some tobacco water. Soon, I became aware of an intermittent metallic hum directly over my head, like the faint sound of an electric fan being turned on and off. I also had the distinct impression I was no longer alone, that there was something alive sitting right above my head. I reached carefully up into the jumble of wood where the saplings came together to form the lodge's peak. I ran my fingers between and over the rough inner weave of the hut's covering. I discovered nothing. But I had been so certain of a presence above me that finding nothing made me feel more alarmed than ever. I wondered if the tipi's shape, which had initially reminded me of a wizard's pointed hat, could be drawing some influx of unknown energy strong enough to be palpable. Had my imagination mistakenly attached solidity to it? That explanation didn't really make sense, but it was the single answer I could come up with.

The hum began again, rose to a high pitch, and tailed off, ending in a strange, sharp noise that I could only describe as sounding like an imploding gunshot. The little hut trembled. Then it felt as though it were levitating, although I was still sitting firmly on the same sandy ground. The tipi rocked like a dinghy in high seas. Since I had no visual evidence or reference points for what was happening, I told myself that it was impossible.

I lost my equilibrium and tilted forward, scraping the side of my face against the saplings. As I grabbed at the poles above my head for balance, I discovered the wood had turned into some kind of horrible, quivering, gelatinous thing. I screamed in shock. I had promised Mary not to leave the lodge, so my options were limited. I hunched over as far as I could, with my forehead touching the sand in a kind of kneeling fetal position. My weight rested on my elbows, and my arms were bent behind me, protecting my back. I shuddered in confusion and twitched uncontrollably in fear.

The vibration came again. The humming sound grew so loud it was nearly unendurable, like pressing on a raw nerve. When I thought I could bear it no longer, it stopped. For the moment all was quiet. I noticed a new sound with a strange wheezing quality. It was like many indecipherable voices whispering at once. It was sinister. I listened intently, wondering what could make such an odd sound. In a terrible instant, I realized the lodge must be full of hissing, slithering snakes. My heart raced. A great knot of horror choked me.

Any thought of remaining inside vanished, but my legs were frozen. I tried to burrow into the sand as a heavy coil of something cool and wet fell across my back. It was as big as an inner tube, and I was certain it was a gigantic snake. I stiffened. Undulations of greater fear rippled through my body. I lost any control. Gagging in terror, I butted my head against the side of the lodge where I hoped the door was. It split and gave way, as if I had broken through a taut skin. The thing on my back was left behind as I scrambled frantically through the hole on all fours. I crawled several yards and rolled over on my back, hyperventilating. Gradually, I became aware of Mary standing over me. Even in the sparse night light she looked furious.

"I couldn't help it," I gasped between deep breaths. "Snakes are in there. Huge ones!"

I was crying and hysterical. Mary pulled me to my feet and shook me.

"Listen," she said. "It's okay. But earlier, even one second, and you would be dead. Believe me. You came out exactly when it became safe again."

I wiped tears from my cheeks. "I'm sorry, Mary. I know I broke my word."

"No matter. Let's go."

She turned on her heel and started off. I called out, asking her to wait while I collected myself. She just said "No" over her shoulder and kept walking. I had no choice but to follow.

She led us on a narrow trail that wound upward through the evergreens along the side of the mountain. Moonlight dappled through the branches and the cold breeze hit my weary body.

Thirty

To my relief, Mary headed straight home. When we were seated at the table inside her cabin, I felt I was in a mental vacuum chamber. I sprawled in my chair engulfed in a deep blue funk. A kerosene lamp flecked the room with shadows. Busy little bees were hidden inside the flecks. I couldn't actually see them, but I vividly sensed their presence. I didn't know what they were up to, and I didn't care.

Mary kept lighting cigarettes for me. I felt so negative that I was on the verge of quitting — just chucking the whole damn business. It was way too much trouble. Medicine didn't fit me. I was balanced as precariously as a possum out on a bending limb. I was treed, and the barking hounds wanted to sink their teeth in my flesh.

Tobacco fasting had gotten me nowhere, or at least nowhere I wanted to be. Instead of starving myself and then being attacked by snakes in some kind of levitating tipi, I could have been back in the city, going to parties and having a good time. I wanted to be angry. I wanted to leave, but either one would have taken more effort than I could muster.

Mary gave me yet another cigarette and lit it. It must have been my tenth or so. As I smoked, I felt an energy twirl up through my stomach, cascade out the top of my head, and swirl around me like a wreath. My mental processes seemed to lock up and stop between one inhalation and the next. I tried to explain this to Mary but found I couldn't speak because my brain was too busy examining the jammed mechanism. Then I discovered I could almost see the labored words that were trying to form in my mind. It was as if my head held a great black pool that contained words. This pool was in the back of my head, at about the level of my earlobe.

Perhaps the pool was memory, perhaps not. I wasn't sure. If it was, then images of the past must also be recorded there. Words had been dumped into this pool all my life. Whenever I had heard a new word and been able to catch it, it had been wrestled and thrown in with all the others. All the words swam around together like fish in a pond.

Many of the words in the pool made me suspicious. Some were definitely troublemakers. Some were malformed and grotesque. Some went deep, and it was a struggle to get them out. Others were perfectly reliable. I realized that I liked some words and despised others.

Words were constantly rising to the surface of the pool's dark liquid. If I gave the proper signal, they would be separated and sucked out. The signal would be transformed into an energy capable of issuing from my mouth, which with the words became my speech. Without my okay, they would plummet back into the pool and resubmerge. If a word went deep enough, it would be forgotten. But if it submerged shallowly, it could easily be enticed to reemerge. Then it would repeat the same process all over again.

I understood with surprise that my mouth was nothing more than a little tube, like a brass bugle with teeth. When I tried to speak, I found I could blow only primal sounds through it, the first basic sounds I had learned to imitate as a child. I was sure there were many other sounds that were hidden from me, and I wanted to create my own language with them. Mary seemed to be encouraging me. I uttered a nonsense word, and Mary answered me with another. This was great fun. I looked to see what the nonsense words were doing in the pool. Yes, they were rising and then racing off to another place, quite unlike the murky word pool. This new place was full of luminescence and cognition. The instant the nonsense word got there, it became perfectly understandable. I saw that the word I had just used, "gurrark," actually meant "pleased with myself."

Mary and I began to communicate in this manner. I quickly became aware that she was more expert at it than me. Her nonsense words overwhelmed mine, many of which were stillborn and got stuck in my bugle. Try as I might, they wouldn't come out unless Mary helped. Mary would coax them, and she seemed to know nonsense words that would release mine.

The more we played this nonsense game, the more I respected Mary's ability. Then she began to say things and behave in a way I didn't like. She started controlling me by her use of sound, playing with my emotions and reactions. I felt like a violin, and a certain quality within the sound of Mary's nonsense words somehow vibrated my strings. I felt like a puppet. I became frightened and wanted to quit.

"No more," I said loudly.

"Yes," Mary replied. Then she picked up a small empty tuna can that she normally used as an ashtray. She held it in front of her, slightly above shoulder height. It reflected the light, and I realized she was using it as a kind of trap to catch my words. The can would collapse them and pong them back to me with their meaning reversed.

"No," I said more loudly than before. The word "no" was caught in the can and flipped back out as "yes."

Mary replied, "Yes," but her word was also caught in the can and came out "no."

"Yes?" I asked.

"No," Mary answered.

We then began another series of word exchanges. All words, it seemed, were shells that carried other words inside them that contradicted the meaning of the outer word. The can functioned as a kind of reverse translation device. Mary could use it to crack open the outer shell and let the inner meaning escape. After awhile, it seemed altogether appropriate that we were saying the exact opposite of what we meant. As we became more accustomed to it, we graduated from simple words to whole phrases.

"Ugly white man," I said. With the can's help, Mary understood this to mean "beautiful Indian woman."

"Monster," she called me. The can bounced this over to me as "prince," and an "intrepid, handsome" one at that.

We went on for quite some time, calling each other every wretched, foul thing we could think of. I was beginning to feel pretty good about myself.

Then Mary turned the can ever so slightly to the side and spoke the word "only." This stopped me cold. I couldn't grasp the reversed meaning, or any other meaning for that matter. I suddenly felt great anxiety.

Why had Mary brought up "only"? What was the opposite of "only"? "Only" what? "Only" meant some unique quality, didn't it? Didn't everything have "only" slightly attached to it? "Only" me. "Only" you. "Only" love. "Only" this moment. "Only" once. "Only" seemed to be a far-off, isolated word, visible only through a magnifying lens. Only by isolation and inspection did one become aware of rare properties and attributes. That was the only answer.

All of a sudden I realized that "only" was the secret of great literature. One had merely to become aware of "only" and use it. All literature that was any good was a kind of manifesto of "only." In another flash of insight, I saw that this was equally true for painting, sculpture, or any art form whatsoever. "Only" was the secret key that unlocked every door. A masterpiece had to leap past imitation and attain the sole flavor of "only." Only then would it stand alone. In the chaos of life, it was just the great artists, like O'Keeffe, Picasso, and Kahlo, who dared to be "only." That was why we loved them. Lesser artists who shrank from the task were cowards unworthy of our time or curiosity. In that sense, "only" became a burden one had to carry around. The more "only," the heavier the weight. I decided to have only a slight amount of this "only" quality in my life. Then I began to feel strange again.

"What's happening to me, Mary?" I asked.

"You are crossing into my world now. This world is much different from the one you have known. My world is mysterious, exciting, and filled with promise. Accept it without resistance. Now is not the time to waste your power trying to get back to that prison you call home. Now is the time to make your escape."

I looked at her, sitting across from me so perfectly contained and spiritually complete. Her image pulled me toward her, and I felt the urge to reach out and touch her cheek. The instant I thought it, she snapped back and distanced herself. I wanted her to come forward into my consciousness again, but instead she remained aloof.

Her face appeared quite long and pointed, and mysteriously broken with shadow. Perhaps she was a witch after all. Right now she sure looked like one. I decided that if she was a witch, I didn't want any more to do with her. Perhaps she wasn't really that important to me. I wished all witches would leave the earth. Who needed Mary anyway? If I had to go it alone, I would.

I became aware of a gnawing sensation in my stomach. I realized that, besides being famished, I was very cold. I began to shiver. Another wave of intense buzzing began to assault my ears. Looking down, I was mildly surprised to see that the tips of my fingers had taken on a decidedly greenish tint. As soon as a particular finger drew my attention, it would seem to melt. I began playing a game of melting finger to see if I could fool them. I would pretend to look at a certain finger but actually direct my attention to another. I found that I couldn't deceive them. Somehow my fingers always knew the truth.

I tried to explain about lying to my fingers, telling them why it was sometimes necessary. The more I explained, the less my fingers liked it. My sincere efforts to illuminate them about life's realities had the contrary effect of turning them into green mush. They were disgusted with me.

Now I noticed that little halos of yellowish light were floating just above my fingertips. This same phenomenon was absent where my thumbs were concerned. Evidently, my fingers had angelic qualities, whereas my thumbs were devilish or at least sinful. I wanted my thumbs to earn halos as well, but even though I tried, I couldn't determine what noble acts my thumbs would have to perform in order to earn this privilege.

Curious about the halos, I began to shake my left hand rhythmically with my palm facing me. This proved terribly perplexing. I couldn't locate the intelligence that was animating my hand. As I tried to disentangle various confusing ideas, the halos were suddenly sucked into my fingers. Further, the dancing motion of my hand seemed to cause it to cover over with multicolored bird plumage. I didn't know how I would ever explain this to anyone and began to despair. Then, when I was overwhelmed with grief about the feathers, my fingers assumed yet another form.

As if they sensed my discomfort with the idea of having a green-, yellow-, and red-feathered hand and wanted to please me by changing to something else, my fingers metamorphosed into snakes. These little serpents were as shocked to see me as I was to see them. I could tell they were uncomfortable with my reaction, as my surprise caused a kind of callus to form — a sort of mossy film somewhere in between animal and vegetable. The snake-beings had formed this callus to shield themselves from my judgmental nature.

"Okay, who are you really?" I thought or said — I wasn't sure which.

In answer, both my hands lost all substance, turning into smoke.

All my life, they had disguised themselves as skin and bone. Now they had full-out honored me by revealing the truth, and I had offended them by being put off by it. No wonder they found it necessary to protect themselves. It was clear they had great powers, which explained how they had been able to keep me hypnotized all these years.

"Ah-ha," I shouted. Again, I wasn't sure if I'd said it aloud or only with my inward voice. "You are made of smoke. Now I know exactly who you are, and you'll never put me to sleep again."

No sooner had I said this than my new smokesnake fingers greatly distended themselves. My skin went translucent, and the bodies of the snakes stretched under the surface of my arms up to the elbows like a series of smoky tubes. As I watched in fascination, my skin cracked open. I was about to shed like a snake. Each finger and thumb was actually a snake with a body winding up the full length of my arm into my chest.

"Return your attention to your fingers," Mary directed me. "They are the important ones. You must learn to charm them. Smokesnakes are great beings, for they open wide the entrance to knowledge." Her voice was steady, soothing. "You have a beginning hand. So soon, you have found it."

"What knowledge? What is it that I am supposed to know?"

"Snakes must be trained to be of use. Just as we control our body, we control the snakes. They exist in a different world. In this other world, snakes are not fingers. They are snakes, like you perceive now. Lay down your flayed skin. Set it aside. Smoke another cigarette. Breathe and sense the world as smoke, as spirit."

Mary lit a cigarette and handed it to me. "Breathe deep," she said.

I began to breathe heavily between my inhalations of smoke, my chest heaving rhythmically. A feeling came over me as if grains of sand were sliding down through my arms and out into my fingers, my snakes. The snakes were getting highly agitated.

"Channel this power. Make the snakes spit. Teach them to be sharpshooters, just like some old codger shooting plug-juice between his teeth. Make your snakes hit a cuspidor across the room."

My swollen-looking forearms were trickling energy even as she spoke. Something was leaving me, escaping. I knew it was happening, but in the wrong way.

"You're leaking," Mary said sharply. "I said 'spit.'"

I mentally connected snake heads with the sensation coursing down my arms. The snakes began to cough, but not exactly spit. It was more as if the energy tingled up into their heads, sputtered, and oozed out.

"Better," Mary said. "You don't have far to go to learn it."

I was tired. I bowed my head and looked down at my lap, noting with amusement that my whole body had vaporized into the same bluish smoke as my hands. Even though I was full of snakes, smoke, and who knows what else, I was holding together. My body belonged to me. Looking back over what had happened, being made of smoke was just another petty annoyance. I was going to have to live with it.

For a moment I thought I had found some firm ground. "It can't get any worse," I said with certainty.

"Possibly not," Mary said. She reached over and pulled my finger, which was, of course, a smoldering snake. It stretched out of me like a long piece of gray-green chewing gum. Then she reached up into the air and tied a strand of floating tobacco smoke to it. When she let go, a flood of swirling, contradictory energies gushed forth and washed back into my body. I wanted to hit the floor, but I couldn't move. Instead I clutched the table, or rather the snakes did.

Mary rose and went around behind me. She took hold of my shoulder and bent forward. Suddenly, she screamed an angry, inarticulate word in my ear, then shouted, "You're so damned slow. Go quickly, I say. Go upward with the smoke."

I had no idea what she was talking about.

"If I go upward, I'll hit the ceiling," I mumbled.

"I said go quickly," she repeated sternly.

I realized there were two entirely different tobacco smokes swirling about in the cabin, Mary's and my own, and I was being pulled between them. Mary had managed to fasten me to the smoke that belonged to me. I was glad she had. My smoke was more flexible, more understanding. Mary wanted me to rise, but I saw that it was her smoke holding me back, pressing against me in a mysterious way.

This realization made me want to protect myself from Mary's smoke, which seemed to be rather forward and pushy. It struck me that there were actually three distinct kinds of smoke in the room. One was mine, one Mary's, and one was mixed — a blend of both mine and Mary's. To protect myself from the other, unwanted smokes, I folded my arms tightly over my chest. When I did this, my connection with my own smoke seemed to strengthen.

A strand of my smoke picked me up. I ascended a few inches above the chair and began to flow with the strand toward the cabin door. As soon as I drifted outside, I began to rise by a series of jumps and starts until I found myself level with the tall top of the chinaberry tree. I looked down at the cabin. Mary had come out and was peering up, waving. I waved back. She smiled at me. I smiled back but rather forlornly, resigned to my fate.

"The tobacco is sending you up," she said. "I can go no farther with you. You are leaving this cold, dead world for a better one. You are now a solitary breath of blue smoke rising in the diaphanous night. Have courage. Be strong. Your purpose now is to gain power. If you come back to me, you will either be very strong or shattered. It is impossible to say which. I will be singing your power song and praying for you. It may help." She pointed toward the heavens. "Now go."

Before I could answer, the smoke swept me upward at a sharp angle. I saw the mountains becoming smaller far below. Then I saw towns, forests, and lakes. The smoke carried me into the night sky until I was among the stars.

I thought I heard Mary's voice, or perhaps it was a distorted form of my own. It said, "Beyond eagle, beyond swan, beyond clouds you are going. Soon you will see a bridge. It is a bridge made from the prayers of our ancestors. It will take some effort, but follow it. Don't fall off, because if you do you will plummet forever. Stay in touch with what you are doing. Cling to this bridge. It leads to the holy place on the roof of the universe."

No sooner had the words been spoken than ahead of me loomed a great smoking bridge. It spanned upward into the starry heights an untold distance, ending in a dark ocean of icy fire. I drifted, and when I reached the bridge its billowing surface buckled, fluttering wildly beneath my feet. I nearly lost my balance, but I knew a fall would be fatal. The moment I realized this, the smoky surface weakened, becoming less dense, and I sank into it. I advanced a few awkward steps.

I discovered it was easier to go slowly. If I went too fast, I had to bend forward and clutch hold of tufts of smoke. It was like trying to claw my way up a soft, rubbery skin. Sometimes, I went hand over hand, straight up. Often, I bounced backward like a rubber ball. The bridge dipped and then was nearly level. I was able to jog at a measured pace. When it became steeper again, I crawled one slow step at a time. My strength diminished. It was difficult to keep going.

I saw an island floating above me, a mysterious sphere. I was climbing toward a tunnel-like opening on one side and had the feeling I was entering a mouth. I stopped at the end of the bridge and stood transfixed for a long moment by the beautiful sight in front of me. Then I continued into the mouth, which seemed suddenly to close over me as if I had been swallowed. There was a shift, as though I had entered and exited at the same time.

The wide sky above me now was filled with drifting orange clouds. Smoke roiled at my feet. Blades of silver light slashed at me from many directions as if refracted from crystalline surfaces. I noticed a woman coming toward me from the distance. As she drew nearer, I realized she was entirely made of smoke. Her body and face shifted constantly, merging and melting into other forms. I felt as if I was in the presence of an infinite number of simultaneous beings. Each of her new manifestations was more beautiful than the last, and her voice changed from one harmonious sound to another as she spoke.

"I am Smoke Young Woman," she said. "I am the guardian of this land of smoke. As you can see, I wear many robes of smoke. I am fed by prayer, and to prayer I owe my existence. Your medicine has brought you here." I tried desperately to fix on one image of her but that was impossible. "I belong to all families and clans — to all nations and peoples. I belong especially to those who send up smoke — to those who drink my essence, and to those who seek my truths." She said this with several new faces and just as many melodious voices. I was about to reply, but my will to speak left me as my attention was drawn in another direction.

We were standing in the exact center of a vast, circular arena. Spaced equidistantly around its perimeter were four gigantic, blindingly bright silver towers. Light shone from them in brilliant bursts, and then the towers changed into terrifying shapes that began to approach us. I fell down at the feet of Smoke Young Woman in fear.

As the shapes drew nearer, they gradually telescoped down in size. I stood back up, trying to grasp what was happening. I saw a monstrous creature that looked like a prehistoric beast contained in a ball of dazzling light. Then I turned and saw another great light. Within it was another hideous beast. Then another and another.

There was a loud roaring, like explosions amplified over a gigantic loudspeaker. As the sound buffeted me, the terrifying figures came closer. Again, I found myself prostrate. This time I made no attempt to rise. My thoughts were tangled in an indescribable agony of fear. I begged silently for mercy as the beasts closed in. But the nearer they came, the smaller they got. Smaller and smaller. The brilliant light around them spluttered and dimmed, finally revealing the forms of four tiny insects — a moth, a bee, a grasshopper, and a praying mantis. The insects flew forward and began to orbit around Smoke Young Woman.

"Let's eat," Smoke Young Woman said. "Follow me."

I stood up, keeping my eyes lowered and saying nothing. I trailed behind the strange procession. Now the sky was a golden amber with spangles of sequined light on the horizon. We passed by elaborate shapes, perhaps dwellings, I couldn't be sure. We approached one of them. It was a cluster of many stories of silvery bubbles haphazardly stacked on top of each other. Each bubble had a hole in the center that functioned as an entrance, opening and closing like the shutter of a camera or the pupil of an eye. We entered a bubble and found ourselves in a cavernous dining hall bounded by shifting, silvery walls.

Smoke Young Woman took her place at the head of the table. I was given the honor of the seat at the other end. When I touched the backrest of my chair, my fingers went through it.

But then I remembered I was smoke myself, so without moving the chair, I floated over the top of it and down into my seat.

The moth and the bee hovered above the table on my left, and the grasshopper and praying mantis hovered to my right. As I studied them, they grew to roughly human size and took their seats too. We were a strange, yet rather formal group.

As Smoke Young Woman metamorphosed into another lovely being, she said, "We have waited for you many eons. In fact, practically forever."

"Yes," said the moth. "You are long overdue."

"Welcome, my son," said the bee.

"How on earth did you manage it?" asked the grasshopper with excessive politeness.

"You're late," said the praying mantis.

The moth placed a gourd calabash in front of me. It was withered and dried-up and had many strange symbols carved into it. "I have come here on the yellow smoke road," said the moth. "I am your great-grandmother many times over. This is my gift that I have brought you. It is the dust of life and the dust of death. You may use it for either, but you may only choose one."

I looked under the lid of the calabash. The dust that filled it was certainly from the moth's own wings. She must have patiently collected it for me. It didn't look very appetizing, but I tilted the calabash and bent toward it, planning to taste the dust with the tip of my tongue. It seemed the sensible thing to do.

"Stop," scolded Smoke Young Woman. "Where're your manners?"

I looked all about me, puzzled. There were no eating utensils of any kind. I was embarrassed and more than a little confused.

"He doesn't know what he's doing," observed the bee.

"Put the gourd down," said the praying mantis. "Eat with your finger, your little finger."

The grasshopper drooled some brown spittle, before saying, "Don't just sit there like an old stump. Eat."

The moth fluttered her beautiful wings and folded them back again. "Touch the dust with your finger," she instructed. "That's all you have to do."

The curious assortment of beings watched as I stuck out my finger and hesitantly touched the little pile of dust inside the gourd. As I did so, the dust was immediately sucked up into the finger. A paroxysm of agony went through me. I groaned with the pain, knocking the calabash off the table. The dust settled inside me, making a small knot in my chest near my armpit.

As soon as I had recuperated, the bee placed another lidded calabash in front of me.

"I am your great-grandmother many times over. I have come here on the red road to meet with you," said the bee. "This is my gift that I have brought for you. It contains both supernatural darkness and supernatural light. You may use it for either, but you may only choose one."

I inspected the gourd container by peeking inside. There sat a small clump of wax. I touched it cautiously. The wax shot up my finger and into my arm, just as the dust had done. I cried out loud and slammed down the lid, crushing the calabash and knocking it to the floor. I writhed in my chair in terrible suffering. Like the dust, the wax also lodged in my chest. In awhile, the excruciating pain abated.

The grasshopper, amused, said, "I too am your relative, your oldest grandmother. Put forth your hand. I have come here on the black smoke road. This is herbal spit. It is my gift to you. It can be used to heal or to poison, but you can only choose one."

Reluctantly, I held out my hand. The grasshopper spit on it.

As soon as she did, the spittle was sucked up my finger and through my arm to lodge in my chest. Another explosive pain wracked me. I slid to the floor, crumpled over, with my knees drawn up to my chest. When the pain lessened, I opened my eyes. The creatures stood in a circle around me, looking down with concerned expressions.

"Is he dead?" asked Smoke Young Woman, peering at me with first one shifting face then another.

"I should hope not," said the moth. "He's come such a long distance."

"Look. He's still breathing," said the bee. "That's always a good sign."

"He wishes he was dead," the grasshopper said.

"Get him up," ordered the praying mantis.

The grasshopper pulled me up, and I now stood in front of the mantis, clutching my arms about me and shuddering. With her dark green blanket folded around her, the mantis reminded me of a stern old grandmother. Her face was in the shape of a V. I was drawn into the glassy interior of her two large bubble-green eyes.

"My friends," said the praying mantis. "I too am a relative. But how negligent of me. I'm getting senile. I have forgotten to bring my gift."

"Then give something else," said the bee. "Why not?"

"Yes," said Smoke Young Woman. "One gift is as good as another."

"Finish him," said the grasshopper. "End it."

The praying mantis stooped forward over me. In the face of her threatening manner, I took a step backward. I could feel her warm breath on me as she spoke. "Don't be afraid of your old grandmother. I have come here on the white smoke road to meet with you. I give you the depth of my ears, so you will be able to hear my way. You will always know when and how to strike the mark. You can use my gift to mend or to rend. But you can only choose one."

The praying mantis drew something out of herself so quickly her movement was a greenish blur. I saw that she now held two curlicue pieces of green hair. They looked like corkscrews. She eyed me coldly and, without warning, stabbed me behind each ear. My head burst in an exquisite light. A sharp-edged pendulum of sound sliced through me, a hideous whine that covered my senses and obliterated everything else. Here was pure pain. I staggered backward, convulsing, holding both ears. I howled, making a new sound that echoed the sound within me.

I heard Smoke Young Woman say, "Sisters, he is ours now. It was close, but we got him."

As I writhed in agony, a pale green light enveloped me and I lost consciousness. For how long, I don't know. I surfaced to consciousness with a wet sensation. My shirt was drenched with sweat, and Mary was wiping my forehead with a foul-smelling wad of cotton fabric she had dipped in one of her concoctions.

"What happened to me?" I gasped out. "The pain . . ."

"You ask, 'What happened?' Well, I'd suppose that you are finally armed, a conjure bowman with some ammunition. You possess newly polished arrows. They're yours. They're deadly. You can use your darts to heal or harm. From now on, you must choose only one way. You must decide to take the bright path or the one of darkness. That is the law, to create or destroy. But remember, there is plenty of room for evil within good. And there's plenty of room for good within evil. On the bright path, darkness always follows you around. On the dark path, you will be stalked by light. This is the nature of things. Don't let it confuse you, especially now. Make your decision. It's up to you, and it must be done immediately. It must be done right now."

Without hesitation, I chose.

Thirty-one

I SLEPT SOUNDLY and when I awoke was in an ultrasensitive state. The bright rays of morning sunlight were pulsing down on me. The light connected with me physically, feeling as real as the press of a hand on my skin. The air was extra fresh and invigorating. The dew sparkled intensely. I was aware of a new luster, a softness, about me and felt a deep kinship with my surroundings that I had never quite known before.

Each morning, it was my habit to go to the well, pull up some cold water, and pour it into a washbasin. I would dip my toothbrush in baking soda and raise my hand to bring it to my mouth. This time, an extraordinary thing happened. To my complete astonishment, my hand and arm were surrounded by an oscillating light extending out about nine inches. I could see it perfectly well. It had various gradations of color, and I soon realized that the same light rippled outward in concentric circles from my entire body. I discovered I could even feel this light with my hands. Apparently, this was what Mary had been talking about — the *shilip*.

"Well, what do you know, Joe?" Mary said, startling me. I jumped about a foot in the air and whirled around to face her, brandishing my toothbrush like a weapon.

She shrugged.

Embarrassed, I put the toothbrush in my shirt pocket. As my eyes focused on Mary, I realized that she too carried a circlet of light around her, a curl of violet smoke inside flowing along her profile and embracing her. Mary emanated far more light.

I wanted to touch her light, but didn't know if it would be too forward.

"I see it," I said, laughing out loud. "I do."

"Did you think I was talking up my hat, David? The shadow is genuine. With proper training, sickness can be viewed within it. Now you can see what disease is approaching. *Shilip* holds it. Here flayeds mingle in the numberless warp and weft of life." She told me to look carefully at all the plants, trees, and animal life and to note their accompanying shadows. She told me to pay attention to my heart, to be grateful and prayerful. "Remember," she said. "When you see the *shilip*, you see the shell of spirit. It has always been there. Nothing has changed except you. It is the tobacco that engenders your sight. And this is just your beginning."

Soon, Mary left me to my own devices. I quickly discovered that all of nature was communicating back and forth with itself — the bugs, the flowers, the sparrows — all of life except us. We humans had given false names to everything, given everything its official taxonomy, all the while feeling enormously superior to it. Now I could see that we had done this at the cost of our souls. Humans had set themselves so far apart from paradise that we could no longer see or communicate with it.

But what Nature revealed was more than beautiful. It was sublime.

Thirty-two

A COUPLE OF HOURS LATER, Mary brought me some food. I told her I wasn't hungry.

"Eat," she said. It was a command.

I chewed obediently on some deer jerky. Seconds later, the peripheral light around Mary receded. It drew into her and disappeared.

"Oh no, Mary."

"It's okay. You're not ready to keep it."

It was surely gone, and in its place a dull ache.

I halfheartedly ate a few more bites. By the time I was done, this new way of seeing was no more.

That afternoon, I took a long walk, climbing up an overgrown trail toward the crest of the mountain. I wanted to be alone to think about the unexpected and frightening things that had happened. My perceptual world had been shattered and would never be the same. I knew that. I needed time to fit it together again in a completely new way. I wondered if I would be able to do it.

Tired from the long ordeal, I found a comfortable place after awhile and stopped. The sky was gray, and the air was wet. Cold air was massing in the north, but I didn't think it would actually rain or snow. I sat down on the edge of a rocky bluff overlooking a steep ravine. Leaning back against a gnarled old tree trunk, I scanned the vista before me. The ravine was about a hundred yards across. Another hundred feet below, a little stream meandered by. The bottom was pebble-covered, and the sandy margin around it was dotted with broken pieces of old rotten wood.

As I relaxed, my eyes became unfocused. I suddenly felt as though someone was staring at me from a spot near the stream. Then I became aware of a strange glass jar, shaped like a bell, sitting at the base of the ravine. To my astonishment, the bell jar was occupied by a little girl no more than two feet tall. I could see her clearly through the glass. She was dressed in frilly blue clothes that appeared Victorian in style. Long ringlets of blond hair fell down her back.

The little girl walked right through the side of the jar, making delicate musical sounds like wind chimes as she exited. Laughing with delight, she danced and pirouetted in a circle around the glass bell. She sang in a voice that matched the delicate music of the chimes, but the words of her song were incomprehensible to me.

When her dance was done, she looked up and curtsied. She laughed, turned, and then walked back through the glass into the bell. Once more she curtsied elegantly to me, smiling all the while. Then the glass, or whatever it was, floated straight up into the air until it hovered not more than a few feet in front of me. The little girl pushed against the surface and leaned forward as though testing it. I couldn't tell its thickness, but the jar resembled an oddly shaped soap bubble. Then it dimmed. In a fleeting second the bell jar, child and all, vanished into the air.

This odd experience both terrified and fascinated me. My heart began to race. The event had been remarkably vivid, yet I had absolutely no idea what it meant. I felt as if I had been sitting in a darkened room that was illuminated for an instant and then not. And here I was stumbling around in the dark once more.

Sitting in Mary's cabin that evening, I told her what had happened. She didn't say anything, so I described it to her again in more detail.

"Oh, her," she finally interrupted me. "Yes, I know who you mean now." She chuckled to herself, bending over some roots she had been washing in a galvanized bucket. She began taking them out and laying them on the counter to dry.

Puzzled by her lack of interest in what I had found to be so startling, I confided the fear I had felt. Going farther, I confessed I was seriously considering quitting my apprenticeship. My latest experience made me think I might soon be meeting up with some men in white coats wanting to help me — help me to the funny farm, that is.

For the first time she showed some interest in what I was saying. Turning to me, she asked, "Don't you think you are being way too self-indulgent? Within any apprenticeship there are always times of wilting. Admittedly, you have become immersed without warning in the inexplicable. No doubt your mind is struggling with these assaults. You must learn at once to be delicately balanced between all worlds, or you're right: you will lose your mind. That's true. This is a dangerous period. But you must learn to swim out of deep water, not be drowned by it.

"I will say this to you. Leave here when you wish without feeling any pangs of conscience. Don't feel like you're so important, because you're not. Perhaps you *should* leave. No one that I know of asked you to come here in the first place. It was you who asked me to teach you. I agreed to it. I am keeping my part.

"What you saw today, the little *bopoli* girl — the bell you perceived around her was her *shilip*. She first appears in a form secreted deep inside the perceiver. She's just the beginning, the first opening of your eyes. You will soon be besieged by the attentions of many hidden beings. Many will be hungry, and courting you for food.

"I can't promise you safe passage from your world into mine. Not at all. I'm not going to lie or prop you up falsely. I do believe in you, or I wouldn't have taken you on. So, no more of this kind of talk. Either walk with me or walk away. But say no more."

Thirty-three

So this was it — my initiation into the practice of the conjure arts. Mary once told me that there is a right time and a wrong time for powwowing. The phases of the moon and stars, the constellations, must be in proper alignment so that the right animal spirit will be present. She would "walk off" the ceremonial space beforehand in order to determine its congruence with the spirit world. If she found it to be satisfactory, she then prepared it. If the powwowing was to be held in a cabin or other place with electricity, it would be shut off. The place was cleared of all furniture. The floor was scrubbed with power water and swept clean with cedar or fir branches. The healing area was delineated by lines of secret powders: tobacco, cornmeal, bird plumage, and other suitable substances.

Mary carefully incensed her body. She burned some sage and broadleaf cedar with tobacco mixed in, and then bathed in this smoke. It was important that her hands be purified, because skilled curer hands had to have the ability to catch sickness and pull it out of the body. Mary blew a plume of smoke on each finger and thumb, and then she was ready.

The night's powwowing began, and I assisted. The first person Mary doctored was a sad and emaciated woman married to a local dairy farmer. The woman's eyes were red and tear-rimmed, and her skin was covered with strange white spots. She seemed broken in spirit.

It took several hours. Mary smoked at least twenty cigarettes, blowing their smoke laterally across the woman's chest and back. From time to time, I caught glimpses of a strange dark area around the woman's midsection.

Afterward, I told Mary what I had seen and asked what she had been doing with the smoke.

She said, "Be aware of attraction and repulsion. For instance, one mountain can feed us while another mountain might diminish us. People are not so easy to unravel. One person might feed us while another devours us, and yet another might not affect us at all. It's complicated only a little.

"The woman was frivolous. She allowed her shadow to lose its vitality. She had elk sickness. I fixed it — for the time being, anyway. The tobacco empowered her to take on more strength. I put a hatchet in her right hand. By that I mean she can now concentrate her power more wisely."

"You blew smoke all around her. Were her problems extended away from her body?"

"No, it may appear to your eyes that this is so. The notion that the shadow is outside the body is false. Both the inside and outside shadow are one and the same entity. Get some doctoring eyes, David.

"When curing, enter the secret doorway. Standing in this hidden world, we are given a fulcrum with which to pry open the lid to the box of mysteries. This fulcrum may be thought of as the adroit use of smoke. From our center, we can realize what is going on. Then can we hope to do something helpful."

"Do you have a story to explain elk sickness?"

"Here is one story.

"One day Yellow Tobacco Boy went up into the mountains. He began to pray, and he prayed for days — seeking a vision. His thoughts flew around in circles until he was blinded by a bright light. He heard a sweet female voice speak his name softly. The figure of an elk came out of the light and walked toward him. Yellow Tobacco Boy tried to focus on the animal. The elk blew a magical breath on him. Before the breath was completed, the elk changed into a beautiful woman with shining black braids. She had blue elk horns painted on her face, beginning from her hairline down her forehead and extending across her cheeks. She was wrapped tightly in an elk skin. Her movements were fluid, and her body curved gracefully beneath her golden robe.

"'I am Elk Woman with a holy voice,' the beautiful woman said. 'I am the love within you. You have received elk's breath. Now I will give you medicines. With these, you will be able to cure elk sickness. Go and heal the sick in my name, and you will become a renowned healer.'

"Yellow Tobacco Boy's heart beat wildly, and he reached for the woman. To his astonishment, she disappeared. At his feet he saw a folded elk-skin bundle. He hesitantly opened the skin and found within it the medicines with which to do his curing. There was also another secret gift."

The story over, I asked several questions about elk sickness, which Mary answered. She told me that certain songs were central to curing the disease. She sang each one for me. When she finished singing, I asked her about another man she had treated.

"That man had owl sickness," she said. "Owl always hovers around in the darkness. Diviners and prophets once wore owl skins with the wing feathers splayed out over the backs of their shirts. Owl can be a powerful medicine for capturing men or women, because owls are beautiful, mysterious, silent, and deadly. Many people are attracted by these things. More often than not, when someone confuses us, we know the truth but simply choose to be in the dark. This is the way of owl sickness. We are not just unsuspecting victims. We are seduced because we want to be. It is the owl who calls out in the night to the willing victim.

"Owl sickness would have brought death. The man's heart was missing, stolen by the owl. I made him a new tobacco heart. There's an old story that tells of this loss of heart.

"It happened at winter's end, when the snow had melted and the new season was near.

"Yellow Tobacco Boy was walking along by the light of a large, full moon. Just then the long, low screech of an owl broke in the deepening night.

"Yellow Tobacco Boy stopped. He knew the owl was speaking directly to him. He turned toward the eerie sound, staring long and hard, but he only saw trees silhouetted against the inky horizon.

"Suddenly, the owl struck. There was a feathery explosion. Talons bit. Yellow Tobacco Boy found himself airborne, being taken up into the wide dark sky. Colossal wings flapped above him. He could not see the valley below, but he realized his abductor was flying toward the high mountain peaks. Far, and farther, the owl took him, and they began to swing upward even above the clouds.

"When they landed, Yellow Tobacco Boy was taken before an enclave of owl grandmothers.

"'Why have you brought me here?' Yellow Tobacco Boy asked indignantly.

"'You were trying to learn the secrets of night,' answered Old Owl Many Generations Great Grandmother. 'These secrets belong to our tribe, not yours. You must die. Take him to the white knives,' she said. 'They will know what to do. Then bring me his heart in a calabash, so that I may examine it and know you have done as I have instructed.'

"This story is very long, but I'll make it short. Yellow Tobacco Boy managed to escape and he sent back a tobacco heart that fooled the grandmothers.

"The patient thought he could use the night to do unspeakable evil. He didn't know what he was getting into, and he quickly became a man without a heart. He didn't realize it.

"Tobacco smoke is what you use to make the owl's arrows

and to force the white knives to drop to the ground." Mary's eyes turned abruptly to mine with a warning. "Owl is watching us even as we speak. Be very careful."

Quickly changing the subject, I asked Mary about another sick man.

"That one? He had mastodon sickness. He had a prejudice against his people, the stem from which his life has been created. He had dishonored the meat and bones of the past. Because of it, he met mastodon. Mastodon keeps the memory. The man will be sick several more weeks.

"Yellow Tobacco Boy once got this sickness. He was sleeping, when the stillness of night was pierced by a gust of howling wind. He woke up. 'I'm cold inside,' said Yellow Tobacco Boy. 'Something bad is the matter with me.'

"Compelled by a sudden urge, he left his village. He walked east. When the blood-red sun pressed against the morning sky, etched against it was a great mastodon.

"'Ancient woolly sister,' Yellow Tobacco Boy said, 'you have awoken me from my dreams. Why have you shown yourself in this manner?'

"'Spears from your atlatl have laid me to the ground many times,' answered the mammoth. 'Now I must teach you how to preserve meat. All meat is holy and must be treated properly. If this is not done, from now on the spirit of sickness will enter it. It will trouble you greatly. Eating dishonored meat insults me. You have insulted me, so I have brought you here to show you the cure.'"

"Mastodon taught Yellow Tobacco Boy the curing and jerking of meat. She also taught him how to put meat into cold streams in order for it not to putrefy. That was her gift."

After a short silence I asked, "What about that elderly man with the bad limp? What was his condition?"

"That was hummingbird. Hummingbird is a deep and destructive disease. Long ago there was a great *minko*. He was much loved by the people. He got sick, and he was going to die. One by one, all the great doctoring experts came. They pow-wowed him. They called on all their conjure powers. They pulled out all their hidden medicines. But still each one failed.

"Doubtless, the *minko* was soon to be of this world no longer. It was then that he had a fevered dream. The *minko* dreamed of twin sisters in the village who had the power to heal him. He saw them bathed in shimmering colors of amethyst, ruby, gold, and emerald. 'We are the twin sisters of the rainbow,' they said in his dream. 'We are keepers of the bridge. We stand at either end and hold it for you to get across. We know your loving heart, and we return it to you. You must cherish your own life as you have cher-ished your people. Send for us, and we will heal you.'

"And so it was that the *minko* woke up and asked for them. Soon afterward, two identical women arrived. They smelled like flowers. They were radiant, beautiful, and happy. There was a stirring and a swift whir of activity. The *minko* felt a strange pres-sure in his ears. The women kissed the *minko*. Their long, hollow beaks were like keen-edged blades that drove deep inside of him. They sucked to draw out his sickness. One of the twins staggered back and spit the sickness into a big bowl. A moment later, the other twin did the same. Both died, but their efforts cured the *minko*. Once again he was robust and healthy.

"Bend down close to the blossoms, and the hummingbird spirit will whisper secrets in your ear. The Maker of Life turned the unselfish twins into rainbow birds in order that they might forever drink the sweet nectar of flowers. They are little eagles, great flower soldiers who teach us the beauty road. That was their reward for healing the *minko*."

"Did the white woman you treated have bear sickness?" I asked.

"No, it was coyote. You only thought it was bear because

you saw that I called upon the bear spirit to aid me. I helped her, but that woman will live only three more years."

"That doesn't give her much time."

"No, but it depends on what she does with it. It was coyote who shot her, and nothing can be done. The death spirit lurks close by."

"How did she get the sickness?"

"Her husband gave it to her unknowingly. He hung a dead coyote on a fence after he shot it. This was a defilement. The eyes of that dead coyote shot him back with a weapon he is unable to understand. Coyote sickness bounded from the husband and bit into the woman. I was able to placate coyote. Three years. After that, she will be his. Coyote claims her soul as revenge."

I asked about a feverish teenager. Mary had used a deer-tail brush to dust powdered yellow root all over her.

"She had a form of opossum disease. Young ones get it. She had snagged her spirit tail on barbed wire, so she had tail-of-the-opossum malady. Opossum conjured and threw a sickness on her. All the guardians of nine flayed who protected her inner fires and watering places fell asleep. Hot winds murmured up inside her. There's many a tale about ways you can encounter this disease."

"So I guess the message is not to pull old opossum's tail, huh Mary?"

Thirty-four

LESS THAN A WEEK HAD PASSED, when Mary took me on a long hike up into the hills. She had her arm through a coil of rope that she carried on her shoulder, and I could only guess that we were about to do some climbing.

Late in the afternoon we came to a steep arroyo. Mary led me right up to its very edge. The wind was soft, and the sky was a powdery blue. The arroyo in front of us plunged several hundred feet to the bottom.

"Hold out your left hand," Mary said. "I want to enter it."

Her choice of words gave me an uneasy feeling. I hesitated and stepped back a bit from the arroyo. Mary seized my left wrist. Looking into my palm, she traced the tip of her finger over various lines. She took a long time, peering as intently as though she were reading a book with small print. "Here your hand is hot, and here is a thin crust of ice," she said. "This fork is not in its proper place, nor is the bowl."

"How about my spoon?" I asked jokingly. "Is that in the right place?"

"No," she said seriously. "It's miles from your mesa."

"Mary," I said, exasperated. "Are you reading my fortune?"

In answer, she pressed her thumb into my wrist. It made a cold shudder run up and down my spine.

"Well, I'm confused. I don't know what you're doing."

"I am trying to protect you from a stalking, malevolent power before it catches you. We must cool your fire and melt your ice.

Otherwise, I can't guarantee your safety. I would regret losing you now. Without my scouts and my women of the bow, you're finished. You might just as well hurl yourself over this rim."

A moan came from somewhere far off as the breeze picked up. I had to catch my breath, looking at the depth of the arroyo. If I fell, it would be sure death.

"Maybe I'll shove you," Mary said, sensing my fear. "Better still, let's both jump."

"Mary, please," I said.

"Listen, I can end it for you right now, and I will if it becomes necessary." Still holding my wrist, she pulled me forward a few inches. I twisted my hand away.

"What are you doing, Mary?" Her eyes were cold and savage. I cringed. "Whoa, you really would kill me, wouldn't you?"

"Yes, I might. You are shaking and weak-kneed. This is a mystery. I thought you were once some kind of killer marine. If we are to die this day, we will do it bravely. You are supposed to be an apprentice in the arts of power doctoring. When death stalks us, we must meet it courageously. But look at you. I don't want to enter the next world with a sniveling coward."

"Mary, if you were a man, I'd kick your ass."

She laughed at me with such horrible venom I thought she was completely delirious. I was inching away by tiny foot shuffling, but Mary stepped abruptly in front of me, backing me right up to the chasm. She stopped and stood still only inches away from me. My heels were as far back as they could go and I knew it would be impossible to move sideways without losing my balance and going over. I felt roller-coaster pangs of fear in my stomach. Mary was the only thing around to cling to, so I decided if she pushed me any farther, she would have to go along with me.

Mary removed the rope from her shoulder and uncoiled it,

looping one end around my waist and knotting it. Then she attached the other end to herself in the same way, leaving some slack between us. We were still standing on the cliff's rim.

"David," she said very softly in my ear, a little above a whisper, "this cord is the snake of a snake-skirted woman. It is my umbilicus. I am a midwife of life, but today I am the midwife of your death." She stuck her arms out like a ballerina and propelled herself violently backward. The rope joining us snapped taut, yanking me forward several steps. Although it took us farther from the edge of the arroyo, Mary's eyes were crazed. I tried to claw and undo the rope, but the knot she had tied was uncanny. The more I clawed at it, the tighter it became. "Mary, untie me," I said sharply.

"There are two ways to power — by luck or by work. Today you work, else you die."

"I don't get this game," I said, pulling on the rope as hard as I could. She was like a slab of granite — I couldn't budge her.

"This is not exactly a game. At least it is not the kind of game you are familiar with, because the stakes are the ultimate. You like to play mealymouthed games where the stakes are crumbs. Do exactly as I say now, or you will fail this contest. This is a death dance, so let's dance. Come on, partner. Move it."

The length of rope joining us was perhaps a dozen feet at most. Mary suddenly spun around and made a beeline for the craggy rim of the arroyo. I backed up as fast as I could, knowing that if she went over, I went with her. As she reached the edge she spread her arms into a swan dive, bent her legs, and sprang forward. I dug my boot heels into the ground and threw myself backward, leaning against the rope for all I was worth. The rope came taut again, and Mary's leap left her on her tiptoes, her entire body hanging far out over the brink. I pulled back with all my might.

"You're crazy," I shouted. "Stop this, Mary. You're trying to kill us both."

Although I did not fail to see some slight humor in my situation, my deeper fright was practically overwhelming. Mary had snuck it in on me. I wondered what people would think if they found us at the bottom of the arroyo, linked together in death. Would they think we'd been climbing and fell? They wouldn't even know that Mary had suckered me and murdered me by a kind of forced suicide pact.

She turned slowly around to face me, then bent forward until she was upright again. She began inching herself gradually toward me, taking small, tottering steps like some kind of spastic, her arms and body jerking in a grotesquely uncoordinated manner. Suddenly, she gave a bloodcurdling howl and lunged forward. The shriek stood my hair on end. I backed farther away, keeping myself as far from her as the rope permitted. Without warning, she snapped the line hard, forcing me to take an unintended step toward her. I pulled backward as hard as I could. She surprised me by moving forward without resistance, and I fell on my back.

"Get up," she ordered.

"I can't," I cried. "You're pulling too hard."

She dragged me on all fours, crawling, right up to her feet. Then she grabbed the rope around my waist and wrenched me to a kneeling position. Bending over me, she said, "You're no dancer. You need dancing lessons. Stand up."

As I staggered to my feet, she pulled the rope taut. I tried to maintain my balance while I dug once more at the knot binding us together. Mary let out another yell — a demented kind of war whoop and battle cry. She quickly bent forward and began a strange high-stepping dance, taking the kind of exaggerated, proud steps a majorette might make leading a band with her baton.

She swung left. She swung right. The rope pulled me around to that side. She made a slow circular turn using me as her pivot. Reversing direction, she made a second full turn. As she twisted me around, I felt an odd sensation, a pressure in my pelvis and hip joints. She moved a bit closer toward me, and the line loosened. Yet another step and the line slackened even more, until it touched the ground. I moved to tighten it again. But as hard as I tried, it was impossible to anticipate her movements. Our union of rope bounced as we danced on.

Mary sprang suddenly several feet, directly at me. Her face was right in front of mine. Our noses were nearly touching, and I could feel her even breath. She blew a long breath directly into my open mouth. It smelled almost like ether. "Merge within my breath, David."

To my astonishment and horror, Mary began to change form. Her hair folded and grew thicker, separating into points. Her nose became a jutting beak. In the same instant, her entire face transformed. It was a shimmering black bird's head tilted to one side so that I saw a fierce eye. Wings sprouted from her arms as though a cape of blueblack feathers had been flung over her.

Up to now I was convinced she was mentally unhinged, but now I realized that I was the one who had gone over. It wasn't rational to believe I was tied up to a bird-being. Surely, my mind had vacated the premises.

I no longer knew who or what I was or who the bird creature was. I became conscious only of our entwined dance. We danced on and on. Now I danced with her, moving and retreating in little jump steps. We were quickly surrounded by many curious animals from the forest that joined us. There were red, blue, and black medicine horses. We danced between them. There was a green buffalo blowing out breaths of smoke. We danced up to her. A great silver eagle alighted nearby. There were dogs, bears, cats, deer, and antelope, and ever more bizarre animals appeared — animals completely unknown to me — froglike beings and great twisted lizards. We all danced together in a frenzied, abandoned dance. And right in the midst of it, the entire menagerie vanished.

Again, I stood facing the bird creature. She beat her black wings high and was lifted feet into the air. Landing, she cawed, scratched the ground, and shook herself, preening. Then she hopped up in front of me and began shoving me backward with her beak.

"Go backward — backward," the bird-being caw-whispered. "Backward."

I backed up until once again there was nowhere else to go except over into the arroyo. I didn't have time to resist. I knew that here was my inevitable end. But this time, instead of fear, I felt outrage. First it had been Mary who had pushed me wherever she wanted. Now here was a human-sized bird doing the same thing. Seemingly, I had no power against either of them. But at least I was finished begging. The world opened up inside me, and something flew out and was gone. It was my spirit. It didn't matter that I was nearing my death, because now I was one with it all — one and the same as the rocks, trees, and rivers. I was sky and cloud. Nothing mattered in the least.

The enormous bird shoved me again, cocking its head. It was imitating Mary. I swung up my arms, trying to maintain my balance. Then I felt my foot slip, and I let go, exhausted. At least it was over.

I felt myself crumpling. I felt myself soaring. In an explosion of light, I heard my mother's voice. "It's important," she was saying to me. "Someday you'll understand these big people things."

I was five years old in a town in southeastern Oklahoma, probably McAlester. My mother had just parked our car on a hill in front of a large white house. She put on the emergency brake.

"Can I go with you, please? Please."

"No, this is not a place for little boys," Mama Opal said. "Stay in the car and don't leave it. And don't touch anything. You could make the car crash."

Standing on the front seat and stretching as high as I could, I watched her approach the house and enter. After awhile, I became bored. I looked at the steering wheel, the gearshift, and the emergency brake. I thought about playing with them but remembered that Mama Opal had told me not to.

I looked at the large house. I wanted company, but nobody came outside. Minutes passed. I got out of the car, went up the sidewalk, and opened the front door. Inside, there was a kind of foyer with black-and-white tiles. Past the foyer, the house looked churchlike and had a sweetish smell, not a pleasant one. Ahead of me, I saw a man lying quietly in a long box.

At five years old, I had no real notion about death. Death was just a word people seemed to use to scare one another. Curiosity drew me toward the man. As I got closer, I saw that he was an old Indian. His arms were crossed over his chest, cradling a beaded pipe bag. I went up to the box, put my hands on the edge, and peered in. I waited a little while for the man to move. When he didn't, I reached over and poked his hand with my finger. It was rigid and cold. I wondered why he was so still. It didn't seem right, and I felt sorry for him. I put my hand on his and held it for several minutes. "Please wake up and do something," I prayed.

Unexpectedly, his head rolled over toward me. His eyes opened, and for a brief moment a bright light shone from them. He seemed to be grinning. Then, the light in his eyes blanked out. I had no idea what had happened, but none of it frightened me in the slightest.

"Good Lord," I heard Mama Opal say. "He's in there with the old man." Another woman was with her, and she said,

"What's it going to hurt, Opal? The old man's gone. Why, I declare. Look at that. He's holding his hand."

I had to let go as my Mama Opal took my shoulder and moved me away. I looked back at the corpse as she escorted me out. I wanted her to let me go back. I tried to pull away so I could be with him. I struggled with her. I screamed, and I couldn't quit screaming.

"Easy," I heard Mary say. "It's over. It's past."

I was startled into yet another state of awareness. I discovered I had been lying with my head in Mary's lap. Her hand rested lightly on my shoulder. I came bolt upright.

"I was a child," I said. "I saw a dead man, an old Indian."

"Yes. Our dance was a remember dance. I wanted to waken him again for you."

"Who was that old man?"

"His name doesn't matter," she said. She told me his Indian name. "I knew him well," she said. "He was a great man. He died with a broken heart, for he could find no one to learn from him and pass on his lineal teachings. From his death, he called to you with an invitation. You made an agreement to take it. This man will always be with you, and it will be your job to recognize him. You may or may not do medicine in this world — it's up to you — but if you should, never let yourself get overblown about it. Take it as a matter of course. You see, it will not be you who does medicine. It will be him. You will be his instrument. It will take you a long time to trust, and perhaps you never will."

I didn't know what to say, since it was all news to me.

"Okay, get up. Let's get going. I've been through the wringer with you, and I'm tired. You're a tough nut to crack."

"Me? Hell. What about you?"

When we were both standing, Mary took a skinning knife out of her pocket and opened its shiny blade with her teeth. She menaced me with it and poked me in the stomach playfully several times — not pressing enough to cut but certainly enough to make me aware of the knife's sharpness. She slipped the blade beneath the rope connecting us and sliced upward, easily cutting it in two. "My placenta no longer belongs to you," she said as the two ends fell to the ground. "From now on, we go it alone like we all must. And it's better so."

Thirty-five

MARY AND I WALKED DOWN A PATH headed toward her cabin. Moonlit clouds appeared in the sky as blue smoke. We came to a water crossing and started across a little bridge. It was made of rope, with wooden planks laid across it to form a walkway. We both sat down in the middle. The stream bubbled and murmured beneath us. Our feet hung down near the water. The dark forms of trees and tangled vines surrounded us. Frogs were croaking down by the little brook, and crickets were serenading us from the woods. The wind moaned, and an owl hooted.

It seemed like a good time to ask Mary about a mystery that had puzzled me for a long time. "There's something I've been wanting to ask you about," I said. "It's about your cabin."

"Yes?"

"The cabin moves around, doesn't it? At first I thought it was just that old stump in your yard, but then I figured out it was the whole building. Am I right?"

"No. Of course not."

"Excuse me, Mary, but I know something is going on. That stump moves several feet in all directions — mainly toward wherever I am. How does it manage it?"

"That isn't what happens. *Shilip* transcends time. I have told you that time is flayed. You can flay it, go into past or future. You can then return to the present or not, as you choose. You have already begun doing a little of this without being aware of it. Of course, it is really your *shilip*, your double.

"There is a way to move beyond the locked door. To most

people, even to some of the great magicians and power doctors, this door stays locked. Sadly, I must tell you most people adore their limitations. They look at the door with satisfaction. They worship their limitations and are so smug about them. The idea of true possibility frightens them to death.

"Intervention by the *shilip* contravenes time. Powwowing and conjuring moves life's components and shifts them, even time. For instance, past events are arranged to balance with future events. This is time manipulation, if you choose to call it that. The ancient calendars were used not only to measure, but also to manipulate. Can't you see that much Native ritual is about time? I know the ancients were able to move around inside the locked house of time. Their bodies burned up with power, but they escaped. They moved into another segment of flayed time."

We fell silent. I didn't know what to say. For a long while we sat there on the rope bridge, looking down at the small light reflected on the hustling water of the stream. A teasing wind played in the darkened treetops, and the owl hooted several more times. It felt like a poignant moment, with the crickets and frogs celebrating the night by singing their familiar songs.

"Well," I finally said. "Your cabin sure is weird."

"No, David. It isn't. Time is like this little creek — fluid. See, it flows on endlessly. But a stream can back up and reverse itself. It can make a sudden rushing, or a slight diversion. Time can do this, believe me.

"The stump and cabin seem fixed to you. In the true fluid of time the stump moved slightly in the current. It may even vanish completely. Don't let it shock you. You had the necessary power to see without understanding. Pat yourself on the back. Only a very few are that attentive. Keep on paying attention. Be grateful."

"Well, Mary, no one can say it hasn't been an unusual day," I commented idly.

Mary replied, "Each day is a gift. You need to know this."

Mary was right, but to me this day had been especially remarkable. Going over it in my mind, I had learned I inherited something — I wasn't sure what — from a dead body, when I was a child. I wondered if I had caught the much-discussed disease, spirit-of-the-dead sickness. I told Mary my concern.

"No, the old man would never do that," she said. "He kept his spirit until he could part with it properly and safely. He didn't give you his spirit. It was only his power — the power that had been given to him by his own teachers. Of course, he gave you a loaded gun. If you are going to go around packing a pistola — and you have no choice — you must do your best to learn how to use it. That's your worry, not the spirit-of-the-dead disease."

"What is death, anyways?" I asked.

"Not what you think. There's a story about it, concerning a dog. They say a dog can prepare the way for death.

"One day a dog named Dog Who Believed Himself to Be a Great Dog barked and went bounding off chasing after a departed spirit.

"Yellow Tobacco Boy yelled after him, 'Hey, come back.' Then he yelled louder. But Dog Who Believed Himself to Be a Great Dog continued barking and chasing the ghost.

"'Wait. Come back,' again cried Yellow Tobacco Boy. He rushed after his dog. He ran swiftly, without thinking, but Dog Who Believed Himself to Be a Great Dog kept ahead of him, leading him down a narrow trail choked with dark foliage. The trees he passed began to look odd and misshapen, and he stopped to get his bearings. He took quick, deep breaths. It was so dark under the trees that there was no clear delineation between substance and shadow. He saw his dog's wagging tail in the distance. A sudden gust of chill wind seemed to pass right through him. He ran after his dog again.

"On a high ridge he came to an abrupt halt. In front of him, a slippery-looking log led over a chasm. Yellow Tobacco Boy peered into the abyss. Thousands of feet down he saw a swirling, boiling river.

"Dog Who Believed Himself to Be a Great Dog had trotted easily across the slippery log and was staring back at Yellow Tobacco Boy from the other side.

"'What is this place?' Yellow Tobacco Boy asked.

"'This is the land of ghosts and supernaturals. It is the land of shadow fires,' said Dog Who Believed Himself to Be a Great Dog. 'I have brought you here to your death. Over here is the land of plenty, where you can hunt to your heart's content and always find game and good food. There are sensual women over here, and they will gladly make you happy. It is dangerous to cross over, but go ahead and try. Come across to me if you can.'

"'What happens if I slip and fall?'

"'You will have to roam the abyss forever with all the other unlucky ghosts,' said Dog Who Believed Himself to Be a Great Dog.

"Yellow Tobacco Boy looked down at the log. 'I think I can,' he said, taking a first tentative step forward.

"'Wait,' said Dog Who Believed Himself to Be a Great Dog. He barked three times in each direction. 'There's a little bit I haven't told you yet. Monsters guard against the unworthy entering this happy place, the good ghost land. When you attempt to cross over, these monsters will rush out. They will throw big stones at you. You must do your best not to get knocked off the log into eternal suffering. The terrible abyss below awaits all those who deserve it. You can only know your fate by the test.'

"Dog Who Believed Himself to Be a Great Dog barked several times more and jumped about in anticipation.

"'Well, here goes nothing,' said Yellow Tobacco Boy.

"Many strange and fearsome creatures appeared on the other side of the abyss. He saw large, hairy beasts with red goggle-eyes and drooling mouths as big as washtubs. The monsters made fiendish slurping noises. They cackled and gibbered in some incomprehensible hobgoblin language. They were every nightmare you've ever had. Walking on their hind legs, they picked up stones with which to hit Yellow Tobacco Boy. For a moment, he was afraid, until his mood changed to one of determination. He ran across the log before the monsters could stop him, dodging the missiles they hurled. Surprisingly, they made only a few half-hearted attempts to hit him.

"This is how you get admitted into the land of the dead. Once you are there, you will soon meet other ghosts and ghost relatives."

"But I don't have a dog to guide me."

"Yes, you do. You just don't know it yet. You have a great dog."

Her remark puzzled me. "You mean a dog spirit, don't you?"

Mary shrugged. "Yes and no," she said.

It was after midnight when we got finally back to her place.

Thirty-six

THE LITTLE HOUSE we prepared was on a farm not so distant from Spiro Mound as the crow flies. Spiro, located in Oklahoma, was said to be the equivalent of Washington, D.C., of the entire Americas before the arrival of Columbus. It was a great trading center and meeting place for the many tribal leaders. Sadly, the mounds were dynamited and ruthlessly looted in the early 1900s. Tens of thousands of ancient artifacts were stolen. Spiro's priceless treasure went over to Europe. The silent land around there seemed to whisper of past glories and untold spiritual truths destroyed by the real barbarians.

The room we occupied for our ceremonies was bare of furniture and illuminated by four candles. Mary stood behind me, and an Indian woman about thirty years old stood in front of me. An altar had been prepared by spreading a cloth over part of the floor. Various items lay on top of it. Mary's doctoring outfit was open nearby, showing the contents. My smaller medicine pack was near hers, also open. Tub was sitting against the wall, playing a hand drum and singing a song. He was chaining the beats, linking each percussive sound with the previous one.

The measured beats, and more particularly, the silences between, pulled me seductively. Under the influence of a fast, one may become aware of a pervasive emptiness, an infinite silence that is deep and dangerous and always abides. Mary had warned us how easy it is to enter this void and become confused and lost.

The woman waiting to be doctored was wearing a halter and shorts. She had been badly hurt in a car wreck, but her injuries could have just as easily have come from being kicked by a mule. Her sides were purple and black. Several ribs had been broken and she complained of a good deal of pain. She was tilted slightly right, her long black hair falling down over her bare shoulders.

Standing behind the woman, Mary prayed softly for her. The words were in Choctaw. When she was done, she motioned for me to begin treating the woman. I reached for a tray of doctoring cigarettes and lit one. I began blowing smoke near her right shoulder.

"Work up, not down," Mary instructed me.

I knelt down and blew smoke on the tops of each of the woman's bare feet and then around behind them on her heels. I jumped the smoke upward in a series of staccato breaths, by degrees encircling her entire body in a spiral of smoke. I couldn't help looking at her angry bruises.

"Your ordinary eyes are baiting you, David," Mary scolded. "Skip the obvious. Observe her *shilip*. Go to dead places in it."

At that moment intertwined blades of radiating color lashed out from her. It came from all around but ended at her shoulders. Her *shilip* appeared healthy on the right but squeezed together on the left, jagged and wavy. There were three holes to the left of center, one of them lower than the others. Another hole was forming on the same side. These were clear signs it was giving way to more serious problems. I saw a dark haze climbing from within the hole. I blew one plume of smoke after another at it, lighting cigarette after cigarette. The holes closed. Then I fanned it with my wingfan and strengthened it.

When I was finished, Mary said, "Good."

The little praise cheered me. Mary began to work on her. She dusted a pink root powder on the woman's ribs with a rabbit-fur mitten and then hung a small medicine pouch around her neck. From her doctoring outfit she gave her a bundle of herbs.

She told the woman her accident had been caused by a hawk, and gave her instructions about medicines and some other steps she would need to take to realign herself to be in harmony with hawk's power.

The next man to be treated was the local deputy sheriff. He was in his early fifties and maybe half Indian. His uniform and shiny star made me uncomfortable. I didn't know if we were doing anything illegal or not, but I didn't want to find out. He took off his gun belt and handed it to Tub.

"Roy Rogers," Tub whispered in my ear.

"Yep, it's Hopalong," I whispered back.

Tub set his black leather rig and hardware gingerly on the floor as the deputy skinned out of his shirt and the T-shirt he wore under it. I noticed that his face and hands were darker than the rest of him. He had a nice beer gut on him. When he stood before me, I held up a cigarette and prayed for vision.

The deputy's *shilip* was translucent and very faint in places. A large portion of its right side was entirely missing, leaving a hole shaped like a large capital C that curved down almost to the middle of his body. A dark, smoky trail crossed the top of it, and there was a black mass at the upper left. A spidery image was attached directly to the area around his kidneys. There was an unusual white luminosity shaped like an elongated egg on his left, just below the middle of his abdomen. Last, and most frightening to me, there was a definite bone intrusion in his chest. It was nearly touching his heart.

I turned and said, "Mary?"

Mary took over because I was alarmed and at a loss. She made a motion to get Tub's attention and then spoke to him in sign language. He quit his soft drumming and left the room, returning soon afterward with an iron skillet full of coals. He set the skillet on a flat rock at the deputy's feet. Mary threw some pieces of dried cactus on the coals, and then some dried bear plant with the root still attached. Tub went back to his place and resumed drumming. To show proper respect for the bear plant being used in the fumigation, he began singing a dream song to the bear maiden. Mary drew the smoke from the skillet over the man with a long, black buzzard-wing fan. She soon surrounded him in a thick cloud. As Mary fanned, the man gave a great sigh of relief and seemed to relax. She continued for a time and then motioned me to remove the skillet.

I took it, along with the smooth rock it sat upon, and placed them both to the side of the altar cloth. The altar was covered with a vast array of gourd cups, colored glass jars, and bottles that contained what was called capture water. Besides this, there were bells, flowers, a mirror, a flute, a rattle, and other ritual objects. I could clearly feel the power emanating from there. Smoke spun upward from the skillet, winging out across the ceiling. Another deep layer of smoke filled the entire room.

When I turned back to Mary, she was spitting jets of power water onto the man's naked chest — several spurts to each side. I could see that this was having the effect of blowing out his *shilip*. It also darkened it and made it more visible — at least to me.

Chanting softly, Tub watched everything carefully, attentive to each detail. Mary handed me the bottle of power water and told me to put it back on the altar with the others. Then she told the man to lie down with his head on a blanket.

"Obsidian lancet," she said to me.

I got it out of her outfit and gave it to her. She made a circle with her spread fingers and then used them to smooth the man's chest over the place where we had seen the dangerous intrusion.

"Do you want your little pump?" I asked, referring to her cupping horn.

"I wish." She smiled. "No, this dart is too delicate. Get the bowl."

The bowl was on the west side of the altar. It was a sort of spittoon and contained chunks of raw beef that served as a catchall for sucked-out blood and any intrusions the wound might contain. After powwowing, the entire bowl and its contents were always offered to the spirits of the west and then ritually buried. I got it and set it on the floor near the man, in a place where Mary could spit into it conveniently.

"I'm going to scratch," she told the man.

He nodded his approval.

It wasn't exactly a scratch. She X-ed a pretty good-sized cut with quick back-and-forth slashes, then quickly bent forward and sucked at the bleeding wound. Each time she removed her mouth to spit into the bowl of meat, the blood flowed freely out onto the man's chest and to the floor.

Spewing out another mouthful, Mary said, "I got it." She made a guttural sound and spat several more times. I handed her a gourd of purifying medicine which she sipped, then swished around in her mouth and also spat out. She motioned for a cloth sack containing a mixture of powdered puffball mushrooms and spider web. I knew what was in it because I had spent several of my visits laboriously collecting the many webs she had needed to make this medicine. She spread a small handful of the mix over the cut marks, completely covering them with it. Then she placed a wide, grayish leaf on top and told the man to hold it in place. She asked me for a small amount of salted bear root, which she chewed for several moments before spitting it into the bowl. After this, she chewed a small piece of sassafras root, which she likewise expelled.

When she was finished, we both tried to help the deputy get to his feet, but he seemed quite chipper and had no problems. Mary told me to join in. We smoked him again, using at least twenty more cigarettes between us. The dark attachment on his kidney slowly dissolved, telescoping down in size with each cigarette. His *shilip* expanded greatly and became clearly defined.

When we were all done, Mary gave him some herbs. She told him thunder sickness had been his problem, along with imbalanced dirts, and that the turkey spirit had also been attacking him. The intrusion had been created by a man he had brought to jail.

"I think I know who that is," the deputy asked. "Is he a witch?"

"No, he was not a witch. Not by heritage or training, at least. He simply possessed a turkey's throwing ability. He kept turkeys as a child, and he loved seeing the wild ones in the woods. Because of this, turkey recognizes him as a brother and shoots its darts when the man dislikes someone. He didn't like you, so the turkey spirit came to lay you down.

"Pin this conjured turkey feather inside your shirt whenever you have to deal with this man. It is a shielding feather. Turkey will see you as a relative, and will not harm you." Mary looked away and then sharply back at him, her eyes glinting. "I must warn you. Don't play any more hoochy-coochy on your wife. You know exactly what I mean."

The deputy was stunned. "Yes, I know what you mean, but I didn't think . . ."

"It's clear to my eyes," Mary said.

Highly embarrassed, the deputy hung his head. Tub helped him on with his shirt and gave him his stuff. When he was all hitched up again, Tub led him outside.

There was still plenty of smoke left in the room, but Mary began making even more by throwing some cedar and sage leaves on the still-smoldering skillet. Then she had Tub carry the skillet about the room while I fanned the smoke in all directions. Mary began to pray out loud again. Then she began to speak in a language I had never heard, in a strange voice that sounded as if it was coming from various parts of the room.

Suddenly, she jumped straight up into the air and spun herself around, gibbering loudly. I thought she had lost her mind and was having a conniption. It put me in a panic, but Tub and I went on around the room smoking up everything. Mary finished by throwing puffs of finely ground cornmeal at the wall, after which she returned to normal — if power doctoring is ever normal.

Mary asked Tub to go get the next patient. He led in an old grandmother, who I guessed to be in her late eighties. She had on a faded flower-print dress and smelled of talcum powder. Age had broken her skin into countless lines and wrinkles, but her face was still happy. She grinned and chuckled at me, as if to say, "I've seen plenty in my time, sonny boy, and it was all very entertaining. Now it's your turn to amuse me."

Holding a smoldering cigarette in my right hand, I raised it, shut my eyes, and prayed another prayer for vision. When I opened them again and looked at her, I saw she had a kind of pear-shaped *shilip*. A dark insect shape was around her right shoulder. Plus, there was something that looked like the nose of a bullet pointed upward, only much larger, like a cannon shell.

When I looked down at her right leg, I was shocked to see what appeared to be a huge bone jutting out from it. I had no idea what it meant, since intrusions normally were no bigger than a finger. I noticed a bunch of dark spots whirling around her like small moons in orbit around a planet.

I let out a breath of confusion and stepped back away from her. Mary said very quietly in my ear, "She's well cooked, isn't she? You better let me doctor her." She pointed at a large object wrapped in an Indian blanket and motioned for Tub to bring it and place it at the woman's feet. Mary unwrapped it, revealing an old horse skull with a large turquoise nugget embedded in the center of its forehead.

Mary told me to get both her horse-skin rattles, which I did. Long hanks of horsetail were attached to their handles. Mary told me to assume a horse position, so I put my right foot forward, crouched at the knees, and threw back my head, holding the two rattles in one fist. She told me to hold the posture, get behind the woman, and rattle on both sides of her. My movements were supposed to embody the proud, flowing force of the horse, and the two rattles together created a one-two galloping rhythm. Tub met my rattling with his drumbeat. I became engulfed in this hypnotically rhythmic sound, and it was easy to find and connect with the horse spirit. I circled slowly around the old woman, rattling up and down her sides.

Tub sang softly and made neighing sounds. Mary blew many tobacco breath plumes and feathers in a way that I had never seen before. Soon an entity appeared in the air from nowhere. I saw it quite clearly. It was about the size of a basketball, and the air around it rippled and flickered like the wake of a boat moving across water. It made me think of a giant, floating amoeba. Whatever it was, Mary seemed to be directing its actions. It drifted over to the huge bone jutting from the old woman's leg and devoured it. Then it left, swimming slowly across the room like nobody's business. I was sure Tub saw it. I could only suppose it was some sort of spirit Mary worked with.

I kept up my rattling all around the woman, shaking the rattles from floor height nearly all the way up to the ceiling. I pawed with my foot and whinnied, shaking my head like a horse just as Mary taught me. Watching the old woman, I could see that she looked nervous and was impatiently tapping her foot to the beat of Tub's soft drumming and chanting. The little dark spots hovering in the air around the woman had taken on colors and were now neon flakes of red, blue, green, and yellow.

"Those headaches of yours," Mary said to the woman. "They come from what is called body-of-stars sickness. They can be ferocious, but I am weakening them." The sprinkling of colored stars began to shatter and vanish — all of them. Mary reached inside the woman's *shilip* with one hand and removed the giant bulletlike thing. When she did this, the *shilip* fluctuated. It made me feel dizzy and disoriented. Mary showed me what she had taken out. It was actually just a little speck of crystal no larger than a grain of wheat.

Rolling it between her thumb and finger, she said, "It carries a form of ghost-campfire sickness." She went on to explain that it had been drawn to the woman magnetically. She told me to place the crystal fragment carefully in the bowl of meat. "Other-wise," she said, "it will spring right back inside her."

Next Mary began to treat an inky area of the woman's *shilip*. This slowly took the new shape of an inverted dark garlic bulb with an odd-looking fringe hanging down from it. All of a sud-den it plunged, then flitted upward like a bird, nearly hitting me as it passed. Then it hit the wall, passing through it and disap-pearing.

I ducked quickly away, almost dropping my rattles. "What in the hell was that?" I gasped.

"Oh, you'll learn to recognize those one of these days. That was a spirit quetzal bird, a spy for the ancestor spirit of the dead. It was inside her, building its nest of doom. With the help of her ghost-campfire sickness, it would have soon blistered and burned her. She would have been completely cooked. This woman should never have left her old family dwelling. Fire is the heart of the home. When she left it, it made her sick."

Mary continued blowing spears of smoke into the old woman's *shilip*. Soon it took a form opposite the pear-shaped one I had first seen. The pear had been turned upside down, with its base at the top.

"This way is to compensate," Mary said. "Her old, unhealthy *shilip* will return soon enough, but this will fix it for now."

She told the old woman she should wear the color red to avert the negative powers of the moon. She gave her some jealous-woman root to chew, to help her *shilip* stay solid. Then she gave her some other herbs for brewing a special tea. Last, she gave her a gourd-root *sabeeha*. The old woman was so happy to get the *sabeeha* that she couldn't stop clucking and chuckling. Mary motioned quietly to Tub, and he led her out — certainly a different person from the one who had entered.

When Tub returned he rewrapped the horse skull and placed it back near his guardian spot. He brought in something heavy and unfolded the covering. It was a huge conjure turtle, made almost entirely from crystal. It must have weighed at least a hundred and fifty pounds. The base, an ancient turtle shell, shone pale green beneath an inlaid layer of large transparent stones. The head, legs, and tail were all carved entirely from quartz. The eyes were red glass beads, perhaps garnet. I felt it centered the energy and held it in place.

Once more, Tub and I incensed all around with smoke. When all was arranged to Mary's satisfaction, Tub left and brought in the next patient. He was a dark and handsome young man of about my own age, with prematurely silvering hair. He seemed to want to speak, but didn't. I prayed and then eyed him as he stood silently in front of the crystal turtle. His *shilip* resembled a flattened orangish pumpkin, with one large green cyclopean eye. A dark area beneath the eye flapped open and shut. A cloudy feline figure was crouched atop his *shilip*.

Whenever the man moved his hands and arms, his *shilip* jumped and shimmered like an infinity of mirrors. Subsiding, it left bands of crimson color that encircled the predominant orange form.

Even more oddly, the man's physical self was not contained at all within his *shilip*. Instead, it floated about two feet to the left of his body. I walked a few feet away so he wouldn't hear me. "What do I do?" I asked Mary in hushed tones.

"This is deer. It is broken love — a broken heart. It is the selfishness of death — an inner willingness to die caused by the offended deer spirit. I have brought the turtle to add power to our conjuring, so perhaps we can help him, perhaps not."

Mary told me to take my small deer antler and put it on top of the turtle's back. "When you do, watch carefully."

I did, and I saw that the man's *shilip* was instantly drawn back more fully around him. However, it was now tilted sharply right. Mary lit a doctoring cigarette and wafted its smoke toward the man, rubbing it on his *shilip*. She kept pushing at it until it righted to its proper shape. Its color altered significantly, becoming much lighter. She picked up the deer antler and handed it to the man, telling him to hold it under his chin between the prongs. She began to work on his dark flapping place with an eagle feather, using it to fan one plume of smoke after another. The spot appeared to be eating the smoke, becoming noticeably smaller with each puff. When the smoke dissolved upward, so did the darkened place. She used the feather in the same way to banish the catlike thing. It too was sucked into itself and disappeared. The man's *shilip* expanded evenly, entirely free of obstructions. Mary had accomplished this with less than five fully smoked cigarettes.

But she wasn't done. She told me to spread a blanket out on the floor. She told the man to take off all his clothes except for his undershorts. When he had stripped, she instructed me to rub him all over with a whiskey-soaked root liniment. I dipped my hand in the mixture and warmed it over the skillet of coals, being careful not to let the alcohol catch fire. The rubdown, which I did in broad circular strokes, lasted about half an hour. When I was finished, Mary put a small wad from the crumpled head of a cattail near the middle of the man's spine. To my astonishment, she took a stick from the burning skillet and lit the wad on fire. The burning little piece of cattail caused a big angry red welt to rise up on the man's back, but he neither flinched nor cried out.

When the tiny fire extinguished itself, she told him to get up. He stood and silently put his clothes back on. He looked alert. Mary gave him a fruit jar containing a thumb-sized purple root floating in a transparent but amber-colored liquid. She instructed him to take a spoonful of it every morning, starting four days before the full moon and ending four days after. Finally she placed a rawhide thong around his neck with a deer's hoof hanging from it.

She told him, as she placed a leather thong around his neck, "This deer hoof I am giving you represents the deer path. You must follow it. You have been eating yourself up with your memories of a recent affair. You only think it is love that you remember. In reality, you were courting death. I ask you to pray now at this altar, that you may follow love's true dance and know the proper continuum of life. No more thoughts of suicide. No more destructive actions. No more self-punishment.

"If you listen to me and do this, you will have many joyous days to come. Remember the fields where you played in childhood. Go to them, and leave tobacco offerings there for the deer spirits who attend them. Use your ears. Do you hear and understand?"

Choking back a sob, the man shook his head to indicate that he did. He knelt at the altar. Turning to Mary, he said, "Until now, I have never prayed. I have only spat at this hateful world."

"You yourself are the one responsible for creating your hateful world, the one that you live in," Mary replied. "Do not blame. If you have not been happy, it is because you have permitted others to lie to you and cheat you. You have been continually striving, reaching, trying to do only what others have instilled in you. This has been your ruin. So quit it. Be still. Find the power of change within you. Now pray, and if you can't pray for yourself, then pray for another."

He didn't just pray. He completely unloaded a boatload, a freight train load of repentance. He wailed like a ruptured duck, blessing everyone since Adam and Eve and confessing to a long list of transgressions. He beat his chest and tore at his hair. It seemed that Mary had opened up a big can of prayer worms, so to speak, and it must have been quite an experience for him — his first big pray. I began to think he would never finish. I was sure he would pray the night into the nubbins, and then go right on into the next century. Mary took note of my growing impatience with a good deal of amusement.

"Amen," I kept whispering underneath my breath. "Amen, brother. Amen, amen."

It didn't help. He went on and on and on, until eventually he ran down like a windup toy. He was tear-drenched but happy. I was grateful when Tub finally led him out. He was our last patient, so when he had gone Mary did closing-off rituals and "broke" the altar. Tub and I packed up everything and put it in the car.

Mary and I drove back to the mountains, leaving Tub in a nearby town with some friends. Neither of us spoke much at first, but my curiosity finally got the better of me, and I asked, "Mary, what language were you speaking tonight? It wasn't like any Indian language I've ever heard. Was that speaking in tongues?"

"Certainly not," she replied. "I was speaking the secret language of the *bopoli*, the little people. Those words have mystic powers. You are very lucky to have heard them."

"Excuse me. Are you saying the little people have a language?"

"Of course. They came tonight," she said. "They were with us. You should be able to see them, or at least be aware of them."

Mary was tired, and she motioned for me to keep silent.

But I didn't want to shut up. So I asked, "So little people have a language?"

"It's secret," she said. "But you can learn it if you can figure out how. That's part of the secret."

Thirty-seven

*T*WO WEEKS LATER I drove down for a meeting to Atoka, on the shores of Lake Atoka in the southern part of the state. Jagged spires of rock and clumps of cattail obscured the shoreline, and I could hear the ruffling water break on it. A large tent had been erected. Mary, Javier, Patricio, and I sat on the ground by the water's edge. Tub had gone off to visit an aunt somewhere in Texas and wasn't back yet. Under Mary's direction, we had just finished preparations for the night's doctoring. This had involved a long ceremony, done in private, for opening a healing bundle. When we began, Javier was to take care of bringing people inside, while Patricio and I were to help Mary directly with the patients.

I was nervous. I was hungry, and already slipping into various vacillating states of awareness. "When can we start?" I asked impatiently.

Mary gave one of her typical answers. "Smoke this," she said, handing me a freshly lit corn-shuck-and-tobacco cigarette.

I didn't understand why Mary was so adamant that I smoke only roll-your-owns made with her special medicine tobacco. "Why can't I just smoke my own cigarettes?" I asked.

"Smoke is the *shilip* curative. When you smoke, you are calling the spirits. Spirits don't like those big-business cigarettes. They want tribal tobacco. Remember, our tobacco was raised in a holy way and in holy ground for generations. Tailor-made cigarettes are coyote tobacco, trickster tobacco. Spirits want our old ancestral plants. They want our old cigarettes. You like to eat the kind of food you are accustomed to, don't you? With them, it's the same.

"Following tobacco will teach you much. It makes you see. That's what the word tobacco means in Choctaw — to see. So here's another cigarette, David. Smoke it. Light up. It will do you some good. Already it has helped you see just a little bit of what is hidden to most. Now we powwow the spirits."

At least twenty people had come for treatment. There were a few whites, but most were Native. One by one, they were brought inside by Javier. Mary had her hands full. I wondered how she could keep so calm in the face of such human suffering and pathos. But she never backed off, and she never gave an inch. She fought for each person as though her own life depended on it. I drummed, led the patients out after they were treated, and assisted and did what I could. I felt impatient and thought the doctoring would never end. For some reason, I made a lot of mistakes, drummed incorrectly, and was generally not being in harmony.

When it was over, Javier, Patricio, and I packed up. Outside the medicine tent a sliver of new moon shone brightly, even though it was still early morning. The air was fresh and cool. The sky was beginning to color in the east. A cold wind was chopping over the lake, and I could hear the water frothing against the banks.

After we had folded up the tent and put it in the trunk of my car, we drove back to the mountains. I made excellent time driving. Tub had returned from Texas ahead of us and was there at Mary's cabin to meet us and to help unload the gear, which now included several beautiful blankets as well as a jar of coins and currency, and various homegrown vegetables, jams, and other groceries that Mary had been given. We put it all inside Mary's cabin. Mary told us we were welcome to stay as long as we liked.

She said good night and went straight to bed. Javier and Patricio followed her example.

Outside the cabin windows, the wind was snapping. I went over and tossed some more wood into the stove. I put a handful of broadleaf cedar on the stove's surface, and the silvery smoke rising from it clouded the cabin with its pleasant odor.

Tub picked up a beaded hawk-feather fan and waved some of the smoke toward him, inhaling deeply. I watched the feathers flex and spread gracefully as they caught the smoke.

"I wish I could fly," I said idly. "Wouldn't that be nice?"

"Well, yeah, sure. You can fly, you know, if you want to," Tub replied. He put the fan down on the table and looked at me with the light from the burning wood flickering on his shadowed face. "You just need the right goodies. That's all it takes."

"What goodies?" I asked somewhat incredulously.

"Mary taught them to me."

"Give," I said. "Give it up, Tub."

Tub explained the recipe to me, and I wrote it all down. He said to take thirty-six pulverized seeds of a certain night-blooming plant, a very small amount of lime, a similar amount of natural tobacco, and grind it all together. The resulting concoction is then mixed thoroughly with a small amount of spring water until it turns into a sticky paste, and it is then divided into four equal parts and rubbed on the feet and hands. Any remainder is then rubbed into the armpits.

"Doing this during a tobacco fast will give you the ability to fly as far as you like," Tub explained. "Your physical body will stay, of course, but your *shilip* separates to roam wherever it wishes. You can see, hear, and know anything that's going on at a great distance."

"Have you done this yourself?" I asked him.

"Yes, I have visited my relatives in Mississippi many times."

"It sounds way too dangerous to me. I'm down for about anything. But for now, at least, I think I'll stick with plain old fasting."

We talked on beside the stove's flickering light until about noon. I clanked the iron door shut. Then I said good night, or rather good morning. Tub and I went to bed.

Thirty-eight

*B*ACK IN THOSE OKLAHOMA HILLS, they have a saying, "Ride fence on your desires." But I had begun to do more and more tobacco water fasts — far more than I was supposed to be doing. This had happened gradually, without my intending it. I knew it was a dangerous sport. At first, I just didn't seem as hungry, so I started eating less at mealtimes. Then I began skipping meals entirely. It happened more and more frequently until I was going days at a time without food. Forgetting about the needs of my physical self seemed to give me a kind of enjoyable freedom. Each day it became a little easier not to eat. It was as if I had visited this amazing foreign country on vacation several times, kept going there, liked it, and then decided to move in. I found that fasting heightened some of my senses and shut down others. I hid the fact that I was going without food from Mary, but her sharp senses soon detected it. She called me on it, and told me to quit fasting unless it was under her strict supervision.

I didn't want to stop, so rather than having a confrontation, I quit driving to the mountains. I had learned the secrets of concocting various fasting waters. Ordinarily, it was difficult to obtain the natural tobacco, but Mary had shown me where it grew and I had stored up a large quantity. I was a happy man.

Often the visions induced by the fasts hatched up great terror. It was like being in the middle of a horror movie that looped, circled around, and replayed without stopping. These frightening spectacles so overwhelmed me that I became purged. I no longer feared anything at all. Even death was okay by me. With the end of fear, courage was born. From courage came love of all creation. I loved everyone and everything I saw. Mary had taught me about the overlapping of dimensions. And in the merging of internal and external, it was easy for me to choose to go between them. The outside world was topical, full of ego conflicts, pretenses, and falsities. It was a miasma of delusion and struggle.

Inner life was different. My old, customary way of seeing people and events was gradually escaping me. People were different. I was aware only of their *shilip*, their shadow self. I had gone over the perceptual edge and splashed down in a phantasmagorically new river. Now the world was full of beauty, truth, and warmth of spirit. It was loving, noncombative, and accepting. This was the world I wanted.

I soon saw people as activity clusters who would sometimes meet in a great clashing. I myself was an activity cluster, but I did my best just to be invisible. I might be talking to a man at work, for instance, when suddenly I become aware of him as an aggregate of his many life experiences. When people had power over others, I saw sticky fibers emerging from the dominant one and latching on to the less dominant one. The fibers leached off energy and lessened the strength of the other's *shilip*.

My fasting didn't have any overt religious fervor. I didn't think of my induced experiences as being on a high spiritual plateau. It was entirely personal. But there was something going on at a deep level that seemed quasi-religious to me. I began to hear music, sublime music. I imagined I was somehow analogous to a radio receiver picking up cosmic harmonies. It was as if the whole of creation was a cathedral, and I was standing inside it during the performance of a mass by Johann S. Bach. Life itself was giving this grand performance. But I could find no human counterpart to this unearthly music — not even in Mozart or Beethoven.

This supersensitivity lasted for weeks. The music became louder, growing from a distant harmony into a near crescendo of ever more ethereal pure sound. I had no control over it, but it didn't bother me. I received this as a great blessing to be enjoyed. But it troubled me that I, who knew very little about music, was apparently the only recipient of this celestial orchestration. I kept thinking that such wonderful music was being wasted on me, that the world should have it. It should be scored and preserved.

I knew one classical musician, a casual friend named Dwight. I decided I would trust him. I would tell him about this music, describe it as it was happening, hum it, and ask him to score it for me. I called and asked if he wanted to compose some incredible music. He sensed my enthusiasm, and we made an appointment. I went to his apartment full of excitement. Just as I was about to knock on his door, the music stopped. That quickly.

I never heard it again.

I missed the music, but soon I found I was able to have visions at will. It was as easy as swimming. I could dive down into a vision anytime I felt like it.

As I was walking along the sidewalk one day, the scenery changed. I saw swimming pools and tennis courts. I knew I was in southern California in a place of spectacular wealth. A blinding light hurt my eyes. The light was glinting off the second-story window of a mansion. There were beautiful flowering bougainvillea vines covering the wall. A winding sidewalk led to the front door, which was flanked with budding jacaranda trees. I was on the lawn looking up at the window.

"Harsh light," I commented. When I said those words, a piece of the light fell to earth. Where it landed in the grass, a man stood. He was wearing a puffy silk shirt and a large gold-and-ruby medallion.

"Who are you?"

"I am a magician. Use me. I can transform you."

When he said it, another piece of light fell from the window to the ground. On the spot was a lovely Native woman dressed in a doe-skin dress. She shook a rattle at me.

Astonished, I asked, "Who are you?"

"I am a conjure. Use me. I can transform you."

Another piece of light fell, and there stood a man.

"And you? Who are you?"

"I am a juggler. Use me. I can transform you."

I opened my mouth to speak, but light chunks instead of words came out. The pieces fell between my shoes, hit the ground, and disappeared. The magician, conjure, and juggler were pulled to the spot. I realized they would be sucked in and vanish too. I tried to shout, "Wait. What are you telling me?" Instead, more gobs of light fell from my mouth. First the juggler, then the magician, then the conjure — the three figures dissolved into the earth at my feet. As I studied my shoes, I became aware, once again, of walking down the city sidewalk.

I had many such brilliant visions. Somehow, I was able to cope with my day-to-day existence, though it had become a great bore. One morning, I looked in the mirror and stopped long enough to focus on the image it reflected. I was shocked. I didn't recognize myself. I was amazingly unkempt. My face was drawn, my cheeks were hollow, and my eyes bulged. I didn't have an ounce of body fat. I suddenly wondered if tobacco water might be some sort of dangerous narcotic. Perhaps I had let myself become addicted. But I was sure I could quit fasting if I wanted. All I needed was to make up my mind to do so. But I was appalled. I just didn't see any reason to quit fasting. I comforted myself that tobacco was an acceptable path to spiritual knowledge, and besides, I greatly enjoyed my visions.

Soon after that I fainted dead away at work one night and

hit my forehead on an iron bar. I woke up lying on the red-tiled floor with my head in the lap of a frightened coworker. Someone was pressing a towel against my head trying to stanch the blood that was gushing from my wound, making a red-on-red pastiche across the floor.

"How long since you've eaten?" asked the man working on my cut.

"A day or two," I lied. I hadn't had a solid bite of food in over two weeks.

Someone left and quickly returned with a meat and cheese sandwich. I didn't feel hungry at all, but he forced me to eat it. As soon as I did, I vomited it right back up. By now the floor ran with a stew of my blood and regurgitation.

They finally got me settled down and helped me sip some broth. When they were satisfied I was mobile, I was sent home to bed. My mom, Opal, came and clucked and fussed over me for a few days. As soon as I was strong enough she drove me to the hospital in Blackwell. I spent five days there while our family doctor ran a bunch of tests. I wondered what Mary would think of my being in this place, going the way of mainstream medicine.

On my last day in the hospital, my doctor came in to talk to me. Dr. Becker was a sweet man and a great old country doctor. He brought the formidable powers of science to the sticks of early-day Oklahoma. I had known him since I was a child, and I felt like he was a revered member of our family.

He ran his hand slowly through his white hair. Old Doc Becker had probably seen every kind of medical condition, but I seemed to have stumped him.

"David," he said, "I have to tell you that in my fifty years of practicing medicine, I have never seen a metabolism as abnormal as yours. It constantly fluctuates up and down, high and low. It's uncanny. I don't know what to make of it. I don't know what you've been doing, so all I can do is tell you to stop it."

"Will I be okay?" I asked.

"I think so," he replied. Then for the next half hour he recited a litany of all the things he'd found wrong with me. He prescribed a lifetime prescription of the drug Ritalin, gave me a diet and nutrition manual, and told me it was important that I eat regularly. He also referred me to a psychiatrist in Norman, a town near Oklahoma City.

Two days later I sat in the psychiatrist's waiting room with several other people. I was early, so I halfheartedly perused a magazine. Down the hallway I could see heavy wooden doors leading to the offices of various neurologists and psychiatrists. I noticed that when the doors opened and the patients left their therapy sessions, their faces were anxious and depressed. Many of them looked as if the wrath of God had struck them.

I became afraid of what might be awaiting me behind those closed mahogany doors. I never saw anyone leave a healing ceremony who didn't look and say they felt better for it. They were empowered by their experience. It was such a stark contrast that I got up and left without a word.

Driving home, I began to reflect that despite my vacillating feelings about my diagnosis from mainstream medicine, this recent obsession and resulting injury from fasting made it clear I had sunk to a low ebb. Maybe I had blown a few shingles off my roof, or maybe I didn't have any front headlights. Mary's work was fascinating, but it bothered me that learning was such a slow process. An apprentice of many years has no certainty of having the ability to practice. I wondered if perhaps I shouldn't strive to do something else with my life that would be safer, quicker, and more tangible.

After all, I had many other interests besides Mary. I was eager to experience the world beyond Oklahoma. My life had reached a serious turning point. I decided that my only sensible choice was to tell Mary it was over. I would leave the conjure road to others who understood it better, respected it more, and were more disposed to it.

I still had several more sick days left before I had to return to work. I used them to give my apartment a thorough cleaning and to call the friends I had neglected for so long, reestablishing my ties. I made a list of books to read. I called a couple of young women I knew and made dinner dates with them. I was a good cook.

A week quickly went by. All the while I was wondering what to do about Mary. I knew I had to tell her my decision, yet I dreaded doing it. I cared about her, and knew how hard she had tried to bring me along. I put it off as long as I could and decided to hide behind my stationery. I sat up late writing her a long, tortured letter explaining why I no longer felt able to continue with her.

When I left my apartment on my way to work the next morning, letter in hand, there was Mary, sitting impassively on the hood of my car. I was so startled to see her that I just gave her a squeeze and sat down on the hood beside her without speaking. I folded the letter and eased it inconspicuously into my back pocket.

After a moment or two of nervous silence, I said, "Mary, why are you here?"

"I thought you might wish to speak to me. I knew you were having some troubles."

"I've been in the hospital," I replied. "The doctors told me to stop what I've been doing, so I haven't come down to the mountains lately."

"Look at you," Mary said. I gazed down at my feet in embarrassment and then back at her again. "You're nothing but skin and bones," she continued. "You look bad. You've let yourself fall to pieces. Why did you stop eating?"

"I don't really know, Mary. For some reason I just wanted to, I guess. Anyway, you told me to fast."

"Yes, I told you to fast. But the fasting road is not the same as the starvation road. Fasting is healthy. Starvation isn't."

The early morning traffic on Shartel Street was already congested, stacking up with lines of cars moving slowly toward the downtown area. The sun was out, but it was a smoggy, gray day. A chill was in the air.

I noticed Tub's empty truck parked at the curb across the street.

"Where's Tub?" I asked.

"He walked over to the drugstore on Classen to get something to eat."

"I'll miss him then, since I have to get going. You know how it is — I can't be late."

Mary smiled at me and put her arm around my shoulder. She gazed steadily into my eyes. "You want to tell me something, don't you?"

"Mary, you have a lot of knowledge," I said. "More than anyone else I know. And I know how hard you've tried to teach it to me. I have learned much from you, but many of your teachings are beyond me. This has been troubling, because it has made me wonder if I'll ever be able to heal people on my own, without your help. And lately, my lack of discipline put me in the hospital. How can I hope to be a curer if I can't even balance my own health?

"I've been thinking, Mary. I still have some rights under the GI Bill. Maybe I'll go to college. I want to learn how to express myself better. I'd like to refine my writing. I'd even like to go to Europe and see what's over there."

"Do as you will, David. But if you are still interested in medicine ways, I advise against going to college. Your true self will suffer."

"How do you figure?"

"Our old ways are laughable to them. You'll soon get all cemented, set in their teachings. And for the rest of your life, you may never be able to escape.

"But look about you. Look at all these people hurrying to jobs they can't stand. Look at the fear etched on their faces. This city you live in is drugged with fear. The people here are not centered. Our way of life is over. That's certain. But theirs stands on a hill of sand, trickling away so slowly they aren't even aware of it. Their lives are choked by hatred and bigotry. Fear is a constant mirror for these people. Most of all, they're afraid of people who are brave. But being brave and centered is the only answer for the difficult road that lies ahead — for all people.

"David, I must ask you to do a last ceremony for me. Not now but someday. Maybe even in the far-off distant future. Someday when your world makes no sense as it inevitably will. Do it then. Go up in the mountains and do it."

"What ceremony?"

"I want you to one day call the little deer man, Kashehotapolo. He is quick to understand dilemmas and quick to act. That's the way it should close between us, with a ceremony. Not here. Not now. You'll know when the time is right."

"I will, Mary. I promise. When it's right."

Mary went on to carefully explain the details of the ceremony, called the seventh ceremony of the peacemaker. I got a notebook out of the car and wrote her instructions down carefully. It was a beautiful but complicated ceremony. She said that in order to see the little deer man, a person must be a "naught" — a master of eternity. "You can only meet him in one of two ways," she said. "By perfect chance, or by perfect design. If you intend to meet him by design, you must first purify yourself. You must be stripped and emptied of everything. Otherwise, Kashehotapolo's power will overcome you and you won't remember. Often, it takes forever to reach zero, a place without before and without after. But it can be achieved. You will meet Kashehotapolo when you are numbered none. Only then will you be able to contact him. Only then can you ask for his counsel.

"When Kashehotapolo first appears, he seems to be just an ordinary deer, a buck. But soon you will notice a strangeness about him. He comes toward you slowly, sensitive to your heart, his black nose sniffing the air. There will be a piercing, high-pitched sound. Then, suddenly, there is a change of color, a swirling of bluish gray, and his image begins to reform. This happens in the blink of an eye. Kashehotapolo's burnished silver figure shimmers before you. He will fill with a strange silver light, dimming and then shining again. In his true form, Kashehotapolo has antlers and he will walk erect like a man."

"Why do you think I should do this ceremony?"

"To heal your heart and keep it, because the world can be treacherous. I have a feeling you will need it someday. You won't know where to turn. Maybe many years hence. Listen, the umbilicus was cut for us. I have borne you, and so too you have borne me. You are leaving my warm conjure nest perhaps never to return to it. Our hidden ring will be broken. It will no longer be the same with us. But don't be too certain about your road. I told you long ago that becoming a power doctor isn't a decision you make. You either are one, or you are not. You have no choice in the matter. And think how far you have already come. You cannot turn around. Backing out is impossible. Are you so sure you do not want to complete your journey? You like to speak of things as if they were finished, but the road stretches on."

"Mary, I'll always remember you."

"David, memory is as ephemeral as a flitting butterfly playing catch-me-if-you-can. If you catch it, how delicate. How sweet its medicine. Such colors. Such beauty. Then you must let go."

I felt hot tears forming in my eyes. I didn't want to cry and was doing my best not to.

"Now, I warn you. It is law that I do so. You must always honor the sacred tobacco. Tobacco is our ancestor, our relative. I have told you before that it came to us from another dimension. The ancient legends tell us that before tobacco we were incomplete, and it made us whole. It was tobacco that hurled us forward.

"There are four hundred and four stories about it. I regret that I didn't make you memorize them. There is no reason you shouldn't hold the stories, even now that you are leaving."

Mary cocked her head. Her salt-and-pepper braids hung down to her lap. "If you have ears, listen to me." I realized I was going to be late for work, but just nodded silently. "Tobacco, like most great spiritual powers, is a paradox. How we choose to use it defines us and the plant. Long ago, it was a gift to be used solely by spiritual persons as a walkway between worlds, as a medicine with miraculous powers. The plant was always used with reverence.

"Used correctly, tobacco has supernatural qualities. When the tobacco is not respected, smoking or any other use of tobacco is a capricious act. A misunderstanding of this plant will surely destroy you. Used improperly, tobacco becomes an impediment to consciousness. Using it indiscriminately will make you less aware. The tobacco will wrathfully and justifiably turn on you. Eventually, you will become addicted to it. Instead of giving you power, the spirit will take power away and ruin you. Either use tobacco spiritually, or stay far away from it."

"Are you telling me not to smoke, Mary? What if I want to pray? Can I smoke then?"

She smiled and laughed at me. "Keep your ears on my words, David. I am not telling you what to do. I'm asking you to stay awake. It is told that Yellow Tobacco Boy died, fell in a hole in the ground, and got covered over. He dreamed, and in his dream he pulled a little and pushed a little and his neck stretched. He started growing, seeking the sun. He began to sprout leaves and became the flowering tobacco plant. Men and women came and danced around him and celebrated him. They knew he was holy.

"So in the end Yellow Tobacco Boy was filled with knowledge and powers beyond imagination. He was strong, and he grew old and wise. Maker of Life said to him, 'For generations to come, the people will know you. When you arise, they will crush you and cut you to pieces. They will always know that you are sacred. You will be filled with the possibility of life and death, for you will be as my own sacred breath. When you are touched with fire, your spirit will be released and returned to Me.'

"Branched lightning comes down from above to touch many places, but it is all one lightning. When you understand power, you are able to visit many exquisite worlds. We humans are a lightning flash on a rainy night. Most everyone can hear the thunder, but not everyone is able to see the light. Fewer still can actually become the light. David, I tried my best to light you up."

Appendix

*I*N THE LAST CENTURY, powwowing and other similar healing
practices have been elbowed aside, and today mostly Western
ideas occupy all the space. These practices, often called conjuring and juggling, are a relic of a bygone era. Ancient and knowledgeable civilizations once flourished on this land we call the
American continent. For whatever reason, many were destroyed,
and the healing techniques and medical traditions that were the
norm in these cultures largely vanished with them. The methods
of powwowing were never examined in any significant way by
the American scientific community. A bridge was never built
across the cultural chasm dividing one set of practices from the
other. The final judgment of history seems to be that all conjures
were charlatans. This is a racist, fraudulent view, and I know it to
be untrue. Conjure practices kept people healthy for untold generations, perhaps even more healthy than we are today.

Powwowing is a healing ceremony conducted by a conjure.
Mine isn't the last word on the subject, nor am I trying to revive
anything. I realize these practices are mostly lost, but I wanted
here to record what little I know as best I can for posterity. I
don't wish to convey that I am an expert on conjure or any sort
of medicine man, for I am certainly not. To become a conjure
takes years of experience, dedication, and study — years of commitment I was eventually unwilling to make. Though I have personal experience with these ancient arts, I am a writer. And I do
not give advice concerning illness.

The idea that each person is analogous to a *shilip*, an inside shadow, is central to conjure. It rests on teachings of the old ones, much of which have been eroded in North America. It has been suggested that the land to the south, Mesoamerica, may still contain much of this same knowledge. I suspect that, historically, such concepts were traded between the indigenous peoples of the north and south. If you examine the allegorical indications of many of the traditional stories, this seems obvious. The impact of colonization and European imperialism greatly fragmented and altered the continuance of this body of knowledge, but it's quite possible that elements of it thrive in enclaves in Central and South America, as the example of Javier and Patricio implies.

Powwowing seeks to reconfigure the *shilip*. Countless variations and permutations exist for every example cited in this book. Since powwowing is visionary, it can be fuzzy at the edges of subjectivity and objectivity.

The purpose of conjure is to rearrange various components of ordinary life into a healthy configuration. For instance, the dead must be sufficiently separated from the living. The winds within the human must be happily married. There is an assembly of protector animals to be nourished. And so on.

The conjurer's realm is firstly spiritual. This means that physical healing is secondary and spiritual refuge for the patient is primary. Strong life is born of strong spirit. Good luck and good health walk hand in hand. They are happy together and like each other.

No two conjures are the same, just as no two healing functions are the same. Each conjure has different capabilities. Some have the ability to cure very specific illnesses, while others are generalists. Each conjure has his personal and familial secrets. To be gifted in curing sick people, conjures often have to have extraordinary power. However, not all conjures have the same degree of training and skill. Some have fragmented knowledge. Innate ability also varies. Sicknesses vary and challenge a conjure's resourcefulness. Events make it necessary to change procedures. And so on.

Curing practices take place within a well-defined model, so it is possible to generalize various aspects of treatment. The feeling and character of powwowing can be described. It should be said at the outset that tobacco and smoking in conjure is considered sacred. Mary Gardener was appalled at the indiscriminate use of tobacco in our world.

If the powwowing cabin has electricity, it is shut off. The cabin is cleared of all furniture and the floor is scrubbed with power water and swept clean with cedar or fir branches. A healing circle is created with an entrance in the south. The circle may be delineated by tobacco, crystals, cornmeal, bird plumage, or other substances. Many conjures have their own secret powders and mixes for this.

When the power doctor makes a doctoring circle, she first blows four puffs of tobacco smoke to the east and implores the daybreak people for help. This direction symbolizes spring and sprouting, eggs cracking open with new life, birth and rebirth. The conjure goes to the sun-nourished south and blows four puffs of smoke. She implores the giants and lightning people for help. This place symbolizes flayed skin or the dropping of old flesh. The conjure goes to the west and blows four puffs, feeding the autumn. She implores the messengers and water beings for help. She acknowledges sacrifice.

The conjure goes to the north. She feeds the cold, icy winter with four puffs of tobacco smoke. She implores the night people, who live alone and are lonely, to come to her aid. She calls any ally wind she may have as a helper.

The conjure goes to the center, where all the roads of the circle convene. She sends four puffs to the centering principle. She implores the tree people for help. She begs these entities to work hard in her behalf.

While in the center, the conjure blows four puffs to the ground, connecting with the world below. Then she blows four puffs to the sky, connecting with the world above.

The conjure must now do a cleansing of her own body. Sage and broadleaf cedar are burned, and occasionally tobacco is added. The conjure bathes herself in the smoke. Most importantly, the hands must be purified. This is done with tobacco smoke. Skilled conjure hands have the ability to catch sickness and pull it out of the patient's body.

The left hand is considered to be female. The right hand is male. Each hand, whether male or female, represents the conjurer's cabal, consisting of a teacher and a group of apprentices. The thumb is the conjure, and the other four digits are the apprentices. The thumb is called the celestial finger. The instructor, it represents the center. The first apprentice finger relates to fire and will. It is called the cane finger. The second apprentice finger relates to air and intellect. It is the flint finger. The third apprentice finger relates to water and emotion. It is the monkey finger. Monkey is the incomplete human who drowned in the great flood, when Creator cleansed the Earth. The fourth apprentice finger, or little finger, relates to earth and dreaming. It is called rabbit finger. This is usually the shooting finger of a witch or wizard or traditional sorcerer. When a plume of smoke is blown on each of the digits, the doctor's hands are empowered.

The conjure might have one, two, or more human assistants, up to four. However, jacks, or spirit helpers, may be countless.

A practicing conjure must never eat pork or salt. Either of these will greatly interfere with the quality of healing that can be achieved. Males must abstain from sexual intercourse, but a female power doctor doesn't necessarily have to.

When the power doctor does powwowing or visits a sick person, she brings a medicine bundle or doctoring outfit with her. If the patient is incapable of standing, he is placed on a blanket with the head a little north of east. It is said this placement asks the bearers for long life. Otherwise, the patient faces north while standing. The conjure shakes a rattle and begins to sing various personal or animal songs before the curing rituals can begin. She prays, sings, rattles, drums, and fumigates the patient with smoke. The conjurer's power song or chant is personal. For example:

> I'm a red pole man (or woman)
> I'm a conjure man
> I'm a shooting hand
> I'm a lynx boy man
> I'm a hidden lynx paw hand.
>
> I'm a powwow man
> I'm an herb hand
> I'm a root hand
> I'm a magic hand
> I'm a ritual hand
> I'm a finding hand
> I'm a getting hand
> I'm a doing hand
> I'm otherworld hand
> I'm a crystal hand
> I'm a seeing hand
> I'm a breaking and setting hand
> I'm a truth hand
> I'm a charm hand.
>
> I'm a flying celestial-star-flying man
> I'm a dizzying earth-below-flying man

I'm a living take-back man
I'm a conjure man.

The conjure's personal power and enhanced ability to perceive in a new way are amplified by singing, and divination can begin. The most common method of divination is the floating of a ball of feathers, which is called measuring. This method is said to be a sort of spirit compass, pointing both the patient and conjure in the proper directions. Since forgotten time, feathers have lent their predictive qualities to divination. They alone can be conjured and speak clearly about life and death. Ancient peoples believed that the spirit came from above and took on density when it descended to earth. The floating of a ball of feathers (birds are at home in the sky, and so are their feathers) represented the spiritualization of matter.

Usually, hawk plumage, along with a tiny amount of beeswax, is used to prepare the ball, but most any feathers may be fashioned by the individual responsible for the powwowing. Each kind of feather has unique qualities. Hawk plumage partakes of the raptor's nature. Hawk sees far, is quick to comprehend, and is willing to share knowledge. Wild turkey down is another favorite because of the bird's humility, sacrifice, and service. In the old days, turkey's spirit was always sought as a divinatory guide.

The patient is given the feather ball and told to drop it out a hand's width from his naked left arm. The area between the arm and an imaginary line parallel to it and about eight inches away is called the ladder. It forms a kind of divinatory avenue. When the patient lets the ball go, its behavior in falling is carefully monitored. As the ball descends, the conjure murmurs a sort of rhythm, pulse, or count, a nine count for women and a thirteen count for men. The course and movement of the feather globe along the patient's arm tells much about the favorable or unfavorable circumstances of his or her life. If the floating ball rises in the air, this indicates that the patient may rise in the world through no effort of his own. Does the ball bear in or away from the patient? If it bears away, the conjure should address spiritual needs. If it bears in, then the body should be examined closely for sickness. The falling feather ball can also speak of sorrow ahead or whether the road is clear for good fortune. This feather tracing may warn of internal or external problems with health.

Now the conjure determines from this divination and from smoke fumigation if a wizard or witch or some other powerful being has caused the sickness. If the conjure believes she can help the patient, there is a binding. A gift is given. If it is accepted, the conjure is honor-bound to help the patient to his or her degree of ability. The conjure agrees to make medicine. It isn't necessary that the gift be of any great value. However, it is said the gift reflects the patient. If the patient thinks very little of him- or herself, the gift given might be of little or no value. Money and tobacco are always appreciated by the conjure. Money, tobacco, blankets, cloth, foodstuffs, and trade beads are the most traditional payment.

I've depicted smoke fumigation and tobacco conjuration a number of times in the text above. Tobacco conjuring is an unmasking and a discovery of the deepest problems of the patient. The process can trigger staggering emotional outbursts. The smoke transfigures or makes manifest various aspects of the *shilip*, the inside shadow. According to Mary Gardener, a Native word used to describe this process means "repaintment." The conjure is said to blow plumes, feathers, fibers, ropes, tendrils, and other varieties of smoke. Often during powwowing, as I watched Mary smoke a patient, the puffs appeared to spring from her eyes rather than from her mouth, suggesting that an animal power was assisting in the conjuration. Indeed, the conjure may treat illness with any one of many animal breaths.

These animal breaths are considered the property of the individual conjures, even though the conjure simply acts as the intermediary between the patient and the animal spirit.

Tobacco smoke is used to aid in realigning disordered attributes contained in the inside shadow. According to Mary, smoke inhaled by the conjure should travel upward until it exits through the closed fontanel and merges with the smoking stars. Mary said that then we become a receptacle of cosmic power.

The conjurer's objective is the general welfare of the patient, more than the cure of a specific disease or condition. Each individual manifests a complex set of adaptations to the disease. In addition, the conjure is nearly always able to observe disruptions in the *shilip* that may well extend beyond the body and into the patient's environment. The power doctor analyzes and engages the forces detrimental to the patient's complete physical, spiritual, and material well-being and confronts not only the immediate primary life energy but all that the patient will ever have in his or her lifetime.

In olden times, the powwower had a special power grounds, cave, or other suitable place for conjuring. Necessarily, powwowing would take place in nature, where the conjure had the direct aid of allies such as boulders, trees, and waterfalls. However, in recent centuries, the arts of powwowing and conjuring have changed considerably, and a make-do attitude has prevailed. Cabins, tipis, and even city apartments have been used. Mary generally held her powwowing circles out of doors near her cabin. The flayed two-lord or flayed two-lady, in other words the male or female patient, would stand or be placed on the earth. Of course, inclement weather would force the powwowing indoors.

Mary told me that conjure grounds were "walked off" and danced beforehand in order to determine their congruence with the spirit world. Powwowing could not be done just anywhere, since it was a port of entry to a different reality structure. A guardian cane with an attached duck feather is traditionally placed outside the entrance door to the structure or the opening of the healing circle. This is a warning, a big Do Not Disturb sign. It means that the conjurer's cabin or other dwelling is protected in the same manner as water rolls off a duck's back.

A typical powwowing begins at around 9:00 P.M. and usually lasts three or more hours but can go on until daylight. The night a powwowing is held should be well aspected, that is, the sun, moon, stars, and various planets should lend force to the venture and not thwart it. This is a study in itself, and I only mention it here. According to Mary, virtually every animal has a celestial counterpart, one might even say "soul." If a person has a disease caused by a certain animal, there exists a line of affinity between the animal and the celestial soul. This affinity or region illuminates the physical and spiritual condition of the patient and the powwowing outcome.

Many animal celebration songs are sung during powwowing. The patient is carefully monitored for clues of an animal attraction or animal rejection. Perhaps the patient has been witched, or pointed. If the witch or wizard who has shot the subject is formally trained, the intrusion will be nearly imperceptible to the conjure. The knowledgeable witch will have used camouflage. The patient is questioned at length about any suspicions he or she may have regarding the sickness. What are the circumstances surrounding the illness? Does the patient suspect bewitchment? Has the patient knowingly offended a particular animal? Is there an indication of an elemental offense? Is the spark or flame angry? Has the patient broken with the good water road? Has he or she stumbled in the dirt or somehow scarred the wind? And so on.

The lighting of a doctoring cigarette or pipe has enormous importance. There is much lore centered around this act. In olden times the tobacco was lit with a coal from a medicine fire or pot of coals. But in recent history, a match or lighter is used. Pipes and cigarettes are living beings. The newly lit tobacco, or fire bug, is the most sensitive feature of a doctoring smoke, because it is a microcosm of the sacred fire. It is a spirit tipster, offering signs and clues for the prospective doctoring. The conception, birth, and health of the fire bug are carefully watched for any anomaly that might communicate a vision or other divinatory message. Remember, this is a dwarf medicine fire circle, and laws of divination apply. For example, if there are failed attempts to light the tobacco, the spirits are sending a negative message foretelling unsuccessful doctoring. Conjures say that there is a strong or weak light and a deep or shallow light, which offer further clues.

When the first doctoring cigarette is lit, the health of the fire bug is determined by color and heat. Does it burn hot or cold? Is it long or short, large or small? If the fire bug is small or short, this is a good indication that the powwowing will be a success. If the bug is long, the powwowing will be of long duration and maybe several powwowings will be necessary. If the fire bug dies, it is an indication of poor preparation by the conjure. It may even signify the death of the patient. The sign is a warning that the animal and other spirits are not cooperating and that the conjure does not possess the necessary power to perform the healing. It signifies conjure power breaths of little significance.

The conjure examines the husk of ash surrounding the bug. Perhaps he sees a cat, bat, or alligator. Any animal may appear, for any animal may have been introduced into the body. It may be a seizer — a hawk. This means that the conjure will have to act quickly. The conjure must hit with finesse and hit hard. Does the conjure see a smokebird, a grouse? This means that the conjure will expend much energy. It could be a hollow ear, an owl. This means that the conjure must go to great lengths to discern the hidden cause of illness. A going-to-the-spirithouse, or swan, might show himself. This means the patient is out of harmony, and the shape of balance must be restored. If a bat appears within the fire bug, it is no simple omen. Death or transformation is approaching, and the conjure is forewarned his own life may be on the line. Fingers-on-the-legs, the lynx, may be seen. This means to keep the conjuring secret. Sharp nose, the badger, means that the conjure will be in for a fight. A snake-related image may appear — smokesnake, deersnake, or sproutsnake. This always signifies great changes ahead for the patient.

Animals have power and can be sent out to do injury to others. Perhaps a dog ally shot at another dog, wolf aimed at wolf, fox battled fox, weasel killed weasel. A witch or wizard can send out any animal familiar, such as a bobcat or wolf, to go hunting for a victim. Other magical animals can show up. An insect intrusion can be shot into the body. When old sneaky, the coyote, is diagnosed, the conjure has to be very careful, because normal conjure laws do not apply for this animal expert at legerdemain.

All animals have enemies. For instance, an eagle may be sent to chase away snake. Bear may be called forth to use its quick reflexes to catch a fish. Lynx may be sent to kill rabbit or bird, lion to destroy deer, and so on.

Certain objects are considered propitious. The conjure may see the face of an ancestor who wishes to communicate with her. A particular organ such as the heart, spleen, or liver may appear. The conjure may see a skull within the fire-bug matrix, or divine past deeds or future events.

There are countless additional conjure divinatory techniques, using animals, beads, stones, water, and plants such as corn, sweet potato, or other roots. The most ancient and effective is tobacco divination. Tobacco ranks first among divinatory plants. Divination can be done at any time, but the optimum is at the new or full moon, for these are gateways and lend energy. It should be undertaken on the fourth day of a tobacco water fast.

The tribal tobacco is rubbed in both hands, but mostly on the left hand of the diviner. Each apprentice finger and the conjure thumb of the diviner's left hand is fed or rubbed with the tobacco leaf. The tobacco is remade for conjure with a special ceremony. It is nine packed, nine rubbed, nine beaten, and nine ground. Nine is the precious plume of the inside shadow. It is the curing number, and it asks the spirit of the tobacco for a positive outcome.

The hand is all-important in this procedure. Here the old ones, the grandmother or grandfather conjures, speak to the diviner. What news from the buried apprentice? What news from the water weaver apprentice? Is the flying apprentice satisfied? And the little smoke maker apprentice — what is the message? What of the center of the hand, the skull or cauldron? Measurement is a constant and has a kind of flow once begun. Divinatory imagery is different from ordinary seeing in many ways. Each revelation is a three count, except the last count on a man, which is a four count. Therefore, the measurement is not actually counted but felt as an adjunct of the tobacco spirit. This sequence of measurement determines a positive or negative outcome.

Tobacco divination by water is a common conjure practice. The patient is provided with a gourd calabash and told to dip water from a moving stream. The conjure watches carefully to see how this is done. If the patient goes deep with the calabash, the conjure should employ deep measures, that is to say, go deep for the divinatory picture. It is also possible that a deep-water calabash means the patient is resisting treatment. If the patient skims water off of the top of the stream, then it will be a surface divination. In other words, the picture is lurking nearby or events relevant to the patient's illness have happened recently.

The patient is told to roll a piece of tobacco around with his fingers and pulverize it. Three pinches are taken from the right palm, one at a time, with the left thumb and pointer finger. The patient places them on the water in the calabash in a small triangle. The conjure watches carefully to see how the pinches of tobacco break up. If the tobacco spreads out, it is a good sign. If it doesn't, it is a bad sign. After the three pinches have been placed, the conjure closes his or her eyes. Often an entire divination will leap to the mind's eye. The conjure relates the vision to the subject in its entirety. However, if nothing appears, the conjure dips the relevant finger in the calabash and sucks the drops of tobacco-clinging liquid from it. This is said to help the tobacco spirit.

The conjure tries again to have a vision. If nothing happens this time, the conjure dips his thumb in the calabash and sucks off the liquid. Again, the conjure tries for a vision. Usually, before this step, the divination has been completed. If by chance no vision appears, the conjure gazes into the calabash until one comes.

Counting in olden times was divinatory in nature. Sacred mathematics told us our future, not simply when to sow and when to harvest. Numbers told of the mantle surrounding us and also within us, in other words, the *shilip*. Spiritual mathematics were used to describe the flayed, the layers of life and being — how one integrates and lives one's life under heaven. Twenty-two flayed, the *shilip*, also has calendrical significance. Nativity determines if one will be lucky or unlucky. Mary often said to me, "Look at shadow man or shadow woman and use measure. It's easy to tell if one is weak or strong by the relative strength of the numbers."

Numbers once had the power to kill. Whether or not they still do, I was never able to clearly understand. Mary often suggested that much of the significance of numbers was imparted in advanced conjure training, training I never received. Generally speaking, the numbers four, seven, and nine are benefactor numbers. Nine is the great healing number. The numbers two, three, five, and ten are enemy count numbers. They are dangerous to be around. Although there are no traditional illnesses of which I am aware associated directly with numbers, all animals fit categorically into an ancient system of geometry.

In addition, conjures understand the dualistic nature of life. Energy is either centripetal, centrifugal, or neutral. Male energy is sky energy and is considered to be centripetal or heavy. Female energy, or earth energy, is considered to be centrifugal or light. If you take a line on a horizontal plane, it is always considered male, because of downward force or heaviness. If you took the same line on a vertical plane, it would be considered female because of lightness.

Each animal has an implied geometry. Although many of these matters reach well beyond my personal understanding, Mary often attempted to explain that the *shilip* was governed by certain principles of sound, such as tones and semitones and even microtones. The tones had a correspondence with the number twenty-two.

Mary maintained that by studying the sounds insects make and bird and other animal calls, one could accomplish seemingly impossible feats of conjure and healing. She once said to me, "With the proper use of sound, all frustration and confusion can be swept away. Clarity is a distinct sound within us. So many people try to find clarity through language, but it can't be done. No matter how precise your language, it will always create a barrier. Experience can also lead you to clarity. It is normal to think of experience as something to do with memory. But experience is flayed, that is to say, clustered all about us, right before our very eyes. Flay it. Measure of flayed is a measure of harmony and disharmony, and ultimately a measure of clarity."

Occasionally, the conjure has lodestones among her curing paraphernalia and uses them during powwowing. Lodestones have male and female healing potentials and can be applied to the body in various positions. Female lodestones are said to be cold, and male lodestones are said to be hot. Lodestones have a strong attracting and repelling ability on the spiritual as well as the physical plane. If placed correctly, a slight electrical shock is felt near or in the area of difficulty. Hot, male stones can alleviate pain. Cold, female stones are untrustworthy, dangerous, and unruly, but they are used to crack very difficult obstructions. They must be tamed and used with caution. The most dangerous female lodestone is said to be pregnant and will impregnate when used. Female lodestones can cause early menstruation in women and hemorrhaging in both men and women. Lodestones are said to be married to their owners. Only big-root conjures with evolved native ability dare marry and use female lodestones.

A word or two about power water: the most potent power water comes directly from the earth, from special springs, wells, streams, underground rivers, and sacred cenotes and from other sources such as rainwater. They are collected and informed with prayer, songs, and sacred intent.

Water has memory and intelligence and is linked with emotion. It seeks to be the lowest and is humble, yet it can cut through a mountain. Power water is utilized to bless and cleanse and for hundreds of other magical purposes. Water was the first mirror and was believed to be able to capture the image and soul of another.

Aside from holy water, the most famous commercial power water is Florida water, so named, I suppose, because of that state's voluminous flora. It is a kind of balmy, citrus-smelling cologne used in rituals. Many other power waters are pungent-smelling.

There are thousands of conjured waters, too many to list

here, and I'm not sure I could if I wanted to. Numerous secret formulas and rituals are used to make them. Many contain roots, herbs, powders, and other ingredients. Power water is always treated with respect and as a living entity, which it is. Life and water are integral. Water can live without life, but life cannot live without water.

Medicine bundles once proliferated throughout Native America, but now are not so common. There was an extraordinary range and variety to these sacred belongings. Dreams, visions, or the possession of a gift from a magical encounter entitled one to make a medicine bundle, which would contain some item infused with supernatural power. To name just a few, there were star bundles, which kept meteorites; elk power love medicine bundles; otter bundles, containing water-related medicines; witchcraft bundles, which held human or animal bone chips or cactus needles to send injury and spirit sickness to an unsuspecting victim. War and hunting bundles were opened to give courage and skill to the owner, and dance bundles would be opened at ceremonial dances.

Coverings were mostly rawhide, painted according to the informing visionary experience with stylized animals or other magical depictions. Other common contents were rocks, arrows, war clubs, feathers, birds, tobacco twists, sweetgrass, corn ears, pipes, animal skins, fetishes, effigies, and horse or animal hair or even scalps. The possibilities were endless. Keeping a bundle always lent an air of mystery to the owner and was a great honor. Bundles had power when tied shut but greater power when opened, and they were untied and the contents revealed with much reverence, with songs, prayers, and ceremonial attention to detail.

Mary's few bundles of this nature were called conjure packs. Early in a powwowing ceremony, a specific bundle might be opened to call a designated healing spirit. Mary was always reluctant to discuss her packs. One time when I persisted, she cut me off with a slice of her hand. "Look, David," she said. "You can talk anything right into the ground. Don't do it with this."

We now come to the altar. The greatest magicians are the great altar builders. There are more altars in this world than you can shake a stick at. When humanity first thought to influence events with the aid of supernatural power, altars were created. At one time, they were set in a geomantic landscape, paying strict attention to the heavenly vault, and served to gather both cosmic and earthly power. Altars are the locus of the most sacred space within a sacred precinct. They alter ordinary reality, transforming it into a reality of multiplied possibility. They create a vortex of energy and are a crossroads that shift one into the land of the miraculous.

Conjure altars used in powwowing are like other altars, except they are geared toward healing, and much healing paraphernalia may be present, such as charms, fetishes, and other power items. Certain conjure altars can be used to call the master spirit of an animal. Others can call down healing power from the planets or star configurations.

Altars can be square or circular or constructed in many other shapes. They are always built with a sense of solemnity. The most common altar is a rectangle, two squares joined together. If you draw an imaginary X inside the rectangle of the altar space, you can visualize four pyramids converging, with their points joining in the center. The four quadrants correspond to the powers of the four directions. Power objects or other meaningful items and tools are placed accordingly.

East is a place of light and therefore is related spiritually to the sun. Objects connected to enlightenment or religious or spiritual beliefs are placed in this quadrant. South relates to the material world and to personal power. Personal objects are placed here, as well as objects relating to material success, growth, and good health. West is the place of sacrifice, so sage or some other incense is usually burned here, and it was once the place where human and animal sacrifice was performed. The west quadrant aligns with ancestor power and the inner territory of sacred dreams and visions. West holds relics, holy pipes, and so on. The north quadrant of the altar references spirit and wisdom, intellect, philosophical beliefs, and higher knowledge. It holds feathers, flint knives representing the cutting power of the intellect, swords, and so on. These four quadrants all contribute transformative power to the center. Altars also have antennae to attract power from the sky. These can be wands or staves of a traditional wood such as chokecherry or willow topped with fluffies or feathers. Oftentimes these antennae have different-colored ribbons tied to them.

Most altars I am familiar with are arrayed on the ground, but the word *altar* can also mean "table" or "mesa." Altars contain deep metaphysical meaning and have a transcendent beauty. All one has to do is to see one out on the prairie to know their holiness and power — perhaps a buffalo skull altar with eagle feathers tied to the horns and stirring in the wind. The sacred skull of the life-giver is stuffed with sage, tobacco, and sweetgrass, then positioned to face west on a bed of sage over mole dirt. I have been to many great cathedrals and seen many a hallowed altar. But to me, there is nothing to equal the simplicity, nobility, and sheer glory of these constructions.

Everything to be placed on the altar and used in powwowing is smoked with bear root or, sometimes, ropes of sweetgrass. A short prayer is said and each item pressed to the heart before being put in its proper place.

Powwowing requires intent and focus. There are many details to attend to, such as requesting permission from the spirits of the place. You are swept along by the currents of events and you must do what is required of you. Otherwise, you insult your helping spirits, and you insult the people who have entrusted you to treat them. Needless to say, one should not practice conjure without years of experience and without a long apprenticeship and the guidance of a teacher. It is bad medicine and eventually brings dishonor all around.

Lastly, the patient need not be sick or unhealthy. Life is manifold, and a myriad of differing enervating conditions can exist. They can exist in the future as well as the present and past, but the momentum of these negative imprints can be slowed or stopped in the early stages. The conjure has an arsenal of weapons with which to restore the balance of health. Future deterioration can be transformed or even halted.

Other generalizations can be made about the practice of conjure. On the surface, powwowing seems ritualized and deceptively simple, with drumming, rattling, singing, and tobacco fumigation of the patient followed by various treatments. Remedies are given and the patient leaves.

In the simplest formulation, a conjure is an agent of alteration. Nothing is assumed to be fixed. There are no moorings, no anchoring in the conjure tradition.

Mary eventually convinced me that a conjure is able to penetrate into unearthly realms. Strange things happen in this context. I have said almost nothing about the conjure's use of spirit helpers and jack powers. Why? Because I don't know how to explain it. Shadow or *shilip* is the same as spirit. You are either well aware of spirits or you're not, and never the twain shall meet. Most people have severed their ties to the spirit world. For them, there is no reciprocity between this world and the other, overlapping world of spirits. Conjure teaches that there are spirits all around us, at every moment. In powwowing, the conjure often calls on particular ones for assistance and help. However, to speak of spirits is to negate them.

I learned the rudiments of Mary's fasting doctor tradition as she imparted them to me. She once said, "When you make a tobacco water fast, you are reaching for holiness and power. There can be no alienation from the divine in conjure. You are seeking the indwelling essence in a direct and simple manner. Now drink this," she said, handing me a gourd cup of the liquid.

She stayed my hand midway to my lips. "The tobacco may not like you. Drink it dry, and we'll see where it takes us. We'll know soon enough."

"And what will we know, Mary?" I asked, after draining the cup.

"We'll know if the mountains will move for you. We'll know what kind of mischief you're capable of. You don't know it, but you can be a troublemaker. If you are, I'll find out while the precious medicine of this tobacco is young." She gave me a slanted look. "Here, have one more cup."

I laughed when I took it. "This stuff couldn't have any power," I said. "This is just some kind or another of Indian soda pop."

The first tobacco water fast is done in a specially prepared conjure hut, as I've described. On the third day of the fast, the leave-taking of ordinary consciousness should be apparent. If not, many cigarettes of an aged Indian tobacco are smoked. Medicine or conjure cigarettes, good ones, are quite strong and can be jolting. I would often feel energy shoot up through my stomach, cascade out the top of my head, and swirl around me like a wreath. Common consciousness collapses, and a state analogous to awake dreaming enfolds one. The inner and the outer merge in a new way. With the help of these conjure cigarettes, the transformation is complete.

At the onset of this experience, one becomes aware of the male and female aspects of all of nature. One becomes astounded at the voluptuous symmetry of being. The most mundane, familiar objects are suddenly remarkable and exotic. An ordinary cup may become suddenly a vessel of female form and energy. A candle becomes the expression of male qualities and force. The tobacco faster is instantly aware that all forms and spaces between are imbued with this simple male and female essence. Categories have to be reconsidered. Human beings arrange events in episodes and epochs and so forth. We assign meaning to various people and objects mainly because someone we accepted as knowledgeable or even the general culture told us what to value and what not to value. But one quickly realizes that centrifugal, centripetal, and neutral manifestations, including our own polarized being, are the big picture.

Mary said, "The form of the *shilip* has been analyzed and mapped by conjures." This information is contained within a mythopoetic oral history. There are twenty-two gradations within the *shilip*. One flayed, the initial shape of the inside shadow, determines the patient's resistance to the powers of fire, which is the yellow man; earth, or many-kinds-of-dirt, the red man; water, or lowly man or woman, the black man; air, or man who went away but sends back relatives, the white man; tree, or green man. This is not hit-or-miss. The proportions of the initial symmetry of the inside shadow are indicative of whatever sickness may be present.

In my opinion, tobacco fasting will not unravel the secrets of the universe, but it may help. It heightens perception. With proper guidance, it frees one from visual conditioning. Tobacco fasting gradually causes immense changes to occur in the visual field, but it also sharpens and refines other senses and perceptions. An unnamed force begins to pour in on the initiate and extends into his or her surroundings. It puts formerly unseen phenomena into sharp focus. The arrangement of light and shadow becomes extremely relevant. Positive and negative envelopes appear that surround every person and object. This energy, projected from within, is the *shilip*, also referred to as flayed, that I have spoken of. Tobacco fasting reveals the *shilip* for the conjure to see and manipulate with tobacco fumigation.

The model of disease I've described here is unknown in traditions of Western medicine. Following is a list of diseases I witnessed being treated: big, little, and chief deer; antelope; dog; prairie dog; creek dog; beaver; wolf; otter; terrapin; mouse; cat, such as jaguar, puma, lynx, bobcat, housecat, and tiger or panther sickness; snail; coyote; cow; hog; elk; moose; bear; toad; horse; lizard; rabbit; snake, especially rattlesnake, water moccasin, and coachwhip; porcupine; skunk; bison; mole; bat; badger; rabbit; weasel; raccoon; opossum; squirrel; muskrat; worm; grub worm; woolly mammoth; cannibal; and white man sickness.

Bird-related sickness are: eagle, hummingbird, crow and raven, chicken, turkey, owl, crane, buzzard, swan, duck, goose, heron, blackbird, partridge, quail, woodpecker, hawk, and parrot. There are many others.

Here are some water people illnesses: turtle, frog, black bass, perch, catfish, crawfish, horned snake, waterbug, merman and mermaid, shellfish, and white water person illness.

Insect-caused sicknesses are: ant, millipede, big and little flea, butterfly, moth, dragonfly, big and little spider, bee, beetle, weevil, mosquito, grasshopper, midge, lightning bug, cricket, and locust.

Other sicknesses are: spirit-of-war, spirit-of-death-and-dying, what's-inside-of-me, tiny-animals-frolicking-about-in-the-water, lightning, rainbow, both what's-in- and what's-by-the-sea, strong man, confused people, living man and living woman, cloud, feather, calumet, birdsnake, television sickness, plenty tall building, little-gray-men-who-run-the-world, rail train, sun, moon, star body, and comet or smoking star sickness. I have omitted some other traditional conjure illnesses, because I wasn't able to understand them as they are caused by mythical beings. Also, there are a number of illnesses that appear to be imaginary in character as they have no manifestation in flayed. I have omitted these as well.

In combination with tobacco fumigation, the conjure uses herbal and other forms of treatment as remedies. The conjurer's materia medica is startling and immeasurable. The ingredients of many remedies continue to be secret. To the conjure, plants have supernatural qualities. In treatment, it is the spirit of the plant that is relevant. The first plant to be discovered is never disturbed. If you dig a plant, proper offerings of tobacco must be made and prayers must be said. Most plants have their own song, which must be sung before harvesting. Treating a plant improperly can cause sickness and misfortune, and disrespect will sap their potency.

Many plants are said to be so powerful that even a conjure dares not remove them. Here are a few of the plants used in conjure remedies. Elk medicine is a bitter and foul-smelling mint. Sweet flag, better known as muskrat plant, is a powerful war medicine. Licorice is called jealous woman medicine. There is also coyote medicine; gray, white, and flat sage; peyote medicine; ghost medicine; wild rose; mullein; bearberry; and many others.

Now, some roots. There is bear root, dog root, yellow root, and blood root, which is one of the most effective love medicine roots if used properly. Woman medicine is called papoose root. Sneeze root is used mostly in divination. Buffalo root is used in many treatments. Many-children root is found growing exclusively in southeastern Oklahoma. Blackberry is sometime referred to as eye root. There is beaver root, gourd root, deer potato, snake root, little white man or ginseng root, butterfly root, crooked medicine or owl root, and mandrake. There are many hundreds of roots not mentioned here.

Some tree medicines are slippery elm, wild cherry, maple,

red and white willow, oak (especially the acorns), cedar, elder-berry, black walnut, hickory, ash, pine, crab apple, wild plum, cottonwood, sumac, sycamore (especially the seed pod), Osage orange, chinaberry or black-red medicine tree, and dogwood, also called arrow tree.

I have said very little about the use of animal ingredients in conjure remedies. The reason for this omission is that I don't want to add to the problems facing animals already. Too many animals are endangered and abused. Generally speaking, the conjure prepared remedies from various animal parts such as hair, testicles, blood, horn, eggs, brains, other organs, and so on. I have never used any of these, nor do I condone this practice.

I have consciously removed from the text medicines and procedures too dangerous or extreme. For instance, bone setting is an art practiced by conjures, but I have chosen not to describe this catastrophic treatment. The cauterization of tumors is an extreme procedure I have witnessed more than once. Similarly, descriptions of other procedures such as herbal enemas and infusions have been omitted. Injections were given using a hollowed bird bone and a bladder containing the fluid to be administered. The bone needle is inserted and the bladder is carefully squeezed. I know this kind of medicine can no longer be utilized in our modern age.

When I was growing up in Oklahoma, the sort of things mentioned in this book were highly persecuted. Yet Oklahoma cradled many streams and lineages of ancient knowledge. In this book, I have tried to pay homage to some of the hundreds of unnamed conjures who lived humble lives and dedicated themselves to the service and healing of others. I still have vivid childhood memories of medicine men and women being led away in chains and jailed for their practices.

My feeling today is that these conjures and medicine people

APPENDIX

were holy. They made do with their ancestral knowledge and with what was available to them. If you had been acquainted with these elderly practitioners, you would agree that it was their intent to help and never to harm anyone. Powwowing, in the final analysis, was an act of love.

As you know, I turned away from the difficult conjure trails, and I have never regretted my decision to do so. Though I learned it in a topical sense, this system of healing was beyond my reach. In a way it has taken me all my life to write this story. Into it I have put memories of my training. I have endeavored to express the everyday character of my life then. I have tried to carefully construct and reflect the things I learned as a young man. I offer this book as a requiem to things past, the passing of a medical practice that is no longer relevant.

I have tried to fix something of Mary Gardener in these pages, but I realize, coming to the very end of this book, that I have veered from the mark. Her character was so much more than I have been able to record. I have failed to capture her patience, her passion for life, her fondness for all of creation, her largesse of spirit, and her ultimate belief in the good of all humanity.

Mary's presence produced in me a sense of timelessness. She was an Indian, but she was also a universal woman. To me, she resembled nothing so much as a natural genius. She integrated an encyclopedic knowledge of a wide range of matter with a precision of mind I admired. Her logic was unique to her worldview. She was an inexhaustible source of information. She bombarded me with bits and rags of instruction that were obscure and fantastic. I had to mature before I could grasp the innate wisdom of her teachings. More than anything else, she was a superb teacher. I loved her. She was a great woman and a great friend.

I often reflect back on my life and the enchantment I fell

under with Mary Gardener. It has given me much to contemplate over the years. I strayed far from the beaten path and don't regret it. Mine is perhaps a strange story in relation to others from my generation. I am not an intellectual man. I simply like to tell stories about animals. Never have I overtly written about myself. This time I've told stories about my own experiences.